GROW BIG IN SMALL SPACES

The Urban Farmer's Practical Guide To Container Gardening & Home Canning Collection

—

BY
LUKE POTTER

THE URBAN FARMER

Luke Potter

DEDICATION

This book is dedicated to the generations of homemakers, especially my grandmother and mom, who grew Victory Gardens during WWII to help the war effort while feeding their families healthy, nutritious food.

And to the home canners who kept their families alive during The Great Depression and The Dust Bowl.

And to the modern-day homesteaders and preppers who prefer a simpler, more sustainable lifestyle.

And to the millions of people around the world who took up gardening and home canning during the recent pandemic.

We take this vow:
"Our families, loved ones, and neighbors will never go hungry because we prepared for the worst of times while praying for the best of times".

My Ancestral Family Homestead in Maine

Proverbs 21:20
"The wise store up choice food and olive oil, while fools gulp theirs down."

Contents

Book 1

Book 2

HOW TO GROW VEGETABLES IN POTS & CONTAINERS

9 Steps To Plant & Harvest Organic Food In As Little As 21 Days For Beginners

———

BY
LUKE POTTER

THE URBAN FARMER

Luke Potter

In The Beginning...

"The love of gardening is a seed once sown that never dies." - Gertrude Jekyll

I started gardening when I was very young. It was a pastime my mother shared with me. It was those early experiences that awakened a lifelong love of teaching gardening. If there is one thing that I could pass on to anyone interested in gardening, it's that this is an exercise in love, patience, thoughtfulness, and dedication. Gardening becomes a time of peace and tranquility - like a short vacation away from your problems without leaving home. Gardening is the perfect opportunity to get some sunshine and take some time for yourself.

Over the many years that I have taught gardening, I have regularly met people who want to have a garden but think they can't. Some simply don't have functional space. For others, busy lives mean there isn't time for gardening. I understand these problems because I have them also.

That's where gardening in containers comes in. It's not exactly the same as in-ground gardening, and it takes some time and effort to get right. It's a smaller, more portable, more controllable form of gardening. Done right, you'll find that a container garden is easy to care for in as little as ten to fifteen minutes a day.

The reward is a personal supply of fresh fruits, vegetables, and herbs for your family. The best part is you'll know precisely where those delicious rewards came from. If you've ever thought about gardening but have put it off, you should try your hand at container gardening.

What This Book is About?

This book will share my experiences and knowledge about successfully growing a garden in pots and containers. I'll discuss essential decisions you'll make before starting your garden. You'll learn the correct way to pick a good spot for your plants and how to arrange your garden for success. You'll learn about mixing your own potting soil, how to water your plants correctly, and even how to protect your garden from pests using organic techniques that actually work.

Growing a garden is only half the fun, and the biggest payoff is enjoying the fruits and vegetables of your labor. I'll show you how to harvest your plants and discuss ways to maximize the amount of produce you grow from your containers. I'll also share my favorite ways to store, can, and preserve your harvest so you can enjoy the organic, delicious food you grew whenever you want.

Who Is This Book For?

If you've tried your hand at container gardening before and came away feeling like you have two brown thumbs, don't despair. You're not alone.

Every person who undertakes gardening will have failed at some point. I could bore you forever with stories about times things have gone awry in my gardens.

The thing that I really want to tell you is that every time something doesn't go right in my garden, it's an opportunity to learn. This book draws on my successes and failures to give you the reliable information you need to grow an organic pot or container garden you are proud of. I hope you find gardening to be an exercise that brings peace. And I hope you share the experience with your family, friends, and neighbors.

I hope that anyone who has always wanted a little garden but thought they didn't have the skills, time, or ability reads this book. Anyone can have a beautiful vegetable garden, and I'll show you how simple it can be in this book. You'll learn ways to choose the right kinds of plants for your lifestyle and how to grow different varieties that aren't available in the local grocery store.

Among the many benefits of growing your own garden is the knowledge about how it evolved. From accidental contamination to the use of unauthorized insecticides and pesticides, even the best organic produce you buy in the store may have a shadowy past you'll never know about. When you grow your own fruit, vegetables, and herbs, you'll rest easy knowing your family has clean and good tasting produce.

Perhaps the most important thing that I hope anyone who reads this book finds is gardening can be relaxing, stress-relieving, and fun. I will teach you how to take gardening one step at a time so that it is an enjoyable experience you'll want to share with others as much as I do.

Who is Luke Potter?

I started gardening as soon as I could walk, and I can't imagine life without having a garden. My first job was working on a farm, and it's my goal to retire one day to farm life. I have been a proponent of natural, organic home-gardening for as long as I can remember. In fact, my love of gardening led me to earn a Bachelor of Arts degree in Environmental Studies from Brown University in 1978.

I teach gardening and life skills classes through a homeschool network today. It's the perfect opportunity to share my passion for eating healthy and growing delicious food at home with kids born in the 21st century.

I started teaching about gardening by helping my family and neighbors with their gardens. I learned that I love talking about gardening, hearing people's experiences, and sharing my own passion and knowledge. I've learned many valuable things over the years, and the learning never stops.

Teaching our children how to grow food is a vital step toward teaching other meaningful life skills. The knowledge to feed yourself and your family with clean, organic produce opens up a world of self-reliance and confidence. Growing a garden is one of the best ways to provide your children with real-life experiences they can use forever.

I had seen many children who started out uninterested over the years but became some of the most eager participants when it came time to tend the garden. They could see the garden growing every day, and it became an exciting game to keep an eye on the sprouting plants. Plus, who doesn't like playing in the dirt?

One of my favorite young students absolutely hated brussels sprouts. I have no idea what possessed this young student to plant brussels sprouts, but I can tell you that they soon became a favorite vegetable. Maybe it was something about seeing the way the little heads grew, or maybe they just taste better when you grow them yourself, I can't say, but what I got to see was a young gardener grow as fast as those brussels sprouts.

Gardening can become more than just an educational experience or a way to find relaxation, too. You may be surprised when you discover how many of your neighbors have small gardens. I've seen many great friendships blossom between neighbors who were strangers until the tomato plant grew over the fence and shared its plentiful bounty. Gardening can be a great way to meet people and share fresh, organic, homegrown produce.

As different as we all seem from one another some days, we are also more alike than we often acknowledge. I like to think that gardening can be a way to bridge many divides we have in our lives, and in the process, help us all find happiness, peace, a little sun on our faces, and a full belly.

I hope this book will inspire you to start gardening at home. It isn't as difficult as it seems, and I'll show you the mistakes to avoid so you can have success. It's okay to feel like having a garden of your own is overwhelming right now. This book will teach you the steps to keep your container garden simple, productive, and easy to care for.

Alright - Let's get dirty!

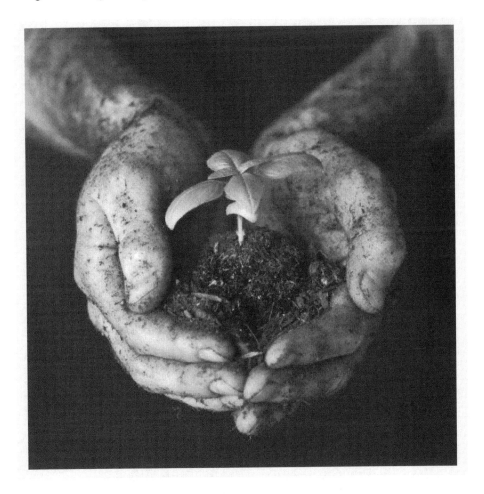

Note: To save you money on this paperback, the photos in this book have been printed in black & white. If you would like to view the photos included in this book in full color, please purchase the Kindle edition or view them on my website www.luketheurbanfarmer.com

And, if you enjoyed this book, please take a few minutes to leave an honest review on Amazon.

Chapter 1

LOCATION, LOCATION, LOCATION...

Life begins the day you start a garden. - Chinese Proverb

You've probably heard the saying that fortunate people find themselves in the right place at the right time. Well, this is particularly true when you're growing a vegetable garden in pots and containers. No matter what varieties of fruit, herbs, or vegetables you plan to grow, you'll need to place them in the right part of the area you plan to garden and at the right time of the year to get the best results. But before you decide what plants you want to grow, before you even open a bag of seeds or soil, you need to make a decision on where you'll place your containers.

Finding the Perfect Location

You may already have a spot picked out for your pots and container plants. It may seem like a perfect spot: easy to access, nothing else is growing there, and you just know it will look pretty when your plants are growing. But before you do anything else, you should make sure that the spot you have in mind is actually the perfect location for growing in pots and containers.

Locating the ideal spot for growing healthy plants isn't difficult - you simply need to walk around your gardening space and pay attention to the natural environment. This is a great way to start experiencing the Zen of gardening. As you move around your yard, take the time to notice where the sun is coming from, how much light hits the ground, what other plants are growing, and generally try to get a sense of whether a vegetable garden will grow happily in your chosen spots.

As you move about your space, thinking about how your garden will look, pay attention to the direction of the sun. A simple compass can help determine the correct direction the light comes to your yard from. Areas with southern light exposure will get the most consistent sun unless there are obstructions like buildings and trees. You may have good success planting vegetables facing east or west if a south-facing planting isn't possible. It usually is not a good idea to grow spring-summer vegetables in north-facing locations because daylight quickly vanishes in these areas.

When you walk around your space, face the sun and put your arms out from your sides. Let the light fall on you and turn slowly. You'll notice that less light will fall on your face and arms as you move away from facing south. As you face north, the sun will barely fall on your face at all, even at high noon. You should think about how much sun your vegetables will get when you plant them facing your chosen direction. You may find that your ideal location is slightly different from the spot you wish to grow in.

While this exercise may seem a little silly, it's an excellent first step to conceptualizing how the natural conditions of your garden will be once it begins to grow. You should spend at least a few minutes in the morning, midday, and afternoon simply slowing down and imagining how life would be if you were growing in that spot. Is it hot in the afternoon sun on a cool day? Do trees and buildings block midday light? Does it take all morning before sunlight hits the spot you want to plant your vegetables? Answering these questions helps to focus your attention on the best location for planting.

It's essential to answer these questions before planting because it's more challenging to move containers with growing plants than to start in a good location. Picking the wrong place for growing in containers is one of the common mistakes people often make when they are new to container gardening. It's an easy mistake because we all have a spot we wish we had plants growing.

One of my first students was struggling to get a garden started. The spot seemed ideal. It was close to the kitchen and had a water faucet right by it. Seeds would sprout but would die before they even had real leaves. What seemed like a mystery at first turned out to be relatively straightforward. The spot my student had chosen as a garden was in deep shade by midday from three massive maple trees growing on the other side of the fence. We moved the garden to a slightly less convenient spot, but one that had a good amount of light all day, and the garden flourished.

Light and Sun Requirements for Vegetable Gardens

Every plant has a particular amount of light and temperature that is ideal. Most vegetable plants prefer bright, direct sunlight and moderately warm places, but that certainly isn't a hard rule. You will find that some of the most popular garden vegetables, like lettuce and most greens, won't grow well in the heat of summer, preferring cooler, shorter days. Other plants, like peppers, won't really start to grow until the days are long and hot.

Most people will find that the best locations for sun-loving plants will be evident by spending a little time in their yard. You may even find that you have ideal conditions for planting spring-summer and fall-winter vegetables simply by changing the location where you place your containers. Selecting the perfect location for growing vegetables is the first step toward providing healthy, home-grown food for your family and friends all year long.

Now that you know what parts of your growing space are sunny and shady at specific parts of the day, you can start picking some of the types of plants you will grow. One of the first things you'll see is that most seeds or small plants will come with instructions that say "plant in full sun." This term indicates the plant requires at least six hours each day of sunlight. All plants need at least some sun, but not all of the plants you want to grow will be successful in full-sun locations. Plants with other requirements like part shade will wither and die in all-day sunlight.

Temperature is also important, and it's one of the most challenging conditions to control when you are growing outdoors. Generally, most vegetable plants will grow well in temperatures below 90 degrees and above 50 degrees. Conditions outside this range can have various effects, from slow growth to seemingly instantaneous death.

For example, I have a friend who lives in Central California, where summertime temperatures often exceed 100 degrees, sometimes for weeks on end. These temperatures are brutal on many plants, and my friend has had to devise all sorts of solutions to reducing temperatures. Some solutions include a pulley-operated shade that blocks some of the afternoon sun when temps are extreme. The garden is also equipped with an irrigation drip line connected to fogger nozzles several feet in the air. Increasing the moisture in the air helps to cut temperatures down, and now the area where nothing would grow flourishes. More work, but worth the effort!

An important fact to remember when planning the location of a garden is that the soil in a container will have a more significant temperature variance than plants in the ground. The type and color of the container you select can affect how great a temperature change the soil in the pot experiences. Suppose you place containers in hot locations, like on concrete that absorbs and reflects heat. In that case, you will need larger containers made from heat-absorbing material to prevent overheating the roots of your growing plants. When temperatures drop, soil in containers will get colder than the ground. Very few vegetables and herb plants can withstand frost conditions, and containers may increase the likelihood of damage to your plants when temperatures drop.

Gardeners who live in areas where afternoon temperatures exceed 90 degrees may need to invest in shade cloth to prevent scorching. Parts of the world with short growing seasons make vegetable gardening difficult since many varieties take 90 to 120 days to fully mature. Using a hoop-house or a greenhouse is the ideal solution to growing vegetables in cool climates. You'll learn some other tricks in this book for speeding up the growing season that can help cool-climate gardeners have as much success as gardeners in warmer regions.

One of the most important decisions you'll make should be locating your gardening area as close to your house as possible. By planting your garden where it's easy to access, it will be easier to remember to water, fertilize, and prune your plants.

Many popular vegetables will not survive if they are neglected during the growing season. So, planting in a convenient spot makes it more likely you will adequately care for your plants. As a bonus, when you plant your garden near your home, you will have an ever-changing tapestry of growing life to enjoy looking at and eventually eating every day.

You'll want to consider some of the practical aspects of gardening when choosing a location. You want to make sure your garden can be easily watered, for example. Watering your growing plants the correct amount will be more challenging when they are far from a hose. As you'll learn later, improper watering is one of the biggest mistakes people growing in containers frequently make.

Various pests that feed on vegetables are less likely near your home. Animals are timid when near human habitation and often pass on a good meal if it means getting too close to people. Locating your containers nearby makes it easier to spot the signs of pests. The faster you react when animals, insects, or diseases appear in your garden, the better chance you have of preventing serious problems.

When you plan your garden, consider areas with good sun and light conditions convenient to visit. You want your garden to be inviting. Keeping it close to home is a great way to encourage everyone in your family to take advantage of the space.

What may surprise you as you start to look for good places to plant are the numerous areas that can work for gardening. Even the smallest apartment, condo, or house has several areas that can be ideal for growing lots of different types of delicious herbs, fruit, and vegetables. There are even some areas you may have never thought of using for gardening that can provide a steady supply of fresh herbs and vegetables in easy-to-care-for pots and containers.

I'm always amazed by the ingenuity many gardeners have to find ways to grow vegetables in seemingly impossible situations. I know quite a few people (including myself) that live in northern parts of the country with short growing seasons and brutal winters. One of the neatest tricks I have seen was shown to me many years ago by a friend. Instead of placing containers on the ground, the containers are on rolling furniture dollies. When unexpected cold weather pops in, it's easy to just move the containers into a sheltered place. It's a simple solution and brilliant in how effective it is for dealing with unexpected weather. Smaller pots can be brought indoors if frost is predicted, or you can invest in a frost blanket to cover tender vegetable plants.

Container Gardening on a Patio or Deck

Patio and deck spaces are among the most popular places for a container garden. Patio and deck areas are natural gathering spaces for friends and family. They can make the ideal place to teach children about gardening. Locating your containers on your patio or deck keeps them close by, and it's convenient to harvest herbs and vegetables as you need them.

As you look at the possible locations for container planting, you should try and factor in how large a container you will use. Ensure containers aren't so large or positioned that plants block walkways when fully grown. You can prevent damage to your patio or deck by planning your container garden so that run-off from watering your plants doesn't pool on the patio surface.

The best location to grow vegetables and herbs in containers on your patio or deck will be the place where you find the sun mostly on your face by mid-morning and throughout the day until at least early afternoon. Remember that vegetables tend to prefer six or more hours of direct, bright sunlight every day during the growing season, the exact conditions a patio or deck cover prevents.

Suppose you have the space to locate your containers just off the deck or patio. In that case, they will be accessible and convenient while getting enough light. Many herb species and some types of vegetables will grow well without direct sun, so all isn't lost if your patio or deck cover doesn't allow optimal conditions.

Depending on your patio or deck design, you can grow in hanging baskets, on plant stands, and even on shelving. When you picture the garden on your deck or patio, start by finding the sun, then try and use as much of the space as possible without creating obstacles for people using the area.

Container Gardening on a Balcony or Fire Escape

Small spaces like balconies and fire escapes can allow you to grow a wide variety of herbs and vegetables if you plan correctly. The first thing you must consider is how the structure is intended to be used. Don't block pathways on fire escapes, for example. Instead, you can use vertical planting methods, hanging baskets, and other solutions that don't create a safety hazard. Also, remember that containers with wet soil can get very heavy. You need to be careful not to exceed the weight limit if you decide to plant a container garden on one.

When you stand on your balcony at midday, notice the direction of the sun. If it is entirely in your face, you have perfect conditions for most types of vegetables. If it faces east or west, you have many options available. Northern-facing balconies may provide you with some vegetables and herbs. Still, they won't be as productive due to the lack of proper light conditions.

Container Gardening on the Driveway

Your driveway may not be the first place you think of to plant a veggie garden, but you would be surprised how well they can work. Most driveway areas tend to get lots of direct sun during the day, making excellent places for containers. Some things to keep in mind if you are going to plant a garden in your driveway: don't grow too close to the street because pollution from passing cars will impact the health of your plants. You should also pay attention to how close you put containers to the driveway if you park your car there. Nothing is more frustrating than realizing you didn't leave enough room to get your car door open once the plants have grown larger. Your driveway can be an excellent location because you will frequently pass by your plants. This makes it easy to remember that they need water or it's time to pick some vegetables. By planting near your driveway, you'll get to enjoy your garden, and it will be easy to care for.

Concrete and asphalt driveways tend to absorb and radiate heat. Larger containers can help to dissipate the heat and make your driveway more comfortable for your plants. You should be careful using smaller containers because they can dry out quickly when the soil temperature is too high. Summer heat on a driveway can cook the roots of plants, so consider using pallets, bricks, or wooden blocks under your containers to reduce heat absorption and enhance drainage. Heavier-duty container boxes made of wood or terra cotta can help reduce soil temperatures.

Container Gardening in a Window Box

A window box is a great solution that lets you have fresh herbs and vegetables when you have no room to work with. Traditional window boxes were wood, but today, you'll find premade boxes in plastic that hold water well and are lightweight, making installation easy.

You'll want to mount your window box at least a few inches below the level of the window. This lets you harvest easier, prevents the plants from blocking your view, and makes it easy to operate the windows. It is essential to locate window boxes low enough on outward-opening windows so that you can use the window.

The biggest obstacle you face when gardening in a window box is the small quantity of soil. These planters will dry out quicker than other containers, so you need to keep a watering schedule. The same sunlight rules apply with window box planters - south is best, east and west are good, north is challenging.

Window boxes work well with many vegetable and herb varieties that don't have deep-running roots. They are a particularly excellent addition to kitchen windows, where a ready-to-use supply of popular herbs is a culinary godsend. Picking the suitable types of herbs and vegetables is essential because some simply need more space for roots and grow too tall to be practical in a window box. Some of the best options include herbs like dill, chives, parsley, and vegetables like radishes, turnips, carrots, and cherry tomatoes.

Container Gardening in the Backyard

There are many excellent reasons you may choose containers over in-ground planting in your yard. Container planting allows you to grow organically, which your yard may not be. We'll get into this topic in-depth later. Because you're able to select the type and quality of the soil in your container garden, you set your plants up for the highest chance of success.

One significant advantage of container planting in your backyard is the ability to prevent pests. Containers are a great way to foil burrowing pests like voles and moles. A container can reduce the chance of certain insects getting into your plants. Using the right kind of soil will ensure that you don't have nematodes, bacteria, or fungus that cause diseases.

You'll want to find the best place with full sun to set your containers. Put the containers so most plants will face the south when you can. This gives you the best chance of success growing vegetables in containers. Taller containers reduce stooping and bending when tending or harvesting your garden, but keep in mind that most vegetables don't have deep roots. Too much soil can be a bad thing in containers because the soil can hold too much water, preventing good drainage.

Pick a location in your yard that is attractive and convenient to access. You'll want to spend time in your garden, so locate it in a spot that is ideal for your plants and for your family. Try to avoid places where your kids play ball, for example, because inevitably, a ball will get knocked into the garden and cause damage. Trust me, I know!

Remember, when designing a container garden in your backyard, you need to put plants with different growing conditions in different areas. Some plants grow well together, while others don't. When you lay out what you will be planting, you should make sure the types of plants have similar care requirements and don't have the same pest problems. Suppose you plan on harvesting seeds to plant next season. In that case, you should consider preventing cross-pollination by growing similar species in different locations.

Container Growing with Grow Lights

You can have a container vegetable garden even if you live in a basement with no windows. The trick is to use lighting intended explicitly for growing plants indoors. You'll use a cool color spectrum light bulb that produces light in the 6500 K color spectrum for vegetative growth. You'll switch to a warm spectrum bulb producing light in the 2700 K color spectrum for flowering. You don't need to buy high-dollar lights, either. Compact Fluorescent Bulbs (CFLs) are affordable and practical for growing herbs, vegetables, and fruit indoors.

There are numerous kits available online, allowing you to quickly and easily start an indoor container garden using artificial lighting. You can also design and build a system to suit your needs. Some types of vegetables will grow in soilless hydroponic systems under 100 percent artificial light and produce copious amounts of vegetables.

An indoor growing space doesn't have to be large. Smaller plants like herbs are ideal for indoor growing. At the same time, slightly larger areas can be used for growing carrots, tomatoes, and other plants. You can use artificial lighting with wall containers and hanging baskets to maximize space in the smallest areas.

Achieving Peace

Most importantly, gardening should be a relaxing experience for you. One key thing I hope you get from this chapter is that gardening is about more than just growing plants. It's also an opportunity for you to slow down from your hectic life and spend time relaxing and nurturing your garden. Picking the right spot is as much about finding a spot for your garden as it is about finding the right place for you to spend time in nature. You'll start the entire process out on the right step if you take the time to find a location where you want to spend time.

Chapter 2

GROW WHAT YOU LOVE TO EAT!

There are no gardening mistakes, only experiments. - Janet Kilburn Phillips

Driveway container garden

Picking out what I'm going to grow each season is one of my very favorite things to do. Even after all my years of gardening, I'm still like a little kid in a candy store as soon as the packages of seeds and trays of young plants show up all over town. There are a few staple plants I grow every year. I always try to introduce something new just to mix it up, too. There are numerous benefits to growing your own food. One of the best is that you can select specific varieties you'll never see in the grocery store.

Have you ever noticed there are only a few types of tomatoes in the vegetable section of the grocery store? Would you believe that there are more than

10,000 varieties of tomatoes in existence? That's a lot of different types of tomatoes you can grow, and it'll take forever to try them all. You may even find that your kids who hate vegetables get as excited about trying new types of veggies as I get when I'm picking out the plants to grow this year. Nothing beats the flavor of fresh produce you pick from your own garden except the thrill of trying something brand-new that you raised. For instance, one year, I even grew cotton in a container. I was amazed that I could grow that in New England and that I was able to harvest organic cotton balls!

Selecting what to grow in your garden takes some considerations. Growing what you love begins with planting what you're able to grow. There are a few practical limitations you should consider before picking out plants. You can usually get an idea of what plants to grow simply by considering the location of your garden. Using the light and temperature characteristics as a guide, you'll have lots of options available to grow foods you and your family will love. Some plants will require full, direct sunlight for most of the day, while others will tolerate some shade.

Once you know what kinds of plants you can grow in your area, you also need to consider the size of an available container. Some of the things we love to eat are simply impractical in a pot or container. I love sweet white corn when it's in season, but the surface roots of corn stalks don't do well in boxes. It's one of the crops you should grow in the ground. Don't lament not growing corn. There are so many more fascinating options open to any gardener willing to put in the love, care, and effort to produce a bountiful garden. But still, if you want to try growing corn, go for it! There are plenty of videos on YouTube showing successful methods to grow certain types of corn in certain types of containers.

Choosing Organic vs. Non-Organic

Organic produce has made a splash in consumer consciousness in recent years. It's considered more sustainable, healthier, and better for the world. Understanding what organic truly means will help you decide if it is worth the extra effort to provide organic produce to your family.

The definition of "organic" the United States Department of Agriculture (USDA) uses to certify produce states that to qualify, produce must be grown in soil not treated with synthetic insecticides, pesticides, or fertilizers for three years. Only certain synthetic substances may be applied during the growing season, which is considered essential and non-harmful by USDA.

Some of the allowed manufactured products make sense. For instance, a newspaper is a non-organic substance that is permitted because it decomposes quickly and provides little to no possibility of harm. In fact, newspapers make an excellent addition to compost. Just don't include glossy ads which are not organic and not allowed. Other synthetic substances must be used in specific ways, like chlorine for cleaning irrigation lines that must meet the standards of the Clean Drinking Water Act. Then there are manufactured chemicals like boric acid, which are helpful for pest control. It is allowed in an organic field provided it isn't used on the plants. Some farmers even use synthetic pheromones sprayed on crops in the field to deter insects, all within the regulations that allow organic produce.

Growing your own vegetables organically gives you the opportunity to know what goes in, so you have confidence that your produce is genuinely organic when you harvest. Organic gardening takes a little extra effort to properly select soil and seeds and pest and weed control. The extra bit of care your organic garden will take will reward you with the best tasting fresh vegetables you can imagine. Plus, you can eat them right off the vine because they aren't tainted with poisons!

Organic Gardening and the Environment

There are a couple reasons we should all be gardening organically. Some of the biggest ones are environmental. We know that certain insecticides, fertilizers, and weed killers can contaminate groundwater and cause a wide variety of potential health issues. We also tend to think of the industrial mega-farms as the culprit of the problem, but we all play a role in the future. Reducing and eliminating the manufacture and widespread use of these control agents begins with the small-scale home farmer who chooses to grow organically.

The widespread use of chemical pest control products has led to the emergence of resistant weeds, viruses, bacteria, and pests. Think of it like a war where every time the gardener begins using a more potent poison, nearly all problems are eliminated. Those that are not killed may reproduce and pass on the likelihood of pesticide resistance to the next generation.

Switching to a different type of control agent has led to weeds that can resist numerous types of weed killer. Some bugs like the Colorado Potato Beetle and the Diamondback Moth have extensive populations and have documented resistance to all known pesticides. The problem of resistant pests is a global problem, and it's something that we must begin to combat in our gardens at home.

The Zen of Organic Gardening

You've heard that organic gardening is more challenging than non-organic, and you probably have a good idea why. The main reason is that instead of spraying your plants and the soil, you may need to manually weed your garden, spend time picking bugs from your plants, and pay close attention to spots on leaves and mushy stems to halt infections and disease. You may even find it necessary, yet rewarding, to hand-pollinate certain crops like cucumbers and tomatoes if natural pollinators are few and far between.

Here's the thing I like the most about organic gardening. It takes time, and that is time I spend touching my plants, feeling the soil, and making sure they are healthy. It's a beautiful, relaxing experience. The extra effort I spend working in my organic garden ends up being one of my favorite parts of the day. I find that it's a great way to let go of stress, take deep breaths and enjoy the odors of the garden, and just relax. There is something soothing and healing about gardening. Knowing that the products I'm using are free of potentially harmful chemicals puts me at ease serving my friends and family. I like to think that I'm doing my small part to preserve the world we live in for today and future generations by gardening organically.

How to Decide What to Grow

The first time you get ready to pick out the types of vegetables, herbs, and other plants you want to grow, it's easy to go overboard. Some plants seem like a good idea until you plant ten eggplants, only to find out that everyone in your family only said they like it because they know you do and don't want to hurt your feelings! Suddenly you have more eggplants than you can give away, and the entire experience isn't satisfying at all.

Take a systematic approach to plan what you'll grow by starting out by looking at what your family likes to eat. Suppose taco Tuesday is a hit three days a week in your house. Some jalapeno peppers, cilantro, tomatoes, and onions are excellent choices. If your kitchen smells best with a roast chicken in the oven, consider potent and flavorful herbs like rosemary, sage, dill, and parsley. One of the best things about a container garden is that even in a home that can only agree that they all like something different, you can provide freshly grown produce to make them happy.

Here's a fun little exercise you should do with your family to get an idea of the types of things you want to grow. Sit down at the table and have everyone think of several of their favorite meals. Write down the answers and compare the ingredients. You may find that some types of produce are in many recipes. Tomatoes are an excellent example of a productive, versatile, and perfect container vegetable. Tomatoes are delicious fresh off the vine, cooked, and are among the best things for canning and preservation.

This exercise is the perfect way to start getting everyone in your family involved and talking about eating healthy. Ensuring that everyone has a say in the decision of what to grow is the best way to keep everyone interested in the process from start to finish. Even your young children will love seeing "their" plant grow up and provide delicious food for everyone. I like to remind them of the story of the Little Red Hen. This keeps everyone involved from start to harvest to mealtime!

The Challenge of the Global Food Supply

Few people today remember a time when the only food available was locally grown and produced. Today, however, we have fruits and vegetables grown all over the world available year-round in grocery stores. One challenge of selecting what to grow involves where you live. There will always be at least a few items that you would love to grow, but it simply isn't practical. In a later chapter, we will discuss the USDA Hardiness Zones in detail, but it's important to know what zone you live in.

You may find that your unique region limits the types of plants you can successfully grow. Some areas have short summers, and you'll need to grow fast-maturing plants to have success. This may mean that your family will need to adjust to different types of vegetables to take advantage of your local climate. Later in this book, I'll discuss some techniques you can use to grow lots of varieties of plants, even in the most challenging climates.

Easy to Grow Vegetables for Organic Containers

Almost any vegetable can be grown in a container, but few superstars do better than average. I like to think of these as categories of plants because there are so many unique varieties of each type.

- **Tomatoes:** Tomatoes are available in a bewildering variety of sizes and colors. Some types of tomato plants can grow quite large. They perform best when given a trellis to climb. Canning tomatoes is a pastime that teaches excellent food preservation skills and ensures you have the best-tasting tomatoes for a perfect marinara sauce even in January.

- **Peppers:** Almost every cuisine the world over uses peppers of one type or another. There are peppers to please anyone from fiery hot, to sweet and mild. These plants are reasonably easy to grow but do best in bright, direct sunlight and warm temperatures. Peppers are excellent fresh and are among the best garden fruits for freezing.

- **Herbs:** Most of your common herbs like oregano, mint, sage, and rosemary are ideal in containers and pots. These plants are excellent candidates for small growing spaces. They'll even do well on a countertop that has bright enough light. You can design an entire herb garden using a handful of small pots and grow enough seasonings to preserve a year's supply every season without taking up a significant amount of space.

- **Potatoes:** This is another fascinating plant that is ideal for container growing. In fact, one excellent budget container for potatoes is a plastic kiddie pool. Potatoes require a very light growing medium to have consistent size and shape, so a large shallow pool is ideal. There are many ways to use fresh potatoes, and they are easy to store and preserve for long periods.

- **Sweet Potato:** Like its more common cousin except around the holidays, sweet potato is an excellent container plant with easy care instructions when the right conditions are met. Sweet potato is a nutrient-packed food that is excellent canned, fresh, and stores easily in cool, dry areas.

- **Lettuce:** Lettuce belongs to a family of plants that includes most leafy greens, including mustard, spinach, and broccoli. These plants grow best in cooler regions and earlier, or later, in the season. Some greens can even continue to grow after repeated frosts. If your family is a fan of those bagged salads, you can grow several varieties of lettuce in shallow containers. Choose leaf-type lettuce to eat a little at a time or heading lettuce to eat the whole thing at once.

- **Cucumbers:** Cucumbers are a delightful container plant and are actually better in a planter than in the ground. A tiny cucumber plant can quickly turn into a massive vine with a seemingly endless supply of tasty fruits. Some varieties grow well in hot climates and cooler regions with short seasons. You'll definitely want to grow these if your kids love pickles!

- **Carrots:** You would never think it by looking at the humble orange carrot in the grocery store, but there is an entire world of great root vegetables out there. The type we see in stores is famous for its color, shape, and consistency. Carrots come in purple, red, white, and yellow, and even mixes of the two. Like potatoes, carrots need lightweight soil that's obstacle-free to grow correctly, making them ideal for planter boxes.

Great Choices for Flower Boxes and Small Spaces

- **Lettuce:** Many lettuce varieties are good candidates for window boxes because they stay small and are easily harvested.

- **Spinach:** Bunches of spinach not only look beautiful growing in window boxes, but they provide an easy-to-grab nutrient boost.

- **Radish:** Radishes grow stumpy, round roots and don't require much space. You can grow a fantastic bunch even in a tiny box. Refer to the bonus section at the end of this book.

- **Carrots:** Several carrots grow short, bulbous edible roots that are perfect for small boxes.

- **Chives:** Chives are a small onion that needs virtually no soil to grow well. Bright green bunches of tubular stems look great in boxes, and they produce lovely purple flowers in the spring. You can even plant the bulbs of your store-bought scallions to have a continuous supply!

- **Bush Beans:** Bush beans make a good choice because they don't require much soil to grow, and they don't tend to vine into monsters, either.

- Herbs: Window boxes are perfect for parsley, dill, oregano, thyme, sage, basil, and many other herbs. The aromatic quality of the herbs creates the most delicious aroma near the window box.

- **Lavender:** Lavender is both an edible plant and a popular dried flower. It will grow well in smaller boxes. There are several varieties of lavender that each has unique fragrances and culinary uses.

Buying Seedlings or Starting Seeds

This one is a serious dilemma sometimes. Seedlings are often easier and more reliable to start but offer limited variety and higher per-plant cost. Seeds are often inexpensive but can require a great deal of additional care to get good results. There are numerous ways to get seeds for almost any type of plant you want to grow. The best way to experiment with new varieties is by sprouting seeds.

Purchasing enough seedlings to fill your garden can get expensive. A single four-inch pot can cost between $2 and more than $6. You're going to want to grow more than one plant of each variety that you plant, so you'll buy several tiny seedlings at a time. The initial cost of seedlings is high, but the ease and convenience factor make up for it. Because the plants are already growing, you just transplant them into your containers and water. First-time gardeners are encouraged to start with seedlings because they will have more success.

Seeds offer more variety but are more work. You may pay anywhere from a few cents per package of seeds to upwards of $10. Each packet of seeds typically contains more than the average person will grow, so only start a few more than you think you want rather than the whole package.

Seed Starting Tips

There are some plants that you can just toss seeds on the ground and sprinkle with water, and they will grow. Others require intervention on your part to have much chance of success. Over the many years I've been gardening, I've learned many things about starting seeds, often the hard way. I've had more than one batch of seeds simply refuse to grow, so I've learned to do a few things to improve my success at starting seeds.

Most seeds you buy will be dry in the package. For the seed to start growing, it needs to rehydrate. Some seeds rehydrate better than others. A technique I learned is called "scarification." This sounds like a horrible thing to do to a beloved seed. Still, it helps them sprout, mainly plants with hard, shiny shells. To scarify, you can use a nail file or a sharp knife and just nick the edge of the surface. All that is needed is to remove the outer layer. You don't need to penetrate the shell. The trick is to avoid damaging the kernel inside. Scarifying allows water to rehydrate stubborn seeds and is particularly effective with plants in the nightshade family, beans, and fruit seeds more quickly.

Many types of plants also require a process called "stratification," which simply means they need a temperature change to begin sprouting. Stratification can be done at home by placing seeds in the freezer for as little as a day or two or as long as several months, depending on the variety. This is an excellent way to stimulate seeds by encouraging natural behavior by providing winter-like conditions that transition to a warmer spring-like environment.

One of the best ways gardeners who live in areas with challengingly short growing seasons can get a jump on the game is through pre-starting seeds. This can be done with any seed and is a great way to start seeds that are scarified or stratified. I like to use regular, unbleached coffee filters. They're inexpensive when bought in bulk, free of dyes and chemicals, and retain moisture very well. The other advantage to using coffee filters is they are easy to fold, making it easy to stay organized.

When I start seeds, I place my seeds on one end of a moistened filter, folding the sides in slightly before folding the other half over. This makes an envelope that keeps the seeds in place and makes it easy to move them around. It's a good idea to label the coffee filters as you go because it's unbelievably easy to forget which seeds are what plant once they sprout. Place the filters on a waterproof tray. Cover the seeds and check at least once a day to ensure the filters stay moist. You can speed up germination rates using a heating pad beneath your seed tray. Warmer ground temperatures signal seeds to sprout.

I transplant my sprouted seeds into a seed starter pod when the roots are at least a half-inch long. If you want to get a significant jump on the season, you can use inexpensive indoor lighting and seed starting trays with warming mats to start your plants. More mature plants will handle a move outside and are more likely to survive sudden, unexpected weather changes.

Direct-Sow Seed Starting

Some seeds are not practical to start indoors and transplant. Tiny seeds, typical of lettuce plants, are too small to start indoors. Some tiny seeds also have delicate roots that won't survive a transplant. You will have more success with these types of plants, directly sowing the seeds in your garden. When you direct-sow, you will need to ensure the soil mixture is ideal for the plant, the soil is at the correct temperature, and the danger of frost has passed.

GMO- What it Means for Your Home Garden

GMOs - or Genetically Modified Organisms - are something you probably hear about and maybe even have strong opinions about. In a nutshell, GMO refers to a seed that has been subjected to gene editing to enhance or restrict certain aspects of the growing plant. The vast majority of GMO crops in the US are engineered to resist chemical weed killers and pesticides. Only a few major GMO crops are approved for use as food for people. The overwhelming majority of GMO products are used for feed for livestock or as ingredients in manufactured products.

GMO plants must be approved by the USDA and the Food and Drug Administration (FDA) to be legally sold to consumers. In the US, maize (corn), soybeans, cotton, papaya, canola, and alfalfa are the most common GMO products. Other countries produce GMO apples, safflower, potatoes, eggplant, pineapples, and sugar cane.

Most people believe that GMO crops produce a more marketable end-product, like larger produce, sweeter flavor, and unnatural growth habits. This is somewhat true but doesn't capture the whole story. For example, a virus that affects papaya plants nearly wiped out the entire production of these tropical fruits. The introduction of GMO papaya, known today as rainbow papaya, eliminated the ability of the virus to kill papaya and ultimately eradicated the problem. Without GMOs, there would be no papaya today.

The Difference Between GMO and Selective Breeding

One of my favorite pastimes is wild-harvesting various crops that grow in my region. One of those wild vegetables I love to find is carrots. It is often surprising to people who aren't familiar with the history of the carrot to see those wild ones are never orange. Wild carrots are usually purple or white and have a flavor more similar to parsnips than commercial carrots. Humans began selectively breeding the root vegetable thousands of years ago to get orange carrots, ultimately creating the orange, tapered, sweet-flavored carrot we see today.

The primary difference between GMO and selective breeding is that selective breeding only involves traits the plant already possesses. Gene editing unnaturally adds or removes DNA to force plants to respond in a particular way. Most scientists claim there is little to no risk of adverse health or ill effects from eating GMO produce. However, consumer concern about food safety has led most companies to avoid using GMO products without labeling their use.

I get the most questions about GMOs. If they are considered safe to eat, why should I avoid planting produce that resists insects, disease, and weed killers? The primary reason comes down to the ecological impact. Eventually, the very problems that GMO plants avoid will mutate and become even more difficult to stop in the future. Here is the good news: unless you're growing very specific plants from seed, you're not likely to find GMO seeds on the market. Generally, GMO seeds are only used for producing animal feed or products that are used to make cooking oils, like cotton and canola. You can always check with the company that packages your seeds for detailed information about their origin.

Open-Pollinated, Heirloom, and Hybrid

More of a concern to the home gardener than GMO plants is selecting between open-pollinating, heirloom, or hybrid varieties. Open-pollinating plants reproduce when pollen is carried from one flower to another. Open-pollinating plants can breed with other, similar plants, creating hybrids. Some of our favorite produce in the US are hybrids, including most lettuces which originated from wild mustard. Hybrid plants won't produce reliable seeds, so they are best when you plan to replant with fresh seed the following season. Heirloom varieties of seeds are all open-pollinating types, but not all open-pollinating plants are heirloom varieties. Suppose you want to keep seeds for next year. In that case, you should grow heirloom varieties and prevent cross-pollination with similar species.

Where to Get Information About Your Seeds or Seedlings

No matter where you get your seeds or young plants, you should get information about the specific needs from the plant tag or seed package. Usually, you'll find information about how to plant, including essential things like spacing, root depth, light and water requirements, and the number of days until harvest. You should always save the plant tag or seed package. Something I like to do with my container garden is to place empty seed packages or plant tags in a sealable zipper-type bag and staple it to the box. This keeps the relevant information right at hand and prevents forgetting which variety is growing in the box.

Having Fun Picking Plants

The entire process of selecting what to grow this season seems pretty complicated. It can get overwhelming if you don't take it in steps. The biggest thing is finding the plants you want to eat that also grow well where you are gardening. I always find that the selection process is more fun when everyone gets involved. When the entire family has a say in what's grown in the garden, it encourages participation. Teaching our children to garden only works when it's fun, so you should always take opportunities to get the young ones involved.

So many choices!

Phew. I know that was a lot of information to digest but deciding what to grow involves more than just a quick trip to Walmart if you want to be a successful gardener. So, make your lists, schedule a family meeting, and consult your kids or friends. Do some research online and on YouTube and maybe join a Container Gardening Group on Facebook. Your fellow gardeners will be a wealth of knowledge and happy to share what they've learned with you! As am I. With the information you've learned in this chapter, you'll be armed with my knowledge gleaned over 60 years of gardening. You'll be amazed at what you will achieve. The bottom line, grow what you love, and you'll love what you grow!

Chapter 3

CHOOSING YOUR POTS & CONTAINERS

Gardening adds years to your life and life to your years. - Unknown

Now that you know how to pick the right location to grow what you want to grow, it's time to select the perfect container. This is one of the most fun steps of planting a garden because you can express your creativity while providing the ideal home for herbs, vegetables, and other plants. While almost anything can be used for growing plants, selecting the perfect pot will ensure your plants have plenty of room to develop large, robust root systems. This will help you avoid some of the more common problems that happen when growing in pots and containers.

I knew someone living the RV lifestyle many years ago - traveling around the country in a converted van. The van was almost totally self-contained - it even had a tiny kitchen and a dining table that converted into a full-size bed. But, living in a van also means you don't have fresh produce readily available. Using old coffee cans and a little ingenuity, this person grew an entire vegetable garden in her van without losing any valuable space.

The whole system was super-compact, but she grew tomatoes, basil, chives, peppers, and several types of root vegetables while on the road. Not only did this little setup provide an excellent source of fresh produce, but it also created an opportunity to barter and share with other road-weary travelers helping to bring everybody together.

Choosing the Right Container

You'll need to consider the main things before planting in a container: size, durability, and drainage. Some pots drain better than others, and many pots out there are decorative rather than functional. When you grow smaller plants like most herbs, you simply won't need the real estate that a larger pot or container will provide. But, some types of vegetables won't do well in a small pot, quickly becoming root-bound which leads to many serious problems. You may even need to start a plant in a smaller container in many cases, then transplant it to something bigger when the plant begins to mature. You'll also want to make sure that the container you choose will stand up to the rigor of an entire season of growing. Some materials simply don't handle exposure to sun and water for long periods, so you'll need to be prepared to repot your garden if the containers you choose can't take the abuse or end up being too small.

The first things that I'm going to discuss in this chapter are the pros and cons of various types of popular containers to help you make the ideal selection for the garden of your dreams. Remember, this is a great time to be creative, but the ultimate goal is to create an environment ideal for growing herbs, vegetables, and other plants.

Choosing the Right Size

Every plant will have specific requirements for how much space it requires when fully grown. It's surprisingly easy to underestimate the size a plant may get. Like many lettuce varieties, some plants need quite a bit of space for roots. The first time I grew bok choy, for example, the roots grew so large they nearly split my container wide open. Other vegetables, like onions and turnips, have tiny roots, and the plants can grow pretty close together.

When you're picking out your plants, you'll see a planting guide that will specify the spacing between plants. You should use this as a guideline for picking the right size container. Herbs that require only six inches of space between plants or less can fit in small pots and containers. You may even have enough room to grow three or four herbs in a small pot. But, if the plant you are growing calls for spacing of ten inches or more, you'll need to plan on providing spacious containers.

Surface area isn't the only consideration, either. Many plants require depth as well. You should aim for a minimum of eight inches of depth in your container for smaller plants and even more room for plants that grow large roots. Avoid getting too deep of a pot, though. Deep containers hold more dirt - leading to a more considerable expense - and often cause more harm to your shallow-rooting vegetables. Larger pots tend to accumulate more water and drain slowly, which is a perfect recipe for fungal and bacterial infections.

Durability Issues

You're likely planning on building your container garden outdoors, so you need to factor in the amount of damage your container can take before it fails. Many new gardeners overlook the effects of sun and regular watering on containers. Regardless of the material, UV rays and frequent exposure to moisture eventually will destroy even the most durable container.

Sunlight causes damage through UV-light exposure. UV is the same spectrum that gives you a sunburn, and it can have adverse effects on your containers. UV causes materials to lose moisture and oils, drying and bleaching in the process. While there are steps you can take to reduce the damage done by UV rays, sooner or later, everything will succumb to the power of the sun. Mother Nature always wins in the end.

Water can cause problems with your containers in numerous ways. Many types of material absorb water, which can cause structural issues. An example is unglazed clay pots which can shatter in cold weather and wooden containers that will eventually rot from moisture. In the next section, we'll discuss the many types of pots and containers you might use and explain the durability of each type. For now, you should simply keep in mind that no matter what kind of container you plan on using, after a few growing seasons, you'll need to replace it.

A good thing to keep in mind when selecting the material for your containers is the amount of abuse it will take from kids playing in the yard, landscaping, and general abuse. If your containers are in locations where it's likely a ball will get kicked their way, choosing a durable, sturdy container is advantageous - no matter what material you choose to use for your container planting. Just make sure that it will be sturdy and robust enough to take whatever your garden can dish out.

Drainage for Containers

This is a topic we'll be talking a lot about going forward. Proper drainage is absolutely essential to growing healthy, happy plants. Too much drainage can prevent some plants from having enough water, while not enough can cause root rot. Finding the balance between too much and too little can be complex.

The first thing to consider is what type of plants you're growing. Some plants prefer to have more moist soil without drying out in between. Other plants must have dry periods to produce flowers or grow well. In the next chapter, I'll discuss potting soil mixtures, but for now, you should consider that any container must have good drainage.

Not all pots and containers you want to use have adequate drainage for growing plants, including many commercially available solutions. At a minimum, small and medium-size containers should have a half-inch drainage hole. Larger pots will require more significant drainage. It is usually better to select a container with multiple, smaller drain holes over a single, large drain hole.

When you're looking at drainage, you should keep in mind that larger holes will also result in more soil loss. You can often use a screen or wire to prevent soil from draining out of the holes, but you may also restrict drainage. Some materials are more accessible to add drainage than others. Fired ceramic pots may be impossible to add drainage without breaking them, but wood and plastic containers are much more straightforward.

Myths about Drainage

It used to be standard to add gravel, rocks, broken pots, and other objects to a planter to increase drainage. Over the years, gardeners learned that following this flawed advice actually hurt their garden. The reason this doesn't work is because of soil compaction. Over time, the gaps and spaces created by oddly shaped additions to the pot provide perfect places for soil to fill. Eventually, the soil will become compacted in the pot, preventing drainage and creating a barrier for healthy roots growth.

Shallow watering is not a workaround for lack of drainage. Most plants won't grow well when you don't water deeply, so it isn't a good idea to simply underwater in the hope your non-draining pot will work out. Instead, transplant into something else that drains or come up with a way to create drainage holes.

Wood Containers

Wood is an excellent material for container planting because it's a simple material to customize and can give you as much or as little space as your garden needs. But, before you break out the saw, you should consider a few things first. Not all wood is created equal. Some types are better than others, and a few types of wood should be avoided altogether. Wood containers can be among the cheapest but most labor-intensive options, or they can end up being much more expensive than some of the other types of containers.

Pre-Manufactured Wooden Containers

These days, getting wooden containers is easier than ever because most prominent home and garden companies sell pre-cut kits you simply assemble at home. These are by far the most expensive options for using wood. However, you end up with a lovely container that is durable and will provide years of use with little maintenance.

Premade wood containers are an ideal choice for designing an aesthetically appealing space. Beyond the initial expense of purchasing a kit, you also need to consider the final size of the container. Wooden containers tend to be substantially larger than other options, meaning you'll need to purchase more potting soil, which can get pricey in a hurry. You'll also need to make sure that the container has good drainage. Many pre-manufactured designs appear to be oriented toward curb appeal rather than functionality, and it's pretty common to need to drill extra drainage holes in wooden containers.

DIY Wooden Containers

Making your own planter boxes from wood is more economical than purchasing pre-cut designs. Of course, it means you'll need a saw and a tape measure, but you can build boxes that are just the right size, depth, and proper drainage for precisely what you are planning.

You can undoubtedly purchase lumber from your local home & garden store and make your own boxes, but there are lots of sources of low-cost or even free lumber ideal for building container boxes. You can consider using old fence pickets when you or your neighbor replace a fence. These weather-beaten boards often make excellent boxes. Another source of lumber for container building is used pallets. Usually, you can ask a local shipping company in your area if they have broken pallets. You might get all the wood you need for free just by asking.

Fruit boxes, construction scraps, and wine barrels are fantastic sources of low-cost or free supplies for building containers. I have even seen planter boxes made from thick branches. Each branch was pressed close to the one next to it and pounded into the ground to hold it in place. A little twine tied the tops together to prevent movement, and the open box was simply filled with soil.

The Downsides of Wooden Containers

For all the upsides to using wood for your containers, there are a few downsides. Wood will absorb moisture and get damaged by UV rays faster than many other materials. Treating wood to prevent damage presents some problems since you don't want your plants absorbing harmful chemicals. Ultimately, wooden containers will rot and fall apart.

Getting the appropriate drainage from a wooden container can also be a bit of a challenge. Most manufactured pots and containers have holes in the bottom to allow moisture to exit. When you are using a wooden container, you may have to devise better drainage solutions since they typically rest on the ground. One of the most effective ways to increase drainage in a wooden container is to drill half-inch holes every ten inches no more than a few inches from the ground. You want holes in all sides of the container to ensure proper drainage, but not so large as to make it challenging to provide enough water. There are some sophisticated ways to build complex wooden boxes that incorporate watering and drainage but building those is substantially more challenging.

Bugs and other pests are more likely to set up shop in the cracks and crevices of your planter boxes when they are made of wood. You'll want to pay close attention to signs of infestations, mainly if you are growing organically, since your plants may be less well defended against hungry bugs.

When you build a wooden planter box, most likely, the container will be stationary. This is important to remember when you live in an area that sees drastic temperature changes between the seasons. Other types of containers may be easier to move indoors, while your wooden planters will work great as long as the weather cooperates.

What to Avoid

One of the best things about building out of wood is that you can access lots of inexpensive materials. Unfortunately, some of the wood you may have free access to isn't a good choice for gardening. You should avoid using any painted or treated wood for building vegetable containers. Many of the harmful chemicals in paint and other products are safe when exposed to air but can break down in the damp, dark confines of your planter box. These chemicals leach into the soil and are absorbed by the roots of your plants. Avoiding these materials is essential for your health and the health of anyone who eats your produce. This especially applies to pressure-treated lumber.

Plastic Pots

The most economical option for most gardeners is plastic pots that come in a broad range of sizes and designs. You'll find attractive designs that look more expensive materials, but you can just as easily opt for black plastic grow buckets. Even though this may be a cheap solution, plastic presents some unique challenges you'll want to consider before choosing this type of container.

A critical factor in choosing plastic is long-term durability. Plastic pots resist impacts, UV rays, and exposure to water better than almost any material. In the right conditions, you'll get many growing seasons out of a plastic pot before it begins to degrade from normal gardening conditions. The durability of plastic makes it one of the most popular choices for home gardeners looking to start growing in containers.

You'll find plastic containers in every conceivable size, shape, color, and style. This makes them ideal for numerous applications. Have a tiki-inspired patio? You'll find plastic pots emblazoned with Polynesian figures, palm trees, and everything you love about the tropics. Are you going for a more rugged, durable look?

Peppers in pots

Plastic pots that look like they are made from stone, metal, and wood are standard and help dress up spaces with lots of concrete. Not only do you find broad designs, but you'll also find unique shapes and sizes in plastic growing containers.

Plastic containers are lightweight, making for ideal choices when you know you'll be moving plants from one area to another or when you need to lift and lower a plant to water, transplant, or harvest. This makes plastic a good choice for hanging baskets, windowsill planters, and boxes you'll move as the seasons change.

Decorative Plastic Planters

The fancier your plastic pot, the more expensive, and some of the nicest-looking containers are pretty pricey. These also look nice, making them one of the most popular choices for gardeners today. You should pay attention to ensure the nice-looking planter you want provides enough drainage. Many decorative plastic pots simply don't have sufficient drainage and are designed to work as a catch-pot rather than a planter.

Avoid using plastic containers that are painted since many of the chemicals in paint can leach into the soil and contaminate your garden. Most of the plastics that manufacturers commonly use today are safe for gardening, but you should still keep an eye out for warning labels indicating that planting in the container is not safe.

Non-Decorative Plastic Containers

We're all familiar with the black plastic tubs that nursery centers sell larger plants in. These are ideal for container gardening. A medium to large black plastic grow pot provides excellent drainage, high UV resistance, and won't leach chemicals. They're also often available for very little money, making plastic one of the better options for budget containers.

These tubs are also quite durable and are easy to move around, even when a large plant is growing in one. When not in use, they often stack inside one another for easy storage. You'll find plastic growing containers in lots of standard sizes. Still, most will be deeper than they are wide and made from HDPE- High-Density Polyethylene- black plastic, a recyclable material that resists deterioration. The little plastic trays your seedlings come in are made from HIPS- high-impact styrene- which will likely degrade quickly and typically isn't recycled.

Other plastic growing containers you can use will take a bit of resourcefulness. For example, a five-gallon bucket will work well for growing larger vegetable plants like peppers and tomatoes, but you need to pay attention to what was in the bucket in the first place. Look for food-grade buckets over buckets you might find at a construction site.

A popular way to grow shallow-rooting tubers like potatoes and yams is using a kiddie pool. These are often available for $5 to $10 and will last at least one season, if not two. The shallowness means you can get the right amount of soil depth for many types of plants without wasting space on a deep planter.

Another option for plastic container growing that is relatively inexpensive is 55-gallon blue water drums. These drums are often available for less than $15 each in used condition, and you can cut them in half to make two large planters. While they do take up some room and require a little work to make them usable, this is a great way to grow in containers on the cheap. I've used everything from plastic storage containers to laundry baskets with great results!

Disadvantages of Growing in Plastic

There are a few things that present problems when growing in plastic. This type of container tends to hold water longer than other types, increasing the likelihood you will overwater your garden. It's crucial to ensure good drainage with a plastic pot or container, mainly if you're using decorative planters or items not initially intended for growing plants, like five-gallon buckets.

Plastic can heat up quicker and retain heat longer than many types of materials, so it's essential to pay attention to temperatures. Plant roots can overheat and die pretty quickly in plastic that gets too hot. Some options to consider are wrapping your pot in a heat-reflecting or absorbing material to reduce temperatures or relocating plants to cooler areas when possible.

Grow Bags

Like plastic pots, grow bags are affordable, easy to use, and simple to store, but not very attractive. You'll find plastic grow bags in a wide range of sizes. They typically are made from a material often called "panda film." This is a high-quality, durable plastic that is white on one side and black on the other. This is an ideal combination of blocking heat and containing warmth for growing.

You can use grow bags in lots of situations. They work particularly well for seedlings you will transplant into larger pots. Most grow bags are rectangular, making it easy to get many plants into a relatively small area.

When not in use, just roll them up and put them away. There isn't any type of container easier to use than a plastic grow bag.

Grow bags are effortless to transport since you can just grab a corner and pick them up. On their own, they have nearly no weight, making them a great choice when you are placing plants on shelves with limited holding capacity.

Disadvantages to Grow Bags

A couple things you should consider - these bags are easily knocked over and spilled. They will not work well if you have a lively growing area since damage to the plants is likely if the grow bag falls. Clustering the bags together or placing them in a box can add stability. The biggest downside is that the grow bag is one of the least attractive options. The plain white exterior and obvious plastic-bagginess of these products don't add visual appeal to the garden. You may want to place them inside a box or container to hide the plastic bag look.

Sustainability and Plastic

I will readily admit that I frequently use plastic pots and grow bags for various aspects of container gardening. Still, I think I would be missing valuable information if I don't mention the danger of continued production of plastic. About 90% of the plastic made every day is from virgin fossil fuels, not recycled plastics. In fact, plastics are one of the more expensive and challenging products to recycle. When you're buying or using plastic pots and containers, try to remember that the finished product in your hands is one of the leading causes of air, ground, and water pollution globally. Try to find every opportunity to continue using plastic as long as possible and recycle it when you can't get any more use to prevent more waste ending up in landfills and the oceans.

Terra Cotta Pots

Terra cotta is a classic and one of the best options for most gardeners. Terra cotta is a type of clay that is not glazed. The porous structure of the pot absorbs moisture well and is very affordable, even when you need a huge pot. The reddish-orange color of terra cotta pots creates a beautiful environment that is visually appealing and relatively easy to care for.

Most terra cotta pots have good enough drainage but don't take it for granted because it's more challenging to add drainage to terra cotta than almost any other material. Large terra cotta pots often have only one drainage hole, which might not be adequate for your garden. Smaller pots usually drain very well.

Terra cotta pots are heavier than plastic, not as durable as wood, and may provide fewer attractive options depending on the gardening market where you live. With that said, a cared-for terra cotta pot will last indefinitely. It is one of the most impervious materials to UV light and will tolerate exposure to moisture better than almost any other potting material.

If you live in an area with high daytime temperatures during your growing season, terra cotta makes a great option. The porous structure of the pot helps to insulate the soil, keeping root temperatures substantially lower than plastic pots. Terra cotta makes an excellent choice for driveway or patio planting when you are concerned about climbing soil temps in the summer.

Terra cotta might also be a great choice for your garden if you plan on using plant stands. Most terra cotta pots are available in standard sizes, so finding a way to display your garden is substantially easier than with other types of materials.

Disadvantages of Terra Cotta

You'll need to consider two significant factors before selecting terra cotta pots. The most important is that these pots are porous, which means water is rapidly absorbed by the pot. This tendency can make it more challenging to keep your potting soil from drying out too quickly. You'll want to get used to how fast the soil dries depending on the weather when using terra cotta.

Terra cotta is also a relatively fragile material that will shatter if it's hit. This makes terra cotta a poor choice if your kids play ball in the yard. Once a terra cotta pot begins to crack, it's only a matter of time before the container fails. If there is a likelihood your plants will get knocked down, terra cotta is a poor choice for container gardening.

On its own, terra cotta is heavy material. Once you add soil, water, and plants, you won't want to move these delicate pots around. If you live in an area where seasonal temperatures require you to move plants indoors or under shade cover, you'll probably have better luck planting in plastic rather than terra cotta pots. These pots also tend to crack in freezing temperatures, making them a less suitable choice for winter gardening in cold areas.

Fired Ceramic Pots

Fired ceramic pots start out similar to terra cotta, then have a glaze applied to the surface. The glaze is most often on the outside only. You will need to treat these pots the same as you would terra cotta. The primary differences are that ceramic is more expensive and maybe less absorbent than terra cotta.

One great thing about using fired ceramic pots is that you can find some stunning, colorful designs to add depth and interest to your garden. It's common for these pots to be hand-made, giving each one a unique individuality. Planting in fired ceramic pots is a great way to express your artistic side by grouping different styles together into one cohesive garden of art. You might even consider using various similar-sized ceramic containers indoors.

Many fired ceramic pots are beautiful but not suitable as gardening containers because of a lack of drainage. These pots are supposed to be used as catch-pots to prevent water drainage from staining the floor. Be sure that if you are using a decorative ceramic pot, you find a pot, preferably plastic, that fits inside to properly water your plants.

Reduce-Reuse-Recycle for a Sustainable Garden

So far, I've discussed some of the most common commercially available options for container planting. Still, we've only just touched on the idea of using various materials for planting that were not intended for gardening originally. The only limit to what you can plant a garden in is your imagination, and there is no "wrong" solution.

You should keep your eyes, and your mind open when you go to garage sales, for example. You may find options you never considered before. Some of the things you may find that work well includes vintage tin containers, old milk jugs or mason jars, wooden boxes and crates, and other odds and ends that work well for planting. I'm not saying a vintage toilet is the classiest planter, but you might be surprised how many vegetables you can grow in the bowl and water tank!

Even discarded items like old car tires make good planters. Just be sure to clean them well before use. Most of the time, tires leach out chemicals at such a slow rate that it will take decades to contaminate the soil. If you are concerned about using tires, but if you have a bunch, try lining them with a plastic barrier, or simply place a terra cotta or plastic pot inside them to provide impact protection.

You can use Styrofoam ice chests and even cardboard boxes for growing. And yes, if you are wondering, a cardboard box will last an entire season. You might benefit from taping the flaps closed and adding a weed barrier or plastic to prevent the box from getting soggy.

Milk jugs and two-liter soda bottles have numerous gardening uses - from DIY watering cans to mini-greenhouses. There are so many ways to reuse plastic in the garden without contributing to waste.

A friend of mine lives in an agricultural part of the country where most of the world's row crops are grown. The nutrient-rich soil in this region is also chock-full of river rocks, also called fieldstones. These nearly round mini-boulders destroy farming equipment and cause problems for growing plants. For well over 150 years, farmers have removed these rocks from fields and dumped them in various locations all over the county. Well, it turns out these same discarded stones are easy to stack and cement together, creating natural stone planter boxes. The best thing- many farmers are more than happy to let you back a truck onto their property and take as many fieldstones as you can get.

Designing Containers with the Family

A great way to get everyone involved in the process of selecting containers and planter boxes. Whether you're heading to the local home & garden center to purchase a premade box or you're scouring yard sales on Sunday afternoon, getting the kids involved in the decisions is a great idea.

Eclectic found object planters are a great way to teach kids about responsible use of items and the actual cost of a throw-away society. It's also an excellent opportunity to get kids to think outside the box - when you create a planter from someone's junk, your kids will see that everything doesn't have to come from a store. In fact, some of my favorite planters literally came out of the trashcan!

Now, we're really getting close. It's nearly time to plant!

Chapter 4

CREATING THE IDEAL GROWING MEDIUM

My garden is my most beautiful masterpiece. - Claude Monet

Now that you have an idea about what you want to grow, where it's going to be planted, and what type of container you'll use, it's time to get seriously dirty! Dirt isn't just dirt, and if you want to get the most from your garden, you'll pay attention to the ingredients in your garden soil. It can be tempting to go to the home & garden center and just buy a couple bags of garden soil, potting soil, or topsoil and toss it into your container. You might have success doing this. You might not. The best way to make sure the plants you're growing are healthy and robust is to provide the ideal growing medium.

Every type of plant will have specific requirements for growing. Still, very few vegetables and herbs grow well in easily compacting, poorly draining soil. The first thing I'm going to do here discusses how soil drains and retains water. We'll take a hard look at the types of materials you'll want to use to make the perfect potting soil mixture. With the proper gardening medium, you'll enhance your success with faster-growing, more productive plants!

How Dirt Works

It may seem silly, but have you ever really looked at dirt? It's not any one thing. Instead, it's a mixture of different minerals and organic matter. The various dirt components determine what kinds of plants can grow in that area. Dirt provides a necessary place for plant life to begin and gives the plant strength, but that isn't the only thing dirt does.

The primary way plants absorb water is through the root system, so the dirt must absorb and hold water long enough to nurture the plant, but not so long as to cause rot. Plant roots also take up nutrients from the soil to feed the plant. At various times of the year, the plant must find appropriate amounts of the correct type of nutrients to grow. These multiple factors are why you see some plants growing in one place but not in another.

Gardening in a container gives you the unique opportunity to provide the ideal conditions for your plant to grow. It's one of the most significant benefits over in-ground gardening. One of the places many novice home gardeners make mistakes. It's an easy step to go wrong with and a difficult one to correct once you've planted your containers. You can save money and provide superior soil for your particular garden by mixing your own using the right ingredients.

Ideal Dirt for Containers

The majority of garden plants require light, nutrient-rich soil that drains well. That means you want to avoid fine sand and clay when filling your planter. What you want is soil with plenty of organic material, provides plenty of water absorbing qualities, and drains well to prevent pooling. There are many products on the market at various prices aimed right at you. Some of the commercial products are high-quality. Others aren't.

There are even bags of potting soil formulated explicitly for above-ground container planting.

Garden Soil, Potting Soil, and Topsoil

The three most common products you'll see in the garden center are garden soil, potting soil, and topsoil. There are specific differences between each. You'll often want to combine several or all of them to get the best results.

The purpose of garden soil is to add to your in-ground garden. Garden soil is an enriched soil that includes organic compost and mulch. This type of soil should be blended into your garden bed to enhance the properties of your native soil. It holds water well and provides good nutrients.

Potting soil is significantly different from garden soil, even though it may seem complicated to tell the difference sometimes. Potting soil includes natural elements that improve airiness, drainage, and retention and helps nourish the plants. Most of these products are heavily based on peat and/ or sphagnum moss with a mixture of coarse sand, vermiculite, perlite, ground bark or coconut husk, and other similar ingredients. This is typically a medium-draining soil that provides excellent nutrients and works well in containers.

You may notice two products on the market - potting soil and potting mix. Generally, there is little difference between the two. You may also see a product called container potting soil, essentially just another name for potting soil. If you are growing an organic garden, be sure to check labels for inorganic additives to bagged potting soil.

Topsoil is a nutrient-rich mixture of aged manure, compost, and mulch. This is an excellent amendment to add to your garden or planter but won't retain enough moisture for your plants to grow in alone. Topsoil is often used as a bottom layer in planter boxes or added to potting soil to enhance nutrient density.

Why Make My Own Potting Mix?

There is an astounding amount of variation in the combination of ingredients used in potting mix. You'll find differences from brand to brand, but also bag to bag. This is because the factories making potting soil use whatever comes in that day. There may be a little more of one thing, something unusual, or simply different qualities of common ingredients. There really is no way to tell that what you are buying is any specific combination until you open the bag and get it in a pot. Then, you may find that one bag of soil drains fast while the other turns to a slurry.

Making your own potting mix is really easy and fun. The kids can dig in and help! It gives you the chance to know how much of any one ingredient is being added, and you'll have more consistent results from one pot to the next. The best part is that you'll often spend less money buying several bags of soil and amendments than you will by buying just enough potting soil to fill your planters. All you need to know is what the different components in an excellent potting soil do, then consider the needs of the plants you want to grow.

How to Tell That You Have Well-Draining Soil

This is a big one, and I realize that it's a little hard to visualize what the difference between fast-draining and slow-draining soil will be. Here is a test for you to use that lets you see the drainage. Fill a pot 12-inches deep with your soil mixture and soak it thoroughly. Set it aside and check it every few hours. Well-draining soil will be moist but not wet after three hours. Standing or pooling water within the soil is an indication that you need to amend with coco coir or sphagnum peat and perlite. Dry soil indicates you need to add peat or coco coir and vermiculite. Anything in between is ideal for container gardening.

Common Ingredients in Potting Mix

There are several different components of potting mix that you'll frequently see. Each has a specific purpose, so you'll need to know what they do before mixing up your planting mixture.

- **Sphagnum Peat Moss:** This is a common ingredient in potting soil that will often represent the product's bulk. Sphagnum peat moss is the dead and decayed sphagnum moss harvested from the bottom of bogs in the Northern Hemisphere. It is a dry, powdery, light brown product that retains water well. It also provides an excellent source of nutrients but is too acidic for most plants to grow in alone. It should be mixed with other ingredients to create an optimum potting mix.
- **Bark:** Most often, pine bark is crushed or shredded and added to the potting mix. Bark adds nutrients, retains water, and improves root growth. Pine bark breaks down slowly, so it acts like a slow-release

fertilizer. The bark is primarily helpful for bulking up a potting mix. Crushed and shredded bark are often difficult to purchase to add to your soil. You can use other materials in place of bark if it isn't available in your area.

- **Coco Coir:** This is a product made from the shredded husks of coconuts. It's a fine, lightweight product that functions similarly to sphagnum peat moss. Coco coir helps keep the soil light and holds water well while breaking down slower than moss. The pH is also close to neutral, making coco coir a good choice for many vegetable gardens.

- **Perlite:** Perlite is a manufactured product made from volcanic glass. When heat is applied to the raw material, small, white, Styrofoam-looking balls form and become what we call perlite. The primary purpose of perlite is to improve drainage. It's an essential ingredient in potting mixes that require fast draining. Perlite absorbs a small amount of water and nutrients. Still, it is useful primarily to aid in the lightness of the soil.

- **Vermiculite:** This is also a product from volcanic glass, but this time it is crushed. Vermiculite absorbs and retains water, balances the pH of the soil, and allows roots to have airiness. Vermiculite is an ideal component to add to gardening soil because of the water holding abilities.

- **Sand:** Sand helps to add drainage. Coarse sand, also called sharp or quartz sand is ideal for creating pockets of air and moisture within the soil. Sand helps to balance fast-draining soil while resisting compacting. Horticultural sand is a perfect choice, but builder's sand, or play sand - available at most home improvement stores - is a nearly identical product.

- **Compost:** Compost is decaying organic material. You can purchase compost, or you may want to build a compost bin to manage your own food scraps. Compost is made from leaves, twigs, and branches, along with vegetables, coffee grounds, eggshells, and fruit scraps. Do not ever add animal proteins to your compost. The purpose of compost is to add organic nutrients to the soil.

- **Manure:** Aged manure is simply droppings from cattle and other animals that's been composted. It provides tons of nutrients to plants, particularly nitrogen. You want to use aged manure to avoid overloading your plants with nutrients. Keep in mind that all manure carries the risk of E. Coli and Salmonella, the bacteria responsible for food poisoning. Don't ever use cat or dog feces as manure. It may contain roundworms.

- **Limestone:** Limestone is useful when using lots of sphagnum peat moss because it neutralizes the pH, preventing harm to sensitive plants. Limestone is a mined material made from pulverized rocks.

- **Vermicompost:** This is a material made from the "castings" of worms. It's an ideal source of essential nutrients for your garden, provides airiness, and encourages root growth. While it's expensive, a little goes a long way in your container garden.

Putting it All Together

You're probably thinking - "wow, that's a lot of ingredients." Don't get discouraged thinking you've got to run out and buy all this stuff. You'll want to mix specific ingredients together to create the ideal conditions for your plants. Some of the ingredients above can be left out, substituted, or made up for by combining other elements to get the same results. When you decide to mix your own potting soil for container gardening, it's essential to consider the growing conditions your garden will need and mix an appropriate potting medium.

- **Soil-Based Potting Mix:** A soil-based potting mix will be moderately heavy and retain water very well. A soil-based potting mix will include sand, peat, and perlite or vermiculite. When you are using a soil-based blend, you should squeeze a handful into a ball. If the ball holds together tightly, there is too much clay or peat. If it crumbles easily, there is too much sand. You can add vermiculite and compost to add airiness and bulk if the soil is too sandy. Add sand and perlite, a little at a time, if the soil is too heavy.

Recipe for Mixing Soil-Based Potting Mix:

- One gallon garden soil
- One gallon pre-moistened sphagnum peat moss
- One gallon coarse sand
- A few cups of aged compost, manure, and/or vermicompost
- Enough perlite and/ or vermiculite to create the correct texture

I've learned by trial and error that this mix is an ideal potting soil for raised beds, containers, and pots. It provides plenty of nutrition, drains well, but also holds enough water to benefit growing vegetables. You should use this mixture for growing plants from seedlings to mature plants.

- **Soilless Potting Mix:** A soilless potting mix is made of sphagnum peat moss or coco coir, vermiculite, and perlite. You'll want to add compost or manure to provide nutrients. Don't forget that peat is an acidic ingredient. While many plants thrive in slightly acidic mediums, too much will cause chemical burns to the roots and leaves. Balance the sphagnum peat moss with vermiculite and limestone if the pH is too acidic. Soilless mixes are often ideal for houseplants, and it's the perfect mixture for starting seeds that need lots of airiness to develop strong roots.

Soilless Potting Mix Recipe:

- Two gallons sphagnum peat moss or coco coir
- Two gallons vermiculite and perlite, mixed and moistened
- A few cups of organic compost or manure. Vermicompost is an ideal addition for garden vegetables.

This makes the perfect mix to start seeds and develop young plants. It also works well when you're growing an indoor garden on the kitchen counter. This is an excellent option for small containers that have a tendency to compact with soil-based potting mix, particularly for aggressive growing plants like potatoes and peppers.

Filling Your Containers

Now that you have the perfect potting mix for your garden, it's time to fill your containers. Remember that your plants will need at least six to eight inches of soil depth for healthy roots, so avoid the temptation to add objects to take up space, even in deep boxes. Remember to ignore anyone who tells you to put gravel, rocks, or broken pots into the containers. In days gone by, this was a practice that was thought to improve drainage but can actually do the opposite and cause compaction and poor drainage. If you must add something to fill bottomless boxes, consider Styrofoam packing peanuts or clean plastic water bottles to take up room.

You'll start by adding your potting mix to the box. Don't tamp it down. Just fill it until you are several inches from the level you want the surface to be. Use a sprayer to moisten the mix as you fill, but don't overdo it. This is the ideal time to make sure your soil mixture drains. If you find yourself having to "lift" the soil to get moisture to drain, your soil is too compact. If water just runs out the bottom but doesn't leave things damp, you have too much drainage. Keep watering the soil until you can see water running from the drainage holes.

Once your planter is almost filled up, it's time to plant your seedlings. Remove them from containers and very gently loosen the roots. Make a hole twice the width of the roots and place the plant in the hole. Carefully scoop your potting mix to cover the roots, gently pressing the soil into place to hold the plant. Don't forget to look at the plant tag and space the plants appropriately. If you crowd the plants, you won't get good growth.

When you're done, you'll want your plant sitting in a mound at least two inches above the soil level. This aids in drainage and helps prevent water from pooling at the base of the plant, which can lead to rot. Immediately water the plants. Use a watering pail or gentle shower mist setting on your spray nozzle.

Some Final Thoughts on Making Soil

There are a few things I want to make sure you know before you start mixing soil for your plants. The recipes I gave you here are general guidelines. This works well for most plants, but you should pay close attention to the plant's needs and add amendments to your soil as necessary. Some plants, like peppers, tomatoes, and potatoes, and most lettuce varieties prefer sandy soil. You'll often hear this type of soil called "loam," which is just a term denoting that the soil is roughly equal parts sand, clay, and silt.

Other types of vegetables like beans, peas, cucumbers, and similar plants prefer heavier soil. These plants need the extra "weight" of soil to firmly anchor roots. You can custom mix loamy soil and clay soil by adding more sand or more peat or coco coir, respectively.

Always make sure to mix all the ingredients for your soil thoroughly before use. Layers of differing soil will give you unpredictable growth habits, and you may end up with plants that either struggle to start or struggle to stay alive. Don't forget to moisten your soil mix well before planting.

Getting the Family Involved

Container filling and planting day are one of my favorite times to get everyone together. It's so much fun, particularly for the little ones who seem to always be looking for excuses to get dirty anyway. Put a couple kids in charge of mixing your soil well and watch them play in the dirt. Not only do the young ones get a chance to have a good time doing something they probably don't get to do normally, but they'll also learn that plants need certain types of soil to grow well.

Showing the kids how roots form, how to plant seedlings, and how to water correctly is one of the best steps toward teaching sustainability. These are the important lessons that kids learn while having fun. I can tell you from personal experience that the hours spent in the garden with the family are some of the most memorable.

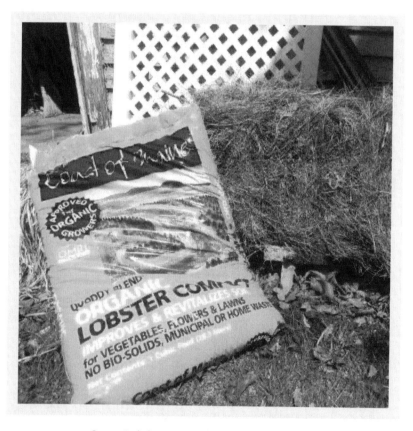

Organic lobster compost & salt marsh hay

Chapter 5

GET YOUR HANDS DIRTY - LET'S PLANT!

When the world wearies and society fails to satisfy, there is always the garden. - Minnie Aumonier

A critical factor in the success of your container garden is planting at the right time of the year. Now, it's easy to say, "plant this in spring and that in summer," but that doesn't always mean the same thing for everyone. Where you live will determine how long your growing season will be. In some areas, certain plants will be more successful than others. Of course, planting at the right time is vital for both plant growth and ensuring the plant matures and is ready for harvest before the first killing frost and your growing season ends.

This chapter will discuss the USDA hardiness zones and explain what that means for you and your garden. You'll learn about when to plant, what garden varieties are a good choice for your area, and some of the lore that may actually work to improve germination rates when growing from seed and seedlings.

Planting Zones in the United States

The United States Department of Agriculture (USDA) provides a national map of growing regions. These regions are defined by the 30-year average annual winter extreme cold. Each zone is separated by a 10-degree Fahrenheit winter-time difference. The USDA zone map "the standard by which gardeners and growers can determine which plants are most likely to thrive at a location," according to USDA.

These zones are not absolute, but they provide you with an excellent guideline of the conditions you should anticipate growing in containers. Each zone is assigned a number and a letter, with colder regions having lower numbers. Letters differentiate between conditions within one zone.

An excellent way to look at the USDA Hardiness Zones for gardeners is to figure that areas with colder winters tend to get cold sooner and stay cold longer than warmer regions. Let's discuss the U.S. regions before discussing what types of plants will thrive in your area.

• Northeastern U.S. Growing Zones

The USDA map considers New England, New York, Maine, and as far south as parts of Virginia to be in this region. Even central states like Indiana and Illinois are considered part of the Northeast Growing region. Zones in this area run from 3b at the farthest northern point (-35 to-30 degrees) to much warmer parts of Virginia at 7a (0 to 5 degrees). There are many variables in this region, including mountainous places, valleys, and northern plains. Massachusetts, for example, consists of five different zones.

• Southeastern U.S. Growing Zones

The Southeastern U.S. is a warmer, humid environment. It is represented by zones 6a through 10b, except for the Florida Keys at 11b. This region is dominated by humid, moist air. Locations in more mountainous areas will have lower USDA zones.

• Southwestern U.S. Growing Zones

This region stretches from the southern California coastline to the peaks of Colorado and as far south as the Mexican border in Arizona and New Mexico. Zones are at extreme ends, with regions as low as 3b or as high as 11b. Coastal areas west of the Rocky Mountains are more humid than inland regions and have varying growing conditions accordingly.

• South-central U.S. growing zones

This region is dominated by the State of Texas. Areas within 100 miles or so of the Gulf Coast have significantly higher humidity, while more northern areas around the panhandle and Oklahoma are at the other end of the spectrum. Zones extend from 7b to 10b in the area.

• Northwestern U.S. Growing Zones

This is another area with massive differences depending on the region. The Northwest comprises Washington and Oregon, and Northern California and extends east to Montana and Wyoming. Zones in this region range from 3a to 9b. Higher mountain elevations are lower, while valleys west of the Rockies are warmer.

• North-central U.S. Growing Zones

The regions from Northern Montana to the Great Lakes and including states as far south as Oklahoma this region includes zones 3 to 5 throughout most of the region, with some areas as warm as zone 6 or 7 in the extreme south.

What the USDA Hardiness Zones Mean for Planting in Your Region

When you select seeds and seedlings for your garden, you'll want to look on the back of the package for the USDA hardiness zone information, and you'll need to know your region. The best way is to visit the USDA website and use the interactive map to find your location. Now when you consider what to plant, you can find options that will thrive in your region.

A limitation of using the USDA Hardiness Zones for planting is that it only describes winter conditions when many plants grow in the spring and summer. Hotter zones from about 8b to 11 will need to account for excessive summertime temperatures. Many plants may fail without some protection.

A benefit to these hot regions is that you can often get two growing seasons by planting in the early spring with a summer harvest. A second planting in late summer can yield a crop before frost sets in during the winter. Warmer regions also benefit by providing a good climate for winter crops that can withstand cold temperatures and even frosts.

Zones 5b to 8a can be highly productive. Still, you may need to take some steps to protect your plants from frost, inclement weather, and extreme temperature changes. These areas make perfect regions for container gardening when your containers are portable.

Portions of Alaska get as low as Zone 2b, indicating an average winter of -45 to -40 degrees. Growing much of anything in these temperatures is a serious challenge but not impossible. Most of the northern and central regions of the U.S. will fall between 3 and 7. A short growing season in these regions can be overcome by planting fast-maturing crops. Later in this book, I'll teach you how to grow a crop of organic vegetables in only 21 days in containers!

Starting Seeds Indoors and Using A Greenhouse

The best way to overcome weather patterns that don't cooperate reasonably with the type of plants you wish to grow is to start indoors and use a greenhouse. Starting seeds indoors means you can have seedlings ready when the appropriate time for planting finally arrives. You'll get a jump start on the season, helping to grow a bountiful harvest before the winter returns.

A greenhouse doesn't need to be a fancy affair. It can be a straightforward structure that simply provides cover and retains warmth. A common way to protect young plants from inclement weather is to use PVC pipe to make a hoop house. This is a simple structure of bowed pipes set like ribs and anchored at the ends with a cover over the top. You can use a cover that permits light but will keep warm to help your plants survive in cold zones. Hoop houses are great ways to encourage seedlings and to help acclimate young plants that started indoors to the outdoor climate.

Common Container Vegetables with Zone Recommendations

When you start to consider the options you have for growing in your region, you may also pay attention to the hybrid varieties of your favorite plants. Virtually all vegetables have hybrid versions, some frost-resistant, not as susceptible to pests or disease, or tolerate drought better than other varieties.

Let's discuss some of the most popular vegetables you can grow in your region and when the right time to plant will be.

Tomato: There are thousands of varieties of tomatoes, many of which will meet your needs, even in the most challenging environments. Zones 5 through 8 can grow a wide variety of tomato types. Colder climates with shorter growing seasons, like those in 3b through 5b, might select fast-maturing varieties like grape tomatoes to ensure a harvest before frost sets in. Gardeners in zones 8 through 11 can choose a wide range of types, and warmer regions will allow year-round tomato production.

Tomatoes prefer warm temperatures between 65 and 85 during the day, with nighttime temperatures in the mid-50s. They'll stop producing fruit in higher temperatures, and many varieties are not frost tolerant. Plant in the late spring in zones 3-5 and early spring in zones 6-8.

Cucumbers & Zucchini: These plants are sun and water-loving but have varieties that are also drought, disease, and pest resistant. The large seeds require warm soil to germinate, making them perfect candidates for starting indoors. There are two types on the market - vining, and bush. Vining types will require a trellis to climb. This can be as simple as pieces of string tied to a fence or as complex as an overhead arbor. Bush types are ideal for containers, with some varieties being perfect for making pickles.

Cucumbers are highly susceptible to frost and can't tolerate temperatures below 33 degrees. Many varieties of cucumber and zucchini are fast maturing, so you can start them indoors and have an edible harvest within two months. Plant outdoors well after the last frost in your region.

Root Vegetables: While specific differences depend on types, almost all root vegetables, including carrots, onions, parsnips, beets, and radishes, have varying levels of frost tolerance. Many of these plants should go in the ground well before the last frost and be harvested after freezing temperatures return. In fact, some varieties require at least two weeks of freezing temperatures to convert starches into sugar.

Not only are root vegetables champions of inclement weather, but they are also ideal for container growing. They have very predictable root growth, making spacing plants easy. You can plant root vegetables two to four weeks before the last frost in most regions. In warmer climates, including zones 8 and above, you can grow root vegetables in the fall for a spring harvest, then plant again to allow a fall harvest.

Squash & Pumpkins: Gourd vegetables are fun to grow as they are delicious to make meals with. They are also versatile enough to grow well in many regions. There are two varieties: summer squash and winter squash. Summer varieties mature quickly and are harvested before they are fully mature. In contrast, winter varieties can take more than 100 frost-free days before they are ready.

The best time to plant summer squash in colder zones is early to mid-spring, well after the threat of frost. You'll have a harvest of yellow squash, crook necks, and whatever other varieties you choose by mid-summer. Those of you in warmer regions can delay planting squash until late spring or even early summer in hot areas. Winter varieties can be planted at the same time or shortly after that in colder regions. Gardeners in warmer areas will want to delay planting until summer temperatures have begun to stabilize.

Beans & Peas: These garden staples are lovely for their incredible variety. Gardeners from the coldest to the hottest regions will have success. This crop also makes an excellent choice for storage. Beans and peas typically flower in the summer and produce fruit through the fall, with some varieties continuing to be productive until the frost kills them off.

Beans and peas also make excellent candidates for starting indoors, particularly with your children. These large seeds develop quickly and put on a great show when they sprout. Starting indoors will often give you a better yield, as beans and peas can be notoriously difficult to start in soil. In cooler regions, beans and peas should be ready to plant shortly after the last frost. Warmer areas can plant as soon as the threat of frost has passed.

Grains: Grains like barley, corn, wheat, and maize can all be excellent candidates for container gardening when in the proper conditions. Many of these plants are frost and drought-tolerant and attractive as well.

Different grain varieties have additional requirements, but most will need 50 to 80 days to mature and require warm weather. Colder climates can start grain types as soon as the threat of frost is passed, while warmer zones can start grains in fall for a spring harvest.

Planting by the Moon

Here's a little bit of superstitious lore that actually works. I'm not going to tell you that you'll have success planting under the light of the full moon, though, if that's what you are thinking. Instead, this planting method considers the gravitational pull of the moon and the way moisture on earth reacts. We know that the moon plays a role in the rise and fall of the tides, making sense that other water bodies would be impacted.

For example, seeds may absorb more moisture when the moon is waning, leading to faster and better germination rates. Some plants may even grow better when started under the right conditions.

Effects of the Moon on Gravity

The moon exerts its most tremendous force at full and new moons. Tides increase as the phase moves through to the full moon and recede as the light decreases, with the waxing and waning having a mid-point called the first and third quarter, respectively.

The rule of thumb is to plant varieties that produce above-ground vegetables, like corn, cucumbers, peas, and herbs during the waxing moon. The waxing moon exists from a new moon (no light) to a full moon (full light). During the waxing phase, the light will always shine on the right side of the moon.

The theory goes that as the brightness of the moon increases, plants are encouraged to grow leaves and stems.

Root vegetables like potatoes, carrots, and onions grow best when planted on the waning moon. The waning moon exists from the full moon to the new moon when light appears on the moon's left side.

Planting from Food Scraps

I love talking about sustainable gardening practices, and here is a great way you can pitch in. When you buy vegetables like lettuce, celery, turnips, beets, carrots, onions, and even tomatoes, you can grow plants from the parts you usually cut off and throw away. This is a simple way to get vegetables you know your family loves growing in your garden.

Leafy green vegetables are among the best for growing from scraps. All you need to do is cut off the bottom "stump" about one inch above where it ends. Place this in a shallow water dish, and it will develop roots in a week or two. This is a great way to show your children how roots form. Alternatively, put the stump in well-moistened soil and water as usual, and it will grow.

You can do the same with root vegetables and regrow them. Onions and garlic will produce a single new bulb, while shallots will multiply. Green onions (scallions) and chives can simply be regrown and harvested as needed. These vegetables even do well in a simple glass of water for an easy, on-hand kitchen container vegetable green.

Many types of root vegetables like carrots will grow leafy green tops but won't form a new carrot root. You can harvest the seeds or grow these veggies for their tasty and underutilized greens, which are edible.

Celery is one of the easiest vegetables to regrow from scraps. Treat it just like lettuce and place it in water until the roots are about four inches long, then transplant it into the garden. Celery will continue to regrow as you cut it down, letting you have a massive, regular harvest all season from just a few dollars' worth of vegetables.

Potatoes and sweet potatoes are among the most entertaining to grow from scraps. Virtually any part of these tubers will regrow, and it will do so at break-neck speed. Simply suspend a cut of potato or sweet potato in water using toothpicks as support. Within about one week, you will see roots. Soon, leafy greens will form and grow. Now, just cut off the leafy portion and place it in water. It will re-root and develop a new potato. This is a fun task to do with your children, and the rapid growth is a rewarding experience.

Plant Good Neighbors

When you plan out which plants to put in containers, you want to make sure that plants with similar needs and wants are placed together. This means putting full-sun, moderate watering, fertilizer-using plants with similar plants. Planting heavy water users with light water users is a recipe for disaster.

You should also pay attention to the height of a plant. When you plant tall crops like corn, tomatoes, or cucumbers, make sure they are not shading smaller crops like herbs, bush beans, and roots. A good solution is to plant smaller plants in their own row on the outside and oriented facing the sun with taller plants at their back. Do you remember our exercise in Chapter 1 about finding the sun? Here is where it starts to pay off. When you plant, you'll have oriented your containers, so they are in the perfect position to let you make easy decisions about where to plant.

Avoid Competition and Cross-Pollination

Most plants with similar needs will grow well with other plants, but there are a few combinations that you may choose to avoid for one reason or another.

Garlic and onions interfere with the root development of beans and peas. Potatoes and tomatoes both share pests and compete for nutrients to the detriment of both.

Make dedicated containers for lettuce, cabbage, spinach, and turnip plants (members of the brassica family). These plants attract numerous insects and cross-contaminate various other plants, including tomatoes, peppers, beans, and strawberries. Basil and tarragon are good companions for brassica plants. These species can also easily cross-pollinate, a problem if you plan on harvesting seeds. You should also rotate brassica planters every year to some other type of plant to avoid contaminating the soil.

Plant Beneficial Companions

Many plants can help other plants. Marigolds, for example, are frequently planted in vegetable container gardens because these delightful flowers deter all sorts of pests. Asparagus and tomatoes make great companions since each deters the pests of the other. Planting varieties that attract beneficial pollinators can also be valuable. Tobacco and sunflowers are both excellent plants for attracting bees, wasps, and hummingbirds, while the sticky hairs on their stalks trap and kill pests like aphids and whiteflies.

Some plants can also play a sacrificial role. Parsley attracts many of the common pests that feed on tomatoes, sparing the more valuable crop from extensive damage. Nasturtiums are excellent for attracting aphids and preventing infestations from happening in your garden. Plus, the nasturtium flowers are edible!

Helpful Planting Tips

When you're filling your planter boxes or containers, be sure to fill the container all the way, but not to the very top. More soil equals more margin for error and reduces the likelihood of overwatering. Many plants you'll grow in container gardens will benefit from more width and depth to expand roots.

Garden the way you live. If you are the kind of person, who feels called to spend time pruning, trimming, and watering, develop a garden that provides you with that experience. Find types of plants that grow what you want and enjoy relaxation and peacefulness. Suppose you are the type of person who doesn't have time for a fussy garden but wants to grow exciting plants. In that case, you might consider drought-resistant varieties, growing a cactus or succulent garden, or developing a more self-sufficient container garden.

Gardening is all about fun, so when you are planting, don't let the sheer complexity of things make you feel overwhelmed. Take things one step at a time, from conceptualization, planning, and finally to planting. The more excited you are on day one, the more likely you will stay enthusiastic about your garden on day 99, mainly after you succeed in caring for your garden through the entire season.

Chapter 6

THE 4 ESSENTIALS: WATER, SUN, NUTRIENTS, AND POLLINATION

Garden as though you will live forever. – William Kent

After all of the planning, the discussions with the family, and everyone's efforts to get a container garden growing, it would be a shame to watch your new plants wither and die. Sadly, that is a fate many container gardens face. Sometimes it's neglect that causes the garden to fail. After all, we all have busy lives, and sometimes it's just easier to put off things that we aren't used to doing. Other times, gardeners get too aggressive with watering and nutrients in the hope of getting faster and more significant results. There are a million ways a garden can fail. Still, only one way it will succeed: your garden needs the right amount of water, sun, nutrients, and pollination. Everything must work together in harmony, or your plants will suffer.

I could tell you a thousand stories about well-meaning gardeners that followed every guideline they were given and still watched as their garden suffered and failed. There is only one trick you can use to keep your garden healthy, happy, and productive: pay attention to your plants. As humans, we are too easily convinced that other living beings don't communicate with us. Still, I believe that we simply don't take the time to learn the language. Your plants will talk to you - not in the conventional sense, of course. But once you know how to understand plant behavior, you'll realize that all the knowledge you need for a successful garden is right there in front of you. You just have to know what signs to look for when your plants are struggling.

Now that your container garden is planted, you'll be able to begin enjoying the most enjoyable part of gardening - tending to the needs of growing plants. I love this phase of gardening because this is when you get to see new growth every day, and you can see the results of your work. It's the ideal opportunity to relax and slow down, something I think we can all use. Take the time every day to spend even just a few quiet minutes looking at the leaves, checking the soil, and paying attention to your plants. In no time, you'll learn to speak the language of plants, and your garden will flourish.

Watering Your Garden

Everyone knows that plants need water to survive. Still, one of the most common mistakes I see novice gardeners - and even quite a few who have lots of experience - is improper watering. Correctly watering a garden growing in pots and containers is more complex than simply spraying some water every day or two. I will discuss proper watering techniques and then discuss some of the signs of watering problems many gardeners struggle to overcome.

Watering Technique

The most important aspect of correct watering is how to give your plants a drink. Many people simply grab the hose, put a sprayer on, and quickly soak the plants. Some plants will do just fine this way, but many varieties will not. You may get okay growth, but you're just as likely to see minimal production, weak growth, and an increase in pests, diseases, and plant death. The problem with spraying water quickly is that moisture only penetrates the very top layer of the soil. This forces the plant to grow roots out instead of down, putting them at a higher risk of problems. Plants cannot absorb enough water before the water drains below the roots or evaporates. A lack of water causes plants to stress, and just like you or me, stress isn't conducive to doing a good job handling what we need to do. For plants, stress can prevent healthy growth.

In a later chapter, I'll discuss pests and diseases. Still, for now, you should know that a quick spray of water left on the leaves of plants is like a giant neon sign begging bugs and fungus to move on in. You definitely don't want that, and one of the best ways to prevent infestations is by watering correctly.

The best practice for watering plants in pots and containers is to pour water slowly at the soil level and avoid soaking the leaves. Add water until it runs from the drainage holes. Watering slowly like this ensures that the moisture penetrates all the way through the soil and encourages roots to grow down and out, maximizing access to nutrients and preventing many common growth problems.

I know it can be challenging to get into the habit of watering slowly, particularly when you have lots of pots and containers to deal with. It's just easier to grab the hose and spray everything down quickly. I urge you to get into the habit of taking the time to water slowly. It's an excellent opportunity to spend a little time with each plant in your garden, look it over, check for other issues, and make sure it is growing well. It may take some time to get into the habit, but once you do, watering your pot and container garden will be one of the times of day you look forward to most.

Dry, Damp, Moist, and Wet - How to Tell the Difference

Unlike many things in life where we get convenient numbers, gauges, and scales to determine the conditions of something, watering is more challenging to gauge. You will often see information on seed packets or on plant tags indicating the watering conditions in terms of relative dryness. Understanding the difference is critical for growing healthy plants, particularly in containers and pots.

Dry soil will be, well, dry. It's pretty easy to tell when soil is dry, but most plants aren't going to be happy in dry soil. Cactus and succulents, along with a few types of houseplants, tend to require dry soil or at least periods of drying out between watering.

Damp soil is slightly wet. If you make a ball of damp soil and squeeze it in your hand, little or no moisture will come out, and the soil won't hold together ultimately. Damp conditions are suitable for many garden vegetables growing in pots and containers. Peppers, potatoes, and many other plants prefer damp soil for healthy growth. Root vegetables prefer damp conditions over moist.

Moist soil is the most common type that garden plants growing in pots and containers will require. Moist soil, formed into a ball and squeezed, will have some water in it, and the ball will hold together reasonably well. The difference between moist and damp is very slight. The two conditions are usually interchangeable once you understand your plants' desires. Moist soil is great for beans, peas, and tomatoes.

Very few plants will survive for long in wet soil. When you make a ball of wet earth and squeeze, lots of water comes out, and the ball stays intact. Wet soil is heavy and is more difficult for roots to grow through. It's also a perfect condition for fungal growth, which will eventually contaminate your soil, kill your plants, and force you to start over. Generally, you want to avoid wet soil.

How Much is Too Much?

Another common mistake that novice gardeners make is thinking that more water is better if some water is good. This is seldom the case, and for many plants, overwatering is a much worse fate than underwatering. Through practice, you'll learn that some plants will need more or less water than others, more or less frequent watering, or more extended periods of drying out in between watering.

There are probably a thousand different tools out there that manufacturers are trying to sell to help you determine how much water to give your plants. Some of these tools are pretty good, others are just gimmicks, and it's hard to tell the difference. The good news here is that the most reliable tool for gauging how much water your plant needs, you probably already have - your fingers.

You'll want to learn to look past soil that looks moist - it often does. Instead, put the tip of your finger in the soil and press straight down. You'll feel the moisture in the soil, and in time, you'll learn to gauge the difference between dry, moist, and wet soil. The trick is to push your finger down several inches and notice when the soil starts to feel damp. That gives you an idea of how much water is retained in the soil. If the soil is dry, it's time to water again.

Checking the moisture in the soil also lets you keep an eye on how the drainage in your containers or pots is doing. Over time, soil compacts, and the tighter the soil compacts, you'll have less drainage. If your pots stop draining well, you'll want to check that the pot is large enough for the plant and that the soil has remained airy enough for drainage. You may have to repot plants once in a while to overcome excessive soil compaction from watering.

Tools for Ensuring Proper Watering

Two tools can help you, mainly when you are new to container and pot gardening. The most basic is a water bulb, otherwise known as a turkey baster. This is a plastic or glass bulb with a thin stem. To use a bulb waterer, you will water your plants, fill the bulb, then press it several inches into the soil stem-side down. As the moisture from the container drains, the level in the bulb will also drop. You will know that it is time to water when there is no more water in the bulb.

Another helpful tool is an electronic probe. These devices typically have two metal rods about 10 inches long. You simply insert the meter into the soil and watch the gauge. It will indicate when the soil is drying out.

Automatic Watering Systems

Setting up an automatic irrigation system for your plants is not feasible for everyone. It involves a significant expense, requires plenty of planning, and needs regular maintenance to work correctly. On the flip side, an automatic watering system reduces the amount of work and effort you'll put in. It also helps ensure your plants get the right amount of water - especially if you go away on vacation during the growing season.

Automatic watering systems use sections of small irrigation pipes and even smaller lines to direct the water where you want it to go. You can set up these systems so that an electronic controller turns the water on and off at specific times, so you don't have to worry about forgetting to water. The downside to these systems is that you'll need to have plants with similar water requirements and similarly sized pots. Otherwise, some plants will get too much water while others won't get enough.

Self-watering containers may also work well for you. These are basically a pot with a water reservoir located in the bottom. As the soil dries, water is absorbed, keeping your plants well-watered. These containers will work well for plants that prefer consistently moist soil but won't do the trick for many types of plants that like to dry out slightly between watering.

Learning to Read Your Plants

Over time, you will get used to seeing your plants behave in particular ways when conditions are not ideal. You'll likely get accustomed to feeling your soil to check moisture levels. While you are at it, learning to look for specific signs of watering issues can help you determine if you are giving too much or not enough.

When the soil is too dry, your plants will tell you about it by curling the edges of leaves up, turning brown on the tips, and the leaves of many plants will feel dry. You can easily confirm by checking the soil. If it's dry, then you know the plant needs water.

When there is too much water, Gauging is a little more challenging since the common signs can also indicate other problems. The leaves of an overwatered plant tend to hang down or even fall off. Leaves may turn yellow or even brown before falling off. Overwatering is a critical situation you need to address right away to prevent fungal growth in your soil that will kill the plant. If your leaves look droopy and the soil is wet, you need to scale back how often and how much you water your plants.

A healthy, happy plant will have upright, evenly colored leaves that feel soft and supple. Finding the middle ground between too much and too little will take practice, and different plants like things differently. Variations in the soil makeup can contribute to how much and how often you water.

The temperature will also make a big difference. Warmer weather will mean you must water more frequently, maybe as much as twice a day. The type of pots and containers you use will also affect the amount of water you give your plants. Plastic pots, for example, hold moisture longer than terra cotta pots.

One of the ways you can improve water retention when you are dealing with containers that evaporate water quickly is the use of mulch. Mulch is made from coarse pieces of wood or bark, and it's used for ground cover. Using organic mulch on the soil's surface in your container will help keep moisture from quickly evaporating in warm weather.

Many people live in places that charge for water usage. There are some ways you can offset the cost of your water bill while still ensuring that your plants get adequate moisture. Smaller pots require less water but will limit the size of plants you can grow. Smaller pots must also be watered more often, limiting the amount you will save. When you plan your container garden, try to get an idea of how much water use costs in your region. This will help you decide how many containers to use and how big the pots can be to still be practical for regular watering.

Another way to reduce your water bill is to collect rainwater. You can often find used water barrels, the big blue ones, for less than $15 each. Rerouting the gutters from your house into a series of containers will provide you a lot more water than you would think, even if you live in an arid region. You want to use a series of containers because you will want to filter the runoff from your roof to prevent accidentally introducing chemicals from roofing materials. But check your local ordinances because some communities prohibit collecting rainwater!

Layers of pumice, sand, and charcoal in the primary container will filter and clean the water. All you will need to do is drain the filtered water into another container, and you'll have a surprising amount of water. This is perfect for irrigating your plants on hand when the water bill is getting out of hand. Setting this system up can vary from gravity-fed and relatively simple to systems that use pumps to move water from one area to another.

Sunlight in the Garden

In the first chapter, I told you about an exercise you can use to determine the best location for your garden. By walking through your space facing the sun, you will understand the amount of light at different times of the day. Now, when you're planting your garden, pay attention to the direction the plants face. Your containers will grow best when they are oriented north to south. An east-west orientation means that taller plants will shade other plants, leading to competition for light and leggy growth.

It's also possible for you to use this to your advantage when your location doesn't provide a good opportunity for north-south orientation. You can plant sun-loving plants to the west of shade-tolerant varieties. Just make sure they have the same water and soil requirements.

Planting this way creates a symbiotic relationship where the taller plants protect the shade-tolerant ones. Planting taller, sun-loving plants west of the others lets these plants get the most sunlight throughout the day and protect the other plants when the afternoon sun is bright.

Many people I know have beautiful yards perfect for container gardening. Still, they lack shade, so the yard is blistering hot in the afternoon. Even sun-loving plants often can't handle intense sunlight and high temperatures. You can help your plants when you have too much sun by using plant covers. Material available online or from agricultural stores called sun cloth or sunshade permits varying amounts of light to pass through while restricting the most harmful rays. A small, portable hoop structure with a sun cloth covering is an excellent way to protect plants that get too much light. A small sunshade structure is affordable to build and easy to assemble independently.

Learning to Tell When Your Plants Needs Different Light

Just like you can learn to listen to your plants for signs of water needs, you can do the same with sunlight. The key things to look for all involve the leaves of the plants and paying attention to the growth rate.

A plant that gets too much light will often show graying or dulling of leaves, yellowing or browning tips, and droopy behavior. New growth may be smaller than earlier growth as the plant tries to overcome the excessive light it gets. You can use a shade cloth to protect these plants, and they will usually bounce right back.

When a plant doesn't get enough light, its growth behavior changes. Suddenly, you'll see the plant growing longer stems with more space between the leaves. Leaves will often turn toward the brightest available light source to boost the plant's energy intake. You should move a plant into a sunnier spot when you see the stems elongating, and it will return to typical growth rates quickly.

Excellent Plant Choices for Partial-Shade Container Gardens

Most plants will have specific light requirements, including vegetables.

Plants require sunlight to create energy through the process of photosynthesis. This is how they turn the sun into growth, and without some light, plants will essentially starve. Suppose you hope to build a container garden on a patio where you simply don't get bright, direct sunlight. There is a wide range of excellent options that prefer indirect light in that case.

You may want to try growing leafy greens like lettuce, kale, spinach, and onions. These varieties prefer cooler temperatures and shorter bright light conditions. You can also have great success with root veggies like carrots, turnips, and potatoes. These plants prefer partial shade locations and will grow well in containers or pots.

Excellent Full-Sun Choices for Containers

Many types of the most popular vegetables we enjoy are sun-loving varieties. These plants require at least 6 hours of bright, direct sun every day. If you have the perfect north-south orientation and a bright, sunny yard, you have many choices for growing excellent plants. Some good options for full-sun locations include tomatoes, peppers, cucumbers, eggplant, and many herb varieties like rosemary, basil, and dill.

You should pay attention to temperature when you have full-sun locations. Daytime temperatures can heat pots and containers to unsafe levels. The openness of the space also means that plants are likely to be exposed to wind, rain, and cold temperatures more than sheltered plants. You may want to make the most sensitive plants portable and try to grow drought-resistant, hardy species in the most challenging hot and sunny spots.

Shade-Tolerant Plant Choices for Container Gardening

Sometimes, you can't avoid a shady growing location. Maybe you are gardening on the balcony, and taller buildings shade your space. Or maybe your neighbor has large trees that block the best parts of the light for gardening. If shady conditions are what you are working with, you have many options available. Some plants like tomatoes and peppers won't grow well, but you can raise a bumper crop of leafy greens, root veggies, and almost all culinary herbs.

You should consider small, shade-tolerant plants for balconies and other small spaces. Try growing mint, cilantro (coriander), chives, or sage. These herbs prefer shady locations and will grow very nicely. If you have a little more room to work with, you might try growing beans, peas, and root vegetables. These plants are about as productive in shady locations as they are in the sun, and many types prefer not to be in bright, direct light for more than a few hours per day.

Try not to forget that even shade-tolerant plants must have some light. Very few plants grow in shady locations, and only a slim minority of those are edible. Your plants will grow best if you try to locate them where they get the optimal light conditions for the particular type of plants.

Nutrients

Nutrients can help boost plant performance during the growing season. When you mix your potting mix, you should include organic material that nourishes plants. Using sphagnum peat moss and compost are excellent ways to provide plenty of nutrients to get plants going. If your soil mix is good, and if you followed my recipe, you'd be able to grow your crops without adding nutrients along the way. Suppose you decide to boost your plants' performance. In that case, you'll want to select the correct type of fertilizer and apply it in the right way because many products can actually kill your plants.

There are 17 critical nutrients that all plants require to survive. Three of them, carbon, oxygen, and hydrogen, come from the air. The other 14 elements must come from the soil so the roots can absorb them. The necessary nutrients are broken down into two categories: macronutrients and micronutrients.

Macronutrients

These elements represent the bulk of a plant's needs. Macronutrients are nitrogen (N), phosphorus (P), potassium (K), calcium (Ca), sulfur (S), magnesium (Mg), carbon (C), oxygen (O), and hydrogen (H). The first three are critical for plant growth and play specific roles in developing a plant. Throughout a growing season, the nutrient needs of many plants change. Providing a nutrient boost during this critical time can help your garden be more productive.

Micronutrients

These are elements that are measured in parts per million in terms of plant use. They show up in the leaves, stems, and shoots of plants. They play various functions, from helping with fruiting, flowering, and pollinating to protecting the roots and stems from harm. Micronutrients are typically available in abundance if you use a good potting mix. Iron (Fe), boron (B), chlorine (Cl), manganese (Mn), zinc (Zn), copper (Cu), molybdenum (Mo), and nickel (Ni) are the essential micronutrients plants need.

Types of Fertilizers

There are several options you have for fertilizing your pots and containers. It's always good to choose organic nutrients to avoid unnecessary chemicals. Still, you should read labels carefully when purchasing any fertilizer products.

- **Organic Compost:** Organic compost is a mixture of decomposing leaves, grass clippings, dead plants, and wood materials. Compost is one of the best ways to provide nutrients to your container garden. You'll have the most success using compost when filling your pots. Putting compost on the soil of growing plants has limited effects and can cause problems. Instead, you can work compost into the top layer of soil somewhat away from the plant. This is known as side-dressing, and it's an effective way to replenish nutrients to the soil when your plants are growing well without disturbing the roots. You don't need to add much. A few handfuls for a growing tomato plant is enough.

- **Kitchen Scraps:** Kitchen scraps make up a significant portion of the trash Americans throw away every year. It's too bad because much of what is thrown out can make nutrient-rich compost. You can put many things into a food scraps compost bin, including coffee grounds, eggshells, fruit, and vegetable portions - even if they are moldy, used tea bags, and even newspaper or shredded cardboard. Avoid meats, fats, and oils, or anything that has harmful chemicals on it. You can make a vermiculture farm using food scraps.

- **Vermiculture:** Vermiculture is a nutrient-dense soil created when worms consume food scraps. The byproduct is commonly known as worm castings, and it's a great source of organic nutrients for container gardens. If you have already started a food scrap bin, just add worms. The worms will decompose the food scraps faster than if they were just in a container and leave behind rich, black soil.

- **Liquid Fertilizers**: This is a product that you mix with water and apply to your plants' roots. Organic liquid fertilizers are made from a variety of ingredients. Common types are fish-based and kelp-based. Liquid fertilizers can be a great way to boost the performance of struggling plants or enhance healthy ones. Still, you'll need to be careful to avoid overdosing the plant. Some liquid fertilizer products can cause chemical burns to the roots, killing the plants.

- **Granular Fertilizer:** Organic granular fertilizers are available even in a slow-release formula that provides nutrients for several months with only one application. These are typically made from one or several types of manure, including cattle, chicken, and numerous other animals. Slow-release fertilizer is generally added to the potting mix before planting.

What the Numbers Mean

One of the first things you will notice when you start comparing nutrients is that they all feature three numbers in an XX-XX-XX format. These numbers represent the percentage of each of the three primary nutrients, nitrogen, phosphorus, and potassium. Varying levels indicate a difference in strength. Nitrogen is the first number, and it is responsible for foliage growth. Phosphorus, the second number, is essential for cell function and energy. The final number is potassium which plays critical roles in numerous aspects of plant growth and development of fruits.

You should learn what concentration of fertilizer your plants will prosper with before using any type of liquid or granular fertilizer. The best way to ensure proper nutrient levels is to mix a good amount of organic compost into the potting mix you make.

Pollination

Pollination is an essential function of the growth and development of fruits and vegetables. Your container garden will attract many bugs that are called beneficial pollinators. This includes bees, wasps, and numerous other insects. You may also attract hummingbirds to your garden, which can help pollinate flowers. Container gardens are often under-pollinated because of the small size of the garden. In many other cases, there just simply aren't pollinators around. In this case, you can take matters into your own hands.

How to Hand Pollinate

This is a great thing to share with your children, even if they don't really understand it at the moment. Hand pollinating means simply that you're going to do the job that bees or butterflies would do in nature. The best way is to remove the petals from a male flower. Using a cotton swab, paintbrush, or even your finger, you gather pollen from the flower center, called the stamen. Then, gently dab the collected pollen onto a female flower. Depending on the variety of plants you are growing, you may need to research the specific traits that denote male and female flowers. You can aid in the pollination of tomato and pepper plants simply by flicking the flowers with your fingers.

Attracting Pollinators

There are some ways you can increase the presence of your garden to pollinators. Plant flowers and nectar-rich plants to attract many types of pollinators. Butterflies, while attractive, are often your worst enemy. Look for plants and flowers that attract bees and wasps. These winged pollinators are also predators of pests they find on the

Busy bee!

flowers.

You can use any number of types of flowering plants to attract pollinators. A good tip is to find varieties that produce flowers when your garden is blooming. This way, the insects flying around pollinate your garden at the right time.

Conclusion

Now that you know how to water and fertilize your plants and your garden is thriving, it's time for you to relax and enjoy your efforts. This is an excellent opportunity for you to spend time with your family in the garden, watching and helping the plants grow. Learning to speak the language of the plants takes time and practice, and there will be mistakes. It happens to everyone, even experienced gardeners. Be patient, look closely, feel the plants, and notice when they look happy. In no time, your garden will be performing miraculously.

Chapter 7

THE 3 DEMONS: CRITTERS, PESTS, AND DISEASE

A society grows great when old men plant trees whose shade they know they shall never sit in. – Greek proverb

After putting in all the effort to select the perfect location for your garden, mixing the ideal medium, and tenderly caring for your plants every day while they grow, nothing is more frustrating than an outbreak of pests, critters, and disease. Trust me, I know how defeating it can feel to see your efforts go to waste when things go wrong.

A few seasons back, I had cucumbers growing on a trellis, and boy, did they produce. Then, one day, I noticed a few little bugs here and there. I didn't really think much about it at the time, but that should have been my first indication there was about to be a problem. Fast forward a few days, and those few little bugs I saw had multiplied into a full-scale infestation. Within days, my cucumber plants turned yellow, wilted, and died. I had no choice but to pull all the plants and throw them out. Had I acted as soon as I spotted the bugs, my cucumbers would likely have kept producing well into the fall.

The good news about pests, critters, and disease is that a bit of preparation and attention can prevent severe problems without resorting to "nuclear" options most of the time. The trick is to learn the signs of an issue and react so that problems don't spread. This chapter will discuss the common problems that can happen, and I will show you how to prevent the issues from wiping out your garden.

Critters

Anyone who lives in areas with large deer populations or ideal conditions for mice, rats, and rabbits runs the risk of growing a perfect garden for animals to devour. Some critters are easier to eliminate than others. Still, there are a few steps you can take to reduce the likelihood of seeing your garden nibbled away before you get the chance to harvest.

Gardening in pots and containers gives you some advantages over in-the-ground gardening when it comes to avoiding critters. Since you can usually move your garden around, it's easy to put your plants in a place that creatures avoid. You can also use various devices, sprays, and fencing to aid in reducing critters from getting into your garden.

Deer

There probably isn't an animal out there that can more quickly destroy your garden than deer. These beautiful, graceful creatures are eating machines that spend their lives seeking out the most leisurely meal possible. Your garden provides the perfect opportunity for deer to get a delicious and nutritious meal - typically without the risk of natural predators. Once deer start coming to your garden for a snack, they can be tough to repel.

The first thing you should do if you live in an area with large deer populations is to install fencing that will deter them. Deer are fantastic jumpers and can easily clear many wood or stone fences and will find highly creative ways to get in when they want. I've even seen deer learn to open gates and exploit weaknesses where fence sections join together. Wire or net fencing makes reasonable solutions, but you'll also need to make sure the fence is tall enough to prevent deer from jumping over. Typically, you'll want at least a seven-foot-tall fence to keep deer out.

Deterrent sprays are an effective and safe method of preventing deer. Many of these products are made from animal by-products, blood, and other ingredients that signal danger to deer. You can spray repellents on and around plants, fences, and other areas. Deterrent sprays are most effective when applying them before deer begin grazing your garden. You should start treating in the early spring when deer are bulking up after the winter. It's advisable to switch deterrent sprays periodically so that deer do not become used to the smell.

Container gardening lets you choose where to plant. If you put your garden near your home, deer are less likely to take a chance on a snack. They are naturally shy animals and don't like taking risks. You may even be able to use bells, tin cans on strings, and other noise-making devices to help prevent deer from getting comfortable. If you have a dog, you've got one of the best deer deterrents around. Let your dog spend plenty of time in the yard to encourage deer to pick a better target.

You might have success deterring deer with natural planting, too. Certain types of deer won't eat some plants like onions, so you can plant things they don't want to encourage them to skip your garden.

Mice, Rats, Skunks, Moles, Rabbits, and Squirrels

When it comes to frustratingly difficult pests to repel, our furry little friends take the cake. Highly adaptable, very intelligent, and always hungry, rodents and other foraging mammals will take any advantage you give them to feast on your plants. Many of these animals are active at night when it's difficult to spot them, and they will carry off your garden in the blink of an eye.

When you position your container garden, putting it close to where you live may help to prevent many of these animals from taking a bite. Unfortunately, some species like mice and rats will just as easily use your house as their new breeding ground. The trick with preventing rodents from getting established is to make sure the conditions are as inhospitable as possible. A dog or a cat in the yard can often be the difference between avoiding problems and a full-scale infestation.

Another trick I've used successfully is to paint small round stones to resemble strawberries. Place these around your plants before they begin producing fruit. One bite into a delicious-looking rock will deter many critters from returning!

Depending on where you live, you will have different pest problems. You'll need to decide how to handle issues with rodents. Traps and poison can be effective, but they are often the least humane way to deal with pests. Deterrent sprays may be effective, but you'll want to switch the type of spray periodically to avoid critters from getting used to the scent.

One of the most effective ways to prevent critters is to use hanging baskets, plant stands, and other structures to keep the pots less easy to access. Keep in mind that squirrels, rats, and mice are not only superior climbers; they can jump a lot higher than you would expect. They are also smart enough to figure out multiple steps to get what they want. So, keep an eye out for tree branches, fences, and other pathways a rodent might discover to get access to your elevated garden.

Burrowing critters are the bane of gardeners everywhere. I know it seems funny when you see a cartoon rabbit sucking carrots right out of the ground, but it's not funny when you wake up to find your containers stripped clean. Preventing burrowing critters is easier in pots and containers because of the natural deterrent of the container. If you live in an area with lots of chewing critters, you might do well to avoid plastic pots. It takes a surprisingly short time for a critter to chew through a plastic pot.

Birds

I have a friend who has the most beautiful cherry trees. Every year when the cherries are ripening, my friend goes to war. From netting to dogs to bells, there isn't a solution my friend hasn't tried, and birds still make an effort year after year.

There are many things out there that birds like to eat. Cherries might be near the top of the list. I have seen my friend's trees stripped of every last cherry overnight by hungry birds that strike within days of harvest when the fruit is ripening.

Deterring birds can be a full-time task, especially right around harvest. Some of the most effective methods are also classic. Birds don't like to eat when danger is present. Things like a scarecrow, wires with cans or silver strips, and even noises they are not familiar with can limit the damage birds will do. You want something

Owl Decoy

that moves or makes noise to limit birds most effectively.

Netting is often the only way to deal with birds. The best way to use netting is to build a structure that holds the net above and away from the garden so birds can't readily get a snack. The netting doesn't damage your garden right when it is the most vulnerable.

Locating your planters near your home may help to reduce many species of birds. Still, quite a few types have become too comfortable with being around people to let the location of your garden be a successful, stand-alone solution.

Every region of the U.S. will have unique critters. You might contact other gardeners, local nurseries, and educational facilities in your area to find out about regionally valuable solutions. It's also a good idea to check the local laws as some methods may be restricted. Suppose you have an infestation of critters happening. In that case, you may want to discuss the problem with an exterminator who has the knowledge to target animals properly.

Pests

Organic container gardening opens you up to an increased likelihood of pests. Since you are not using chemicals to kill and prevent insects, you are sure to find bugs at some point. The trick to handling insects is acting quickly and staying consistent. Many types of insects only live in particular conditions. So, you may be able to adjust watering or move plants to other areas of your garden to eliminate or reduce pests.

There are tens of thousands of types of bugs in the U.S. that will devour your garden. Each region will have some more common insects than others, so it's a good idea to find out the most likely problem if you are new to gardening. Keep an eye on the types of bugs you encounter each year and record effective elimination methods.

It's impossible to describe every bug out there that may harm your plants. So instead, I will break this down into three categories: Sap-Suckers, Leaf-Chewers, and Root-Borers. While there are tons of different types of bugs, most of them can be easily managed when you know what they eat and the best way to treat them.

Ants

Ants get a special category because they can affect plants in numerous ways. Some types of ants cut and eat leaves, fruit, and roots. Perhaps the worst thing about some types of ants is that they actively "herd" colonies of aphids and mealybugs to harvest the sweet "honeydew" these sap-suckers secrete.

Ants can be tough to control. They often build extensive subterranean homes that protect the queen and larvae. At the same time, the marching lines of ants you see are just sterile workers. Creating inhospitable environments for ants will reduce the chances of problems.

You can use petroleum jelly applied to a piece of masking tape and wrapped around the base of plants to stop ants from climbing. You should trim leaves from the bottom of your plants, so they don't touch the ground.

Ants don't like mint or cinnamon. You can put pieces of cinnamon gum, mint, or even a healthy sprinkle of ground cinnamon around the base of plants. Cinnamon is also effective for preventing root rot.

You can also use ants' behavior against them by mixing equal parts of cornmeal and sugar. The cornmeal will expand when ants consume the sugar, killing them.

Sap-Suckers

There are many types of insects that feed on the sap of plants. Some of the most common sap-suckers you'll find in your garden are aphids, thrips, mealybugs, and mites. These pests multiply rapidly and grow from a few individuals to an unstoppable horde in what seems like the blink of an eye.

- **Aphids:** Aphids are tiny insects that cluster in large groups on flower buds, leaflets, and other parts of the plant. There are around 400 types of aphids that impact crops in the U.S., and many species affect only one kind of plant. Aphids penetrate the surface of your crops and suck the sap out. As aphids grow, they secrete a chemical that hardens and holds them in place. When an aphid infestation happens, you may see your plants begin to wilt and yellow. Eventually, aphids will deplete a plant so severely that it won't survive. They then move on to the next plant. Aphids reproduce very rapidly and can take over an entire crop or a whole garden.

- **Thrips:** Thrips are tiny, cigar-shaped flying insects that spread at least 20 viruses to plants. On their own, thrips damage leaves and stems when they suck the sap. Thrips leave bleached, discolored spots on leaves. Infestations of thrips are difficult to control since these little bugs can easily hide in cracks and crevices. They have a unique, circular flying motion and swarm in warm, humid weather. Thrips commonly cause viruses that damage crops like tomatoes, potatoes, and tobacco.

- **Mealybugs:** Mealybugs are small, fuzzy-looking insects that primarily live on the bottom of leaves. Mealybugs rapidly reproduce when conditions are warm and humid. Mealybugs cause leaf drop, yellowing, and wilt. They frequently spread diseases among various plants. These sap-suckers are less common in many gardens. Still, they will be attracted to tropical and subtropical plants like mango and pineapple.

- **Spider Mites:** Spider mites live on the bottom of leaves and create small, spiderweb-like structures for protection. They are often difficult to spot until a significant infestation occurs. Like other sap-sucking insects, spider mites damage the surface of leaves and can cause leaf drop, yellowing, and plant death. They prefer hot, dry conditions and can reproduce in as little as five days. Generally, spider mites do not spread diseases.

Leaf-Chewers

Leaf-eating bugs are widespread and can cause an unbelievable amount of damage in short order. You will find both insects and larvae that eat leaves. Among the most damaging to your garden are caterpillars, Japanese beetles, flea beetles, slugs, and snails. It can be challenging to identify which pest is eating your leaves. It's even more frustrating when you start seeing lots of damage in your garden.

- **Caterpillars:** Butterflies are beautiful, but you'll quickly see them in a different light when a caterpillar outbreak chews through your leafy green crops, tomato plants, and cucumbers. Both moths and butterflies produce larvae that become caterpillars. Damage to plants is typically focused on the leaves, where large portions of the margins of the leaf will be eaten off. Nasty infestations will kill the plants. Many caterpillar species also feed on growing produce, particularly the Tomato Hornworm, which decimates the leaves and fruit of tomato plants.

- **Japanese Beetles:** Japanese beetles are flying, scarab-type insects that feed on flowers, leaves, and fruit of numerous types of plants. You will often find large, white grubs with orange or redheads in the soil in spring. Japanese beetles are an invasive species now found throughout the Eastern U.S. You will often notice leaves skeletonized when you have an infestation. Japanese beetles feed on many crops, including peppers, tomatoes, okra, corn, and many berries.

- **Flea Beetles:** Flea beetles are tiny, black insects that live on the bottom of leaves. They chew small, irregular holes in leaves. In the most frustrating fashion possible, they will often chew holes in numerous leaves throughout a feeding session, damaging multiple plants in the process. Flea beetles thrive in hot, dry conditions. Adults feed on leaves of many plants, including all types of lettuce, tomato plants, peppers, and the greens of onions, radishes, and turnips.

- **Slugs and Snails:** Slugs and snails are voracious eaters and can cause significant damage to garden crops. They feed on leaves, stems, fruit, and roots. Most of the time, slug and snail problems are relatively small-scale - these pests are a delicacy for predators - but populations can get out of control and kill entire plants.

Root-Borers

Several insects feed on the roots of plants. The larvae of many of the pests listed above begin life by eating the roots of plants. Plants with root-boring insect infestations exhibit poor growth habits, yellowing, and dropping leaves, and often die. Common root-eating insects that can affect your container garden include root grubs, fungus gnat larvae, root aphids, and root weevils.

- **Root Maggots:** Root maggots (grubs) are the larvae of the root maggot fly. These destructive root-eating larvae hatch in spring and immediately begin eating into roots. Root maggots are often crop-specific and target cabbage and lettuce crops, along with onions, garlic, and turnips. Root maggots cause a decline in overall plant health and can kill the plant before they emerge from the soil as flies. You'll find root maggots in the main root ball or burrowing into young onion bulbs.

- **Fungus Gnat Larvae:** Fungus gnats are tiny, black flying gnats. They tend to swarm in warm, moist conditions. The larvae feed on tender roots until they mature. Mature plants are only minimally harmed by the larvae, but seedlings can quickly die from fungus gnat larvae. They are a common nuisance when container gardening indoors.

- **Root Aphids:** Root aphids infest the stem and root of plants at or below the soil level. Because root aphids are challenging to see, their population can often get out of control. Root aphids leave plants yellowed, withered, and stunted. Plants that suffer damage from root aphids are more likely to get other diseases like root rot.

- **Root Weevils:** Root weevils hatch at the roots of plants, where they spend the first stage of life feeding on roots. Adult root weevils emerge at night and eat angular notches from the edges of leaves, then returning to the soil before daybreak. Root weevil larvae will feed on many different types of plants, frequently chewing holes in roots. Plants are more likely to contract diseases when damaged by the larvae. A common garden pest is the strawberry root weevil.

Organic Pest Control

Organic gardening means that you'll never be able to use a synthetic chemical insecticide. Your container garden will be a tempting target for all manner of insects. The best thing you can do is prevent problems in the first place. You can do this by using clean, sterile soil mixes free of eggs and larvae.

There are a few organic methods of pest control that are easy to use and more effective than synthetic treatment in some cases. One key point, regardless of the way, you want to catch pest problems early and take even a minor infestation seriously. Once an adult population of insects is established in your garden, it can take years to completely rid yourself of them.

Plant Natural Deterrents

Numerous plants like mint, marigolds, basil, and chives can repel insects, making them excellent additions to your container garden. Chrysanthemum flowers provide the natural form of permethrin, a commonly synthesized ingredient in many insecticides. Natural deterrents are the best way to prevent harming beneficial insects in your garden.

Stimulate Natural Predators

One of the most effective and natural ways to control insects in your garden is to create hospitable conditions for beneficial predators. Ladybugs are heavy feeders with an affinity for aphid larvae. Lacewing will also actively hunt aphids, mealybugs, and other insect larvae. Flowering plants, fennel, dill, and yarrow are effective plants for attracting ladybugs, lacewings, and many types of bees and wasps that feed on insects. You can order Ladybugs and Lacewing larvae online.

Effective Homemade Insect Soap

Most insects that feed on the leaves and stems of your plants can effectively be controlled using a simple homemade insecticide soap. This recipe kills soft-bodied bugs, including aphids, mealybugs, and thrips. But, keep in mind, it will also kill ladybug and lacewing larvae. Simply combine two-and-a-half tablespoons of castile soap and two-and-a-half tablespoons of vegetable oil in one gallon of water. Shake vigorously to mix and pour it into a clean spray bottle. This will immediately kill bugs while it is wet but is ineffective once it dries.

Inexpensive Beetle Control

Beetles are not affected by insecticidal soap, though they may be deterred. A readily available product called diatomaceous earth- DE for short- is a practical, natural method of controlling many types of leaf-chewers, including flea beetles and caterpillars. It also works on spider mites and other soft-bodied insects, slugs, and flies. DE is the powdered remains of fossilized shells. The tiny grains prevent insects from breathing. Treating insects with DE will require that you periodically reapply, as watering will reduce the effectiveness of DE.

Avoid Contamination

One of the most disappointing things is when a plant suddenly dies from a pest infestation that gets out of control. A mistake too many people make is to reuse the plant's soil. Most harmful pests lay eggs in the soil that can last for more than a year until the right conditions exist to hatch. It is incredibly easy to accidentally spread numerous pests from one container to the next by combining soil. As much as it is frustrating, the soil should be discarded. Don't put the remains of plants that died from pests in your compost, either. The eggs can survive unbelievable conditions and continue contaminating your garden.

Diseases Common in Container Plants

There are a handful of common diseases that can strike your garden at any time. Often, you'll find that the only option is to destroy the plant before others are infected. Most of the common diseases can be prevented with proper technique.

- **Root Rot:** By far the most common problem for novice gardeners and experienced ones alike, root rot is typically the result of water accumulating at the roots and stem of plants. Poor drainage, heavy soil, and excessive watering generally are present when a plant shows signs of rot. You will notice plants looking yellow and weak. Eventually, stems and stalks will feel mushy and turn brown. Roots are often enlarged and soft. Once root rot sets in, you must cut the infected part off the plant and put the remainder in new, clean soil. Root rot is easily spread to other plants, so do not cross-contaminate your planters.

- **Blight:** Blight is a broad term that describes damage to plants caused by fungi living on the leaves. Blight appears as spots and blotches that rapidly progress, eventually killing the plant. Blight can be spread by pollinators, the wind, and mishandling, so you should remove any plants you suspect of having signs of blight. Blight is often found when plant leaves are left damp or wet for extended periods. It is most common when daytime temperatures create warm, humid conditions.

- **Wilt:** Wilt is caused by outbreaks of fungi, bacteria, or nematodes. There are many different types of wilt disease that affect plants. Common types found in the container garden include verticillium wilt and bacterial wilt of cucurbits. Wilt often appears as a sudden yellowing and death of plants. It can affect trees, branches of trees, and hundreds of vegetable and fruit crops. Wilt can come from various insects that feed on your plants, infected soils and spreading from nearby infected plants. The damage from wilt can look a lot like root or crown rot. There is no cure for most types of wilt disease.

- **Anthracnose:** This is a fungal infection that shows up as yellow or brown spots that turn into sunken lesions. It is common for outbreaks to happen when leaves get wet while watering. It thrives in warm, moist conditions and is easily spread among plants. There is no cure. Infected plants must be removed and destroyed.

Avoiding Common Diseases

Many diseases are prompted by excessive water or inadequate drainage.

Ensure that your containers or pots have excellent drainage and that your potting mix doesn't get heavy or hold too much moisture. When you water, make sure you give your plant deep watering with periods of mild drying out in between. Root rot, fungus gnats, and many other problems need warm, humid conditions to thrive, so correct watering can prevent many common diseases. I prefer watering my plants in the morning so that moisture on the leaves dries during the day. Watering at night is generally a bad idea unless your plants are exceptionally thirsty.

Conclusion

Learning to spot the early signs of critters, pests, and diseases will ensure that your garden thrives. There are many organic methods of preventing problems. You'll most likely find a combination of techniques that works for the type of plants and containers you garden in.

Everyone will deal with insects, critters, or diseases at one point or another. Don't despair if it happens to you. Just follow best practices to deal with the problem as quickly as possible. It can be hard to cut down plants you have nurtured for months but doing so can save the rest of your garden. Good luck and consider joining my Facebook discussion group to answer your questions and concerns immediately.

The Urban Farmer Gardening & Home Canning Advice for the 21st Century

https://www.facebook.com/groups/501585191212408

Chapter 8

HARVEST TIME!

A weed is a plant that has mastered every survival skill except
for learning how to grow in rows. – Doug Larson

It's been many long weeks of patient work and care, and your garden has blossomed. Now it's time for the best part - harvest time! Every plant you grow will mature at different times. Some vegetables can be ready for harvest in less than one month, while others will take several months. This chapter will give you tips on how to harvest your vegetables correctly and increase your yields.

I think everyone loves harvest time the most. It's such a great time to enjoy the product of your efforts and to reflect on the entire process. I love walking my garden in the morning, picking fresh and ripe vegetables for my table. Harvest also brings me together with many friends and neighbors as we share our bounty and trade for varieties we didn't grow. It's a beautiful time of community building, and it's the most delicious time of the year!

How To Get a Bigger Harvest

Let's get right into the best part - how to get the most from your containers. One trick that experienced gardeners use is called succession planting. Essentially, succession planting is simply a continuous planting of the same crop weeks apart. When you harvest the first plants to mature, the next harvest will be weeks away, giving you time to use your crop or store it.

Succession planting is a great idea for many fast-maturing plants and plants used up after harvest.

This sounds strange, but one secret to getting bigger harvests from many of your favorite container plants is actually preventing the plants from producing fruit early in the season. This trick works great with tomatoes, peppers, eggplant, cucumbers, and summer squash. You can pinch off the flower buds before they become fruit for the first month or two. Doing so forces the plant to produce more flowers. Once you begin letting your plants set fruit, you should harvest it early and often. Your plants will respond by giving you larger harvests. Don't forget that many of your favorite plants have edible flowers. Squash blossoms, in particular, are delicious when stuffed with chorizo and fried.

Determining When Your Garden is Ready

It may sound a little corny, but I always say that if it looks good enough to eat, it probably is. I like to walk around my garden when I know plants are reaching maturity and sample things. There were few better flavorful experiences than that first ripe cherry tomato of the season when it came right off the plant you're growing.

Seed packet and catalogs will give you an average of the number of days until the plant is ready to harvest, presented as the average days to maturity. This is valuable information because you'll get an idea of when you need to be ready to harvest. The maturity days should be counted from the day you put seedlings in the ground or the day that seeds sprout.

Some of the everyday things that can alter the amount of time until your plant is mature include sudden weather changes, too much or too little rain or watering, pests, and incorrect lighting. Many plants will produce best when conditions are kept stable. However, a few types will react to specific stressors by producing fruit and vegetables. For example, pepper plants will produce larger yields and more flavorful fruit when they are periodically stressed for water once the fruit begins to develop.

While many varieties of popular crops are available as quick-maturing types, there are many plants you can grow and harvest in less than two months. These are excellent for keeping kids engaged in the process, filling in parts of the garden after harvesting other crops, and providing a steady, regular supply of delicious and fresh produce.

Fast-Maturing Summer Crops

If you want to grow some fast-maturing summer plants, look at the snap pea varieties. These delicious little guys are ready to harvest around 50 days for some types. They are delicious raw, cooked, and used in Asian recipes.

Bush beans also make excellent fast-maturing choices. Many varieties will be ready for harvest in as little as 60 days. They will continue producing beans until fall sets in. Bush beans are also ideal container plants because they have a compact growth pattern that's easy to maintain. Some of my favorite varieties include Slenderette, Top Crop, Top Notch Golden Wax, and Provider. All are excellent for home canning.

One of the most satisfying fast-maturing summer plants is summer squash.

Common varieties like zucchini often mature in less than 60 days, and you can harvest immature fruit for tasty snacks. Zucchini is a fun choice because it grows so fast you can almost watch it reach for things to climb on.

Carrots can also be a good choice for fast-maturing summer veggies. You can harvest lots of types of carrots when they are 50 to 60 days mature for delicious, sweet, and crunchy baby carrots. Carrots make an excellent succession planting veggie. Don't forget that carrot greens are edible and delicious, and they add a unique flavor to salads. Try growing Nantes, Little Fingers, and Early Scarlet Horn.

Long-Maturing Summer Plants

Plants that take longer to mature need to be planted earlier in the season if you live in areas that experience frequent early frosts in fall. Tomatoes, peppers, corn, and many squash plants take more than 60 days to mature, with some types taking longer than 120 days to fully mature. Many types of peppers, potatoes, and full-size carrots can take all summer to develop and may not be ready until well into the fall. Most of these plants are also vulnerable to frost and will begin to decline as soon as the weather starts to cool.

Container planting long-maturing varieties is an excellent trick to ensuring a good harvest when you live in northern climates that simply don't have a long growing season. With your plants in containers, you can more easily move the plants indoors or undercover when an early frost strikes. This enables you to preserve the plants and extend your growing season.

Fast-Maturing Cool Weather Plants

Lots of the fastest maturing crops prefer cool weather and make excellent choices for succession planting. Among the fastest maturing plants are any of the brassica plants. This is a large family that originates from wild mustard. The group includes all lettuce varieties, turnips, spinach, Asian leafy greens like tatsoi and bok choy, and broccoli and cauliflower. Many varieties will mature in 40 to 50 days, and immature plants are delicious as micro greens added to salads. You can harvest brassica varieties for microgreens as soon as they have true leaves, usually within three weeks.

Identifying Ripe Fruit and Vegetables

One of the stressful aspects of harvesting your garden is when to pick. When you buy produce in the grocery store, you tend to look for flaws like bruises, insect damage, and rotten areas rather than whether the produce is ripe. That's because the farmers harvest the crop when ripe or just before. It seems like it would be easy to tell when your garden is ready, but it can be quite confusing to determine if it's actually time to harvest. Over the years, I have developed a system for determining if my fruits or vegetables are ready.

- **Color:** Most varieties of fruits and vegetables will change color as they ripen. Tomatoes, peppers, and squash change from green to orange, red, or even purple when they mature. Fruits and vegetables change color because the starches in the fruit break down into sugars, so ripe produce tastes sweeter than unripe vegetables and fruit.

- **Sheen:** Many varieties will change in their appearance, becoming shinier as the fruit or vegetable matures. This is typical of many melon varieties, cucumbers, zucchini, and other types of fruit. These plants become shiny because tiny hairs, called guard hairs, are no longer necessary for the plant to protect the fruit once it matures.

- **Texture:** Many varieties of vegetables and fruit you grow change how they feel as they mature. This is particularly prevalent when you grow beans and peas. Immature pods will be flat, but once the seeds start to develop, you'll see the pods swell, and you can feel the beans getting larger. Other plants, like tomatoes, will exhibit softening of the fruit as it matures. When you gently press on a tomato, there should be some give but still some resistance. A hard tomato isn't ready yet, and a squishy one has gone too long.

- **Size:** Size is an excellent indicator of maturity. Plants like cucumbers and zucchini need to be harvested when they are of medium size. Waiting too long with these plants will produce almost inedible and massive fruit. Cucumbers and zucchini become bitter, and the skin becomes tough as they mature. Like peppers and okra, many plants are best when harvested at a medium to small size for the same reason.

A great way to find out if your plants are ready for harvest is to pick one of the most advanced fruits or veggies and take a bite. If it tastes good, has a good texture, and has good color and sheen, you know that your plant is ready. If the veggie you pick doesn't taste good, it may not be ready yet. Remember that many vegetable varieties become bitter as they age, so you'll want to harvest early and often rather than let fruit set on the plant.

Just because your veggies aren't as big or bright as those you see in stores doesn't mean they aren't good. Most of the produce you buy in the store is treated to make it appear riper than it is actually.

Edible Flowers

Many people don't realize that many of our favorite vegetable plants have more than just edible fruit. The greens and flowers of many plants are edible. You can add carrot greens, turnip greens, and beet greens to salads, and they make a healthy juice, too. Flowers from cucumber and squash plants, onions, chives, and herbs like dill and fennel are delicious raw or cooked. They are often useful for making infusions which we will discuss in the next chapter. You should avoid eating leaves and blossoms from any plant in the Nightshade family, including eggplant, tomatoes, and potatoes. These plants can be poisonous.

How to Harvest the Right Way

When you are picking fruits and vegetables in your garden, you'll want to pay attention to the right way to do it. Some fruits, like tomatoes and peppers, pick easily by hand when ready. Other varieties like eggplant and zucchini should be carefully cut from the plant to prevent opening the opportunity for pests and diseases. Squash, including pumpkins and plants in the melon family, can usually be harvested when the vine shrivels and turns brown where it meets the fruit.

You'll want to research the particular plants you're growing to see what the best-accepted practice for harvesting is. An excellent way to get an indication is to look at produce in the grocery store. If the type of produce looks like it was cut, you should also cut your veggies when you harvest. Often, you'll learn to feel the best way to gather. Some things come off easily by hand. Others may break branches and damage the plant.

A vital tip to remember about harvesting: Always remove damaged fruits and vegetables. Sometimes, you'll see damage from bugs, weather or watering, or rot that happens when plants are growing. You should remove these unusable parts as soon as you see a problem. Doing so conserves the plants' energy for producing new, better fruit. It prevents creating an ideal situation for pests and disease.

Tips for Succession Planting

Succession planting is the ideal way to extend your harvest season. We touched on the topic earlier in this chapter. Still, I want to expand on some of the popular concepts so you'll have a good idea of how succession planting can be helpful in pots and containers. There are a couple ways you can take advantage of succession planting both for larger harvests and more diversity in your pot and container garden.

Same Crop, Different Planting Day

This is the most common way to use succession planting to your advantage. Rather than plant all your seeds or seedlings at once, simply wait one or two weeks before planting the next batch. I like to do this in rows in bigger containers, growing a second harvest in between the first harvest. This gives more room for the older plants to develop while keeping everything reasonably compact. Crops like lettuce varieties that make heads are ideal for this type of succession planting because you will harvest the entire plant once it's ready. If you plant all at once, you'll get one harvest and may end up throwing some of your crops away before it gets used.

Different Crop in Succession

A great way to take advantage of your container garden is to plant fast-maturing varieties early in the season with later developing types. This works really well with cool-weather crops like lettuce, spinach, and broccoli ready for harvest in the spring. This leaves the perfect amount of time to plant tomatoes, peppers, and eggplant that take longer to grow. Fast-maturing beans and peas make for excellent early harvest plants. You can follow up with squash or melons that require the hot summer weather and a little more time to develop. This is often called companion planting, and it's a great way to take advantage of naturally beneficial plants.

Same Crop, Different Maturation Date

One trick for successfully extending the harvest is to plant similar plants with different maturity dates. There are many early - and late-harvest varieties out there for plants like tomatoes and peppers you can grow together and harvest as the plants develop. This is a great way to get biodiversity in your garden without having to dedicate container space to lots of similar plants.

The Three Sisters

Our native American ancestors introduced Europeans to a type of planting called the Three Sisters. This is a form of companion and succession planting that maximizes the amount of harvest you can achieve from the smallest space possible. In essence, the Three Sisters method relies on different plants that complement one another.

The classic example of this method plants corn, peas or beans, and squash together. Corn is a fast-growing plant that leaves a sturdy cane after harvest. Beans and peas use the stalks of the mature corn to climb and grow. Beans and peas are in the legume family of plants known to be "nitrogen-fixing" plants. This means that these plants absorb nitrogen from the air and store it in the roots. When the legumes are harvested, the squash is growing and can take advantage of the nitrogen release from the beans or peas.

Planting the Three Sisters gives you a late spring corn harvest, an early summer bean harvest, and a late summer or fall squash harvest. You can plant several containers spaced a week or two apart to maximize the results from planting in this method.

There are literally thousands of combinations you can make to take advantage of the natural growth characteristics of different types of plants. While many varieties play well together, some combinations should be avoided. Heavy feeders like tomatoes and corn can quickly deplete the nutrients in the soil before either plant is ready for harvest. Onions and other allium family members do not grow well with beans and peas. However, planting beans with carrots, cucumber, eggplant, or strawberries benefits both plants.

If you combine interplanting, companion planting, and succession planting in your container garden, you'll be able to grow a large number of numerous types of fruits, herbs, and vegetables in a relatively small area. You'll even find that many types of plants can deter insects from one another, provide nutrients and shade, and even enhance the crops' size, color, and flavor.

Harvesting Seeds

I always try to harvest enough seeds from the plants I grow to plant another season. It usually takes only one or two plants to get enough seeds to make sure you always have a ready-to-grow garden. Most vegetable varieties produce seeds in the base of the flower. The seeds mature after the flower dries and falls away.

The best way to harvest seeds is to snip off the entire flower being careful not to shake it. Then, place it crown side down in a paper bag. Let the flowers dry for a few days in a warm, dark place. You can then shake the bag, release the seeds, and remove the stems. You'll have seeds and chafe - the leftover husks and flower petals. Sift to remove the seeds.

Some plants I harvest seed for growing, others I gather for seasonings. Dill, parsley, onions, fennel, and celery produce flavorful and nutritious seeds that complement many meals.

One note on seed harvesting: many plants you'll grow are hybrids. Hybrid varieties frequently will produce seeds that develop different plants. That means that sometimes, the delicious, beautiful plant you grew one year may have plants that struggle to survive. I think that it's always worth a try.

Sometimes, you'll get lucky, and the seeds you gather will carry on good traits.

Tips for a Successful Harvest

A successful harvest begins with ensuring your plants have the best opportunity to thrive. Gardening in containers gives you the ability to control every aspect of what your plants need. I think this is both a responsibility and a pleasure. When I see plants thriving in my garden, I know that the time and effort I put in will be rewarded with a bountiful harvest. Indeed, you shall reap what you have sown!

Succession planting is a great way to get a great harvest. Ensure that you have enough seeds to sprout over a few weeks. If you sprout too many in the beginning, you'll end up thinning a lot of plants out, and you may run out of seeds before the season is up.

Try sprouting enough seeds to put two plants in each area according to the spacing but add spacing as needed for the next round of plants. Growing this many gives you room for error since some seeds won't sprout, and others will die before becoming seedlings.

A great way to help boost your harvest is to add well-aged compost after your plants have flowered. Work it into the top one or two inches of soil and water well. This will boost nitrogen and other essential nutrient levels and help the plant produce abundantly.

Cool-weather crops mature relatively quickly, so you can often take advantage by planting in the summer. The trick is to plant in a well-watered container, then cover the top with a thick piece of wood. This insulates the container and keeps cool moisture deep in the soil. Check the container every day for moisture and see if any seeds have germinated. Once you see sprouts, you can remove the board. The young plants will be ready to put in the ground as the summer heat fades and the nights become cooler and longer.

Summary

Harvest time is the best! I just love seeing all the different colors of vegetables and fruit, seeing all the plants blooming, and the smells and tastes of the garden. Container gardening makes harvesting much simpler and more accessible than in-ground gardens. You can position your containers so that you aren't stooping and bending to harvest. Your plants are easier to examine, particularly in the critical stem to soil region. And best of all, your compact container gardens give you a plentiful supply of homegrown, organic, and delicious produce that you know exactly where it came from.

I know that the first time you taste a juicy, sweet tomato from your own garden, you'll never look at store-bought tomatoes the same again. Container gardening is a peaceful,

Harvest Time

relaxing, and thoughtful experience that results in a flavorful and nutritious ending. Harvest time is one of the most enjoyable to get together with family and participate in. The kids love picking strawberries and tomatoes. Everyone is fascinated watching peppers change from green to orange to red before picking. Harvest is a wonderful opportunity to share your garden with others and let them enjoy the taste and texture unique to lovingly homegrown produce.

Chapter 9

PRESERVING THE HARVEST TO LAST ALL YEAR

"The wise store up choice food and olive oil, but fools gulp their down." Proverbs 21:20

No matter if you plant one plant or fifty, sooner or later, you'll harvest more than you can use before it goes bad. The good news is that food preservation is as old as farming, and there are some effortless ways you and your family can store your harvest. The best thing about food preservation is that when your favorite fruits and vegetables are not in season, you have a steady supply at hand.

There are different methods of preserving different types of fruits, vegetables, and herbs. I'm going to give you some helpful tips I've learned over the years for successfully keeping my own harvests. I know I have said that every part of the gardening experience is my favorite part, but this is one of my best experiences.

It brings together the entire family, friends, and neighbors to celebrate the harvest. We swap stories over bubbling pots and whistling pressure cookers, talk about what we want to do next season as the dehydrator hums away. We remember the warmth of the summer sun in the slowly drying hues of hanging chili peppers. You'll find **99+ *Easy Home Canning Recipes*** in Part Two of this collection.

Pickling Vegetables

Pickling is a traditional way to preserve many types of vegetables. It's an ideal way to keep cucumbers, beans, cauliflower, okra, onions, radishes, and many other vegetables. Pickling is also very simple to do at home. It gives you lots of opportunities to be creative by mixing and matching flavors for unique combinations.

Quick pickling is also called refrigerator pickling. It will preserve your vegetables for five to six months in the refrigerator. You only need a few basic things to get started. You'll need vinegar, water, and mason jars to pickle your harvest.

Simply pack your vegetables into the jars, filling them as much as possible without smashing your harvest. In a saucepan, bring equal amounts of distilled white vinegar and water to a boil and add one tablespoon of kosher salt and one tablespoon of granulated sugar. Bring to a boil until the sugar is dissolved, then pour the brine into the jars, leaving one-half-inch of space at the top. Gently tap the jars on the counter to release trapped air, then screw the lids on tightly. Place the jars in the refrigerator for 48 hours before sampling. Flavors improve with time.

Some ideas for making unique and interesting pickling flavors might be to use different types of vinegar. White wine, rice wine, and apple cider vinegar will work as well as regular white vinegar. Avoid malt vinegar and balsamic, as these won't provide good flavor or texture due to the acid composition. You can include fresh or dried herbs like dill, parsley, oregano, and thyme, along with spices like whole peppercorns to add intrigue to your pickling recipe.

Two Ways of Canning

Canning is one of the best ways to preserve food easily and quickly. It's also a low-tech operation that requires only a few standard kitchen instruments to be successful. The most important thing about canning is to make sure you select high-quality mason jars that have seals and lids in good condition. Ensure the jars have no chips or cracks, as these can cause breakage during the canning process. At a minimum, clean your jars thoroughly with dish soap and hot water. I like to use a food-grade sanitizer. Or, I run them through the dishwasher cycle using hot water before canning to ensure no fungi or bacteria will contaminate my preserves.

Steps for Hot Water Bath Canning

Hot water bath canning is a suitable method for preserving high-acid foods. This includes most fruits and pickled vegetables. Low-acid produce runs the risk of developing the bacterial spore that causes botulism. You'll need to add citric acid to safely can or use a pressure cooker for canning low-acid vegetables.

The first step is to place your clean, sterile jars in a large pot of hot water deep enough to fully cover the jars. Fill the jars and kettle with water and put them on low heat. Place the lids and pressure rings underwater over low heat in a saucepan until you are ready to use them.

Preparing Fruit and Vegetables for Canning

There are two ways to preserve your harvest using the hot water bath: raw and heated. The raw pack method is self-explanatory. You'll simply chop the fruit or vegetable up enough to fit in the jar and fill the remainder with water or syrup. Heating the fruits and vegetables to boiling before putting them in the jars tends to yield a better flavor and color. You can use the liquid from heating to fill the canning jar. The heating process reduces the risk of your preserves shrinking and leaving too much space at the top of the jar.

A canning rack keeps the bottom of the jars from touching the kettle, which can cause excessive heat and may break your jars. If you don't have a canning rack, you can use a pressure cooker insert, a cake cooling rack, or even a folded kitchen towel to prevent the jars from breaking.

You will want to find a recipe specifically for the type of fruits and vegetables you're canning. There will be a recommended headspace in the jar that prevents over-or under-filling. Using a jar lifter, remove one jar at a time from the hot water kettle and drain the water back into the pot. Immediately fill the jar, making sure to use a rubber spatula to scrape around the inside of the jar to free trapped air bubbles.

Put the lids and pressure rings on the jars and tighten until just finger-tight. You don't want to overtighten the bands because the jars can explode. Air needs to escape during the canning process. Set the jar on the canning rack before getting the next jar from the hot water. Don't let the jars touch on the canning rack.

Once the jars are filled, you'll lower the rack into the canning bath. This can be a large kettle or pot with a snug lid, but it must be deep enough for the jars to be fully submerged by at least one inch without touching the bottom.

If you are canning raw fruit and vegetables, start with the water hot but not boiling. Fruits and vegetables heated first should go into softly boiling water. Add enough water to ensure at least one inch of depth above the jars.

Raise the temperature to a steady, rolling boil, then cover and set a timer according to your recipe. When the scanning is finished, turn off the heat and gently remove each can from the water. Place them on an elevated rack at least one inch apart. This will prevent sudden temperature changes that can result in dangerous explosions. Do not touch the pressure rings or metal lids. Let the cans cool before handling. Don't forget to label and date them!

Pressure Cooker Method

The pressure cooker method of canning is the only safe way to can low-acid foods like many vegetables. In fact, this is also how you preserve meat, poultry, and seafood. You'll prepare for canning in a pressure cooker just the same as for canning in the hot water bath. The difference is that you'll put only two or three inches of water in the pressure cooker rather than submerging the jars.

Once the pressure cooker is filled with jars ready for canning, lock the lid in place. Turn the heat on high and let the temperature rise quickly. This will rapidly increase the pressure in the cooker. When steam begins to hiss from the vent pipe, set your timer for 5-10 minutes, then place the gauge in place. Most recipes call for 10psi (sea level). Lower the burner slightly until the gauge "jiggles" 3-4 times per minute. This lets the pressure build gradually, making it easier to settle the pressure at the proper temperature.

Follow the guidelines in your recipe for the length of time to cook your harvest in a pressure cooker. Most fruit and vegetable recipes will require 30 to 45 minutes per pint - longer for quarts. When the time is up, turn off the heat and move the pressure cooker off the burner if possible. Do not remove the vent cap or try to open the lid. Pressure will gradually decrease. You'll leave the cooker alone for 30-45 minutes or longer, depending on the style, size, and thickness of your particular cooker. Once you remove the lid, gently lift the jars from the canner using a jar lifter. Arrange them on a cooling rack, or dry dish towel, at least one inch apart, and let cool. You'll hear a "ping" as the jars cool, indicating you have a successful seal. After the jars are thoroughly cooled, check the seal by gently pressing on the metal lid. It should not pop up or down. Refrigerate any cans that didn't seal properly. You can remove the bands and label your jars. It's a good idea to write down the date you can. That way, you are practicing proper food rotation when consuming your harvest.

Freezing Your Harvest

One of the most convenient ways to preserve fresh produce from your garden is to freeze your harvest. As a rule of thumb, any herb you can eat raw from the garden can be frozen uncooked. You'll want to experiment with different herbs to test whether you prefer them air-dried or frozen. My preferred way to freeze herbs is to wash them thoroughly and pat them dry. You don't want to freeze a bunch of water onto the herbs.

Layer the herbs between sheets of parchment paper and then put them in a plastic sealing bag. Remove as much air as possible before you seal the bags and freeze them. Don't forget to label what the herb is and the date that you froze it. You can also chop the herbs into salad-size pieces and put them in an ice cube tray. Fill with water and freeze for instant-use flavors. You can even mix herbs together for a savory addition to many recipes. I've frozen fresh basil in a freezer bag with some extra virgin olive oil recipe-ready for my next pasta dish or marinara sauce!

Blanching and Freezing

Almost all other vegetables aside from leafy greens must be blanched before freezing. This includes onions, broccoli, okra, artichokes, carrots, beans, and many other vegetables. Blanching is a really simple process to do at home.

Start by getting a large pot and a large bowl ready. Boil one gallon of water per pound of vegetables. Bring the water to a vigorous, rolling boil before adding the vegetables. Many charts provide you with the proper amount of time required to blanch different types of vegetables. Under-blanching is often considered worse than not blanching since it can introduce the opportunity for bacteria to develop. Over-blanching reduces the color, taste, and texture. Larger produce like artichoke globes and large onions will require longer boiling times.

While the vegetables are boiling, fill the bowl with ice and water. When the timer is up, immediately immerse the vegetables in the ice water. Keep adding ice and cold water to stop the cooking process and cool the vegetables. Cooling should take the same amount of time as boiling.

Once your veggies are cool, pat them dry, place them in sealed plastic bags, and ensure that the air is removed from the bag before freezing it. Label your bags with the date and the contents.

Cold Storage

Many types of root vegetables are best stored at moderately low temperatures. If you live in a place where you have a root cellar or any kind of dark, consistently cool place, storing roots is easy. When you harvest potatoes, onions, turnips, kohlrabi, and other root crops, brush the dirt off them, but do not rinse them clean. Instead, pack them in a large wooden box and surround them with sphagnum peat moss or damp sand. Keep them cool and in the dark, and your roots will stay fresh all winter and well into the spring. This method only works if you can keep temperatures consistent and low. Warming temperatures will trigger the roots to begin growing again and may encourage bacterial and fungal growth.

Drying and Dehydrating

Drying and dehydrating is the simplest form of preservation. If you live in a warm, dry place, you can preserve many of your favorites simply by hanging them from the stems right after harvest. Other types of fruits and vegetables can be dried in the oven or in a food dehydrator. Dried fruits and vegetables offer a unique way to eat many items. Dried okra, peaches, kale, and green beans are favorites around my household.

- **Sun Drying:** Sun drying is an excellent option if you live in a place where you have high afternoon temperatures (85-100 degrees) and plenty of sunshine. It's only appropriate for fruits that are high in sugar, though. You'll use different methods for drying vegetables. Simply arrange your fruits in thin, even layers on a drying rack. Cover with a screen to prevent insects while allowing heat and moisture to exchange. Periodically test the drying fruit and vegetables. When they crack when bent, they are ready. Sun-drying can take several days to complete, so keep an eye out for dew that can lead to spoilage. Some fruits and herbs are best hang-dried in a warm, indirectly lit place. A popular traditional way to dry peppers is to string them through the stems and hang them. This allows airflow around each individual pepper and makes it simple to use dried peppers as needed.

- **Electric Dehydrator:** Electric dehydrators are simple devices that combine a heating element with a fan to circulate the heat. They typically are a series of racks that stack together, letting you get lots of different things on at once. This is a highly efficient method of preserving vegetables and fruit at home and making jerky. The key is to slice your fruit and vegetables in equal, thin slices. This lets the circulating air have an equivalent effect on all the fruit or vegetables at once and allows them to dehydrate at the same rate.

- **Oven Drying:** To dry vegetables and fruit in the oven, you'll need to set the range to the lowest possible temperature. The ideal temp is 140-150 degrees. Higher temperatures risk "cooking" the food, which gives a hard, inedible exterior to your harvest. Like other dehydrating options, slice fruit and vegetables in consistently thin slices to ensure consistent dehydration. Place your harvest on a cookie sheet lined with parchment paper and put it in the oven. It will take anywhere from 8-12 hours to dehydrate many types of fruit and vegetables, so this is a method best used on cooler, fall evenings.

Tonics and Infusions

Making tonics and infusions is an excellent way to create unique flavors and provide culinary seasonings using your fresh harvest. Many different things can work for infusions and tinctures, but flowers are among my favorite to use. A white wine vinegar infusion with chive blossoms makes an excellent alternative to standard oil & vinegar salad dressings.

Infusions

An infusion is simply herbs steeped in water or oil to extract the beneficial properties and flavors. A good general rule of thumb is to use 1 teaspoon of herbs in each cup of liquid. To make an infusion, simply add dried or fresh herbs to very hot water and steep for 10 minutes to one hour. Then, simply strain into a jar, and you have an infused liquid. This is a great way to preserve and use the flavors of many aromatic herbs like mint, chamomile, and turmeric.

Tonics

A tonic is different from an infusion because it usually uses alcohol and takes a more extended period to complete. Many brews can rest for several days or even several weeks before straining. Making a tonic is no more difficult than making an infusion. You'll add dried or fresh herbs to 100 proof alcohol and allow the mixture to steep. The longer it steeps, the more potent the tonic will be. You will want about a 1:2 ratio of herbs to alcohol. Using 100 proof alcohol ensures that you will have pure flavors from the herbs without added flavors from other types of alcohol. Tonics are usually administered by the drop, so you don't need to be concerned about the alcohol content. Once the mixture has steeped for the necessary amount of time, strain the herbs from the liquid and store them in a glass jar with a tight-fitting lid. Tonics will keep for more than five years.

Conclusion

There are lots of great ways to store your harvest. From quick pickling that you can enjoy in a few days to canning and freezing, which let you enjoy your harvest well into the next season, there are ways you can preserve your harvest on a budget at home. I find pickling and canning to be particularly

A well-stocked pantry

enjoyable when I get my family involved. The younger members have fun picking out different flavors and combinations of vegetables. At the same time, the adults get to appreciate the sights, smells, and sounds. In my house, we often gather together with our friends and neighbors and preserve our harvests together. It's a great way to celebrate the months of hard work and careful planning that grew you a delicious and healthy garden from just pots and containers.

BONUS: FROM SEED TO TABLE IN 21 DAYS!

If you've never experienced the joy of accomplishing more than you can imagine, plant a garden. – Robert Brault

Some radish varieties

This is one of my favorite exercises to give to younger people who are learning about gardening, and it's something I hope you'll share with your little ones. You can use this exercise in a single pot, even indoors. It's a great way to show children how a seed develops, and since the entire process takes only 21 days, they are more likely to stay involved.

Successfully growing vegetables at home in 21 days helps to get kids thinking about other things to grow and understand where the produce at the grocery store comes from. Later, the experience of this quick gardening lesson may help them make better food choices, picking healthy fruits, nuts, and vegetables over-processed, unhealthy options.

About Radishes

I selected radishes for this exercise for a few reasons. They grow compact and do very well in even the smallest of containers. Radishes are one of the fastest maturing vegetables. Many options mature in 45 to 60 days, but very few options will give you satisfying results in less than one month.

Radishes are also a hardy plant, so young gardeners and novices with two brown thumbs will have success. They also make an ideal plant to learn about the importance of proper soil, water, and light conditions without the risk of accidentally killing a valuable, expensive plant that takes months to grow.

Types of Radishes

Radishes have been around for a long time and are among the first domesticated root vegetables. They come in a wide range of sizes and shapes. Radishes come in shades of red, pink, and white. Some even look like tiny watermelons!

There are two types of radishes, spring, and winter. We will focus on spring radish varieties for this exercise because they are the fastest maturing type. Suitable spring radish varieties include early scarlet globe and Old French radishes. These fast-growing radishes grow different shapes with the heirloom French radish "18 Jours" type growing a narrow, tapering root in as few as 18 days. Globe radishes are small and round and take about 22 days to fully mature. Red radishes are the variety commonly sold in stores. Varieties of red radish can take as few as 22 days or more than 70 days to mature.

Growing Radishes in 21 Days

This is a fun container garden project you can do with your kids or as a project to learn about gardening in the classroom and see results in record time. Radishes are fun to grow and have many delicious uses. Later in this bonus section, I'll share some of the ways I like to use radishes.

Things to Gather Before Day One

You will want to gather a few supplies together before beginning. There are several ways you can improve the process by having some supplies. At the same time, other things aren't always necessary for success.

- You'll need to have radish seeds of an early harvest, spring variety. Look at the seed company recommendation for days to maturity information and select one that is less than 30 days. French Breakfast Radish varieties tend to be the earliest maturing type.

- You should select a location for growing your radishes that receives at least 6 hours of direct, bright light every day. You can start radishes indoors well before the last frost, so consider the amount of light in early spring when choosing a location.

- Mix a well-draining potting soil that is airy and light. Use an appropriate mixture of potting elements to get a nearly neutral soil. Radishes will grow best if you use a screen to filter out large pieces of bark, clumps of clay or sand, and incompletely decayed compost items.

- Select a container that will provide you with at least eight inches of depth and has good drainage.

Day 1:

On day one, you will fill the container with soil and wet it down well. Let it drain until it is moist and workable. Ensure the potting mix is well mixed and moistened, then create shallow furrows about one-half inch deep. Radish seeds are relatively small but try to place one or two seeds every inch in rows three inches apart. Lightly cover with potting mix and water well.

Days 2-4:

Check your radishes every day to ensure the soil stays moist but not wet. Radishes will not grow well in wet potting mix and are likely to rot. You'll see seeds sprouting after a few days. Some varieties may shoot in two or three days. Others will take four or five.

Days 5-9

Continue to check on the growth of your radishes. Watch every day to see how much they are growing and make sure to keep them watered. By day nine, your radishes will be several inches tall. You can thin the seedlings to have one radish every three inches. Use the seedlings in a microgreen salad or a quick snack while working in the garden.

Day 10

Your radishes are doing great - now it's time to plant the second round. This is how succession planting works. You can simply make a divot one-half inch deep and place another seed. You can plant the same variety of radish, or a totally different type, depending on your goals. Remember that white and purple radishes mature slower than red varieties.

Days 11-20

These are the glorious, relaxing days. Monitor the water, keep an eye out for pests, and make sure your young radishes get plenty of bright light. By Day Nineteen, your second planting of radishes will be nearly half-grown, and your first planting will be nearing time to harvest.

Day 21

Begin checking the size of your radishes every day. Red, globe-type varieties are ready for harvest when the greens are about four inches tall, and the top of the root is around one inch in diameter. Tapering varieties like the 18 Jours radish will be about three-quarters of an inch across when ready. On Day Twenty-One, select an average-size radish and harvest it.

To harvest radishes, grasp the greens at the top of the root. Pull gently and steadily straight up without twisting. The radish will slip out of the soil without disturbing the delicate roots of radishes nearby.

You'll know your radish is ready when it has the right color for the variety, it's evenly shaped, and it has no signs of problems. Radishes should have a crisp texture and be moist inside. Cut off the thin tail and add it to your compost. Cut off the leafy greens, make a salad, or sauté them in garlic and butter. They are quite tasty and a little spicy. Young spring radish greens are more tender than other varieties and older radishes.

Brush off the soil from your radishes and put them in a plastic bag in the refrigerator's crisper drawer. You shouldn't wash them off because it can increase the rate of dehydration and make the radish taste dry.

If you find mushy, yellow, or brown spots, the root has a fungal infection and needs to be discarded. You may have to discard the entire container if root rot has spread throughout your plants. You should also look for signs of root-boring pests. Many insects can transmit bacteria and disease to plants that may make you sick, so don't eat bug-ridden vegetables.

My Favorite Ways to Use Radishes

When I first started doing this exercise, someone asked me, "Why radishes? They're so gross, and no one eats them!" I was shocked. I love radishes, and I thought everyone did, too. Then I realized that many people simply haven't had the opportunity to try fresh, homegrown radishes prepared correctly in a delicious meal. Here are a few ways even people who swear they hate radishes say are pretty good.

- Thin-sliced pickled radishes: These are such a delicious snack. Simply use a sharp knife or mandoline to slice the radishes into thin pieces and place them in a glass jar. Mix equal amounts of red wine vinegar and water in a saucepan and add one teaspoon of salt, one teaspoon of honey, and several sprigs of fresh dill, rosemary, parsley, thyme, or oregano- or a savory mixture of your favorites. Add 20 or 30 whole black peppercorns and bring the mixture to a very gentle boil. Pour the brine into the jar, seal, and refrigerate. The pickled radishes are ready in 48 hours. They have a beautiful pink hue that looks delicate and delicious on a serving platter.

- Marinade for Asian-Inspired Dishes: Radishes feature prominently in many Chinese and Southeast Asian recipes. You can marinade radishes in soy sauce, vinegar, and honey for thirty minutes, then use them in stir-fry recipes or over white rice as a delicious side. They also make excellent additions to soups and stews.

- Chopped in Slaw: Grate radishes with the coarse side of a cheese grater and mix them into potato salad, egg salad, or coleslaw to add a spicy, earthy kick. This is particularly delightful when you use one of the colorful radish varieties.

- Salad Topping: Thin-sliced radishes are at home on top of a fresh garden salad. You can grow many varieties like arugula, spinach, and other lettuce varieties you can harvest as you need rather than the whole plant. Nothing sets off a fresh salad like fresh sliced radishes.

- Tempura-Fried: Tempura is a light batter that is extremely crispy. It's delicious with carrots, radishes, turnips, and many other vegetables. You can make a simple tempura batter by combining one cup of cornstarch with one cup of ice-cold water and an egg. Whisk the egg until the yolk and white are combined. Strain the ice water into the egg in a large bowl. Then add the cornstarch and stir gently until almost combined. The batter should be lumpy, and some dry spots are even okay. Overmixing will make the batter dense. Heat oil in a skillet and dust slices of radishes and other vegetables in cornstarch, then dredge in the batter. Drip off the excess and fry until golden, turning to get both sides.

There are numerous other ways to use delicious radishes. They have a wonderful flavor, and I highly encourage you to try growing different varieties, especially if you don't like radishes. Like many homegrown veggies, radishes from your own garden taste totally different than those you buy in the store.

You Did It!

I love this exercise because of how fast it goes. It's lots of fun to see the little radish plants grow, and they sprout so quickly you can almost see it happen. This is also an excellent exercise to help children learn about how things grow and where food comes from. It might even be an opportunity to get a picky eater in your family interested in growing vegetables they want to eat. Starting a radish garden in a container is fun, easy, and inexpensive. You get quick results and a vegetable that is versatile and delicious. Try it and share your results in my Facebook discussion group!

THE END, FOR NOW...

Gardeners, I think, dream bigger dreams than emperors. – Mary Cantwell

We've come to the end of our journey together, at least for now. We've had fun learning about gardening in containers. I hope you can see how much more efficient and straightforward a small garden can be while still being productive and easy to care for. I've included many tips and tricks I've learned over the years that can help you avoid some of the mistakes that are easy to make.

As you garden, you'll find that certain things work better for you than others, and you'll adapt yourself and your garden to accomplish your goals. Every season brings new challenges and new rewards, and I know that you'll come to look forward to those moments you spend in your garden just like me. For me and many others, gardening isn't even all about the plants - it's also about the mental well-being that gardening provides. Getting out in the sun and working in the soil seems to chase away clouds of doubt and depression. There are few experiences so simple in life as gardening that provide you with the self-esteem and confidence that you'll discover growing your garden.

In this book, I've shared the right way to pick a good spot for gardening by finding the sun - and now you know what the best types of plants for your garden will be. When you go to a nursery or garden center, you won't have to wonder about the different kinds of soil and the best choice for containers because you know how to pick the proper materials to make your own potting mix. We've learned about water and about the pitfalls of too much or too little. It's time to go and pick some pots or containers, or maybe it's time to get creative and build something unique that fits your personal tastes.

As your garden grows, you'll learn to listen to your plants and anticipate their needs and desires. You'll be able to quickly identify things that are going awry, and now you know what to do about it. Everyone who has ever had a garden has dealt with some type of problem at one point or another. So don't be dissuaded if you've struggled in the past. Take each step one at a time, breathe deeply and enjoy the moments you have.

When it's time for the harvest, you can use the lessons in this book to know when and how to collect the fresh fruits and vegetables you've grown. You even know the best ways to preserve and store your produce. I'll be honest; the chapter on storing, canning, and preserving your harvest is one of my favorites. I really hope you and your family get to have as much fun as mine when it comes time to store our garden for the season.

I hope you've enjoyed the lessons and experiences I've shared in this book. I sincerely hope you take the opportunity to start a garden of your own, especially if you've been unsuccessful in the past. You should never let go of the desire you have to garden - whether it's for the peace and tranquility or for the bountiful harvest of fresh produce you'll grow.

Over my years of gardening, I've learned that each step in the process has its own special place, and I look forward to every part of gardening. I hope this book inspires you to try something new, whether it's a type of vegetable you've never heard of before or a variety that you can't buy in the store. I hope you learn to love each step of growing an organic garden, too. You'll never have such fresh, safe, and delicious fruits, vegetables, and herbs as those you grow in your own garden.

Maybe gardening has been stressful in the past - believe me, you aren't alone on that - but I hope you take a chance to see how relaxing and refreshing it can be. Even if you simply set up an Adirondack chair in your garden and spend a few minutes each day watching the plants grow, the flowers bloom, and the bees going about their busy day, I know you'll find a place of Zen in your garden if you take the time to let it happen.

The final thought I would like to leave you with before we bid farewell is this: even the smallest countertop herb garden is an opportunity for greatness. Treat every situation in life as a new container garden. Give it the attention it deserves. Keep it in the sun, and don't forget to water. No matter what insurmountable task you are facing, with a bit of love, a little patience, and a little time, you can succeed in anything you do.

I want to give a big thank you to all of you who read this book. I hope you find the content enlightening and that you are motivated to get your hands dirty in the garden. If you enjoyed reading this book, please share it with your friends. Leave a review on Amazon so that other gardeners can find the inspiration to grow a bountiful crop of fresh, organic produce. I hope to see you in the garden center or at the farmer's market, enjoying the fruits and vegetables of your labor. Remember, life is abundant!

Stay Connected! Facebook discussion group link
https://www.facebook.com/groups/501585191212408

RESOURCES

Ch.2

USDA "Organic 101: What the USDA Organic Label Means"
https://www.usda.gov/media/blog/2012/03/22/organic-101-what-usda-organic-label-means
The University of Florida, "Chapter 15: Resistant to Most Insecticides"
http://entnemdept.ufl.edu/walker/ufbir/chapters/chapter_15.shtml#:~:text=Two%20of%20the%20most%20striking,like%20Bacillus%20thuringiensis%20(see%20Results)

Ch.3

GardeningKnowHow.com: "Growing Vegetables in Tires"
https://www.google.com/url?q=https://www.gardeningknowhow.com/edible/vegetables/vgen/tires-as-planters-for-edibles.htm&usg=AOvVaw258OtPoepGg-e6L53Y5HJi
Bonnie Plants: "The Many Different Types of Tomatoes"
https://www.google.com/url?q=https://bonnieplants.com/gardening/what-are-the-different-types-of-tomatoes/&usg=AOvVaw1V-3VnzZ0Qysz0CL3H9rb3A
University of Florida, Gainesville, Department of Entomology & Nematology: Chapter 15: "Resistant to Most Insecticides"
https://www.google.com/url?q=http://entnemdept.ufl.edu/walker/ufbir/chapters/chapter_15.shtml&usg=AOvVaw2gltI56up6Te0AExSTxOLj
United States Department of Agriculture: "Pesticide Registration Requirements"
https://www.google.com/url?q=https://www.epa.gov/pesticide-registration/data-requirements-pesticide-registration&usg=AOvVaw3xXJ77syguTdkjKdlEsYQN
GMOAnswers.com "What GMO Crops are Currently on the Market"
https://www.google.com/url?q=https://gmoanswers.com/

gmos-in-the-us&usg=AOvVaw1ACR3SuGXnAfMBusdkB-7I

United States Department of Agriculture "Organic 101: Allowed and Prohibited Substances":

https://www.google.com/url?q=https://www.usda.gov/media/blog/2020/10/27/organic-101-allowed-and-prohibited-substances&usg=AOvVaw2-cII3muOHw5YARuUydb1b

Ch.4

FlowerShopNetwork.com "What is the Difference Between Soil-Based and Soil-less Potting Mix":

https://www.google.com/url?q=https://www.flowershopnetwork.com/blog/soil-based-soil-less-potting-mixes/&usg=AOvVaw0tEbiiBvGwa-3DzAv7EuaXN

EpicGardening.com "Perlite vs. Vermiculite: What is the Difference?":

https://www.google.com/url?q=https://www.epicgardening.com/perlite-vs-vermiculite/&usg=AOvVaw0CsqMVirxty5JbEvIKrC8z

ProvenWinners.com "Best Potting Soil- The Dirt on Dirt"

https://www.google.com/url?q=https://www.provenwinners.com/learn/dirt-dirt-potting-soil&usg=AOvVaw31t2V5cUHXFMtTyeyCBC-K

GardeningKnowHow.com "Is Sphagnum Moss Peat Moss?"

https://www.google.com/url?q=https://www.gardeningknowhow.com/garden-how-to/soil-fertilizers/sphagnum-moss-vs-sphagnum-peat-moss.htm&usg=AOvVaw19AQNmXfLrf4rmoK4_sLwU

TheDirtBag.com "Topsoil vs. Garden Soil: What's the Difference?"

https://www.google.com/url?q=https://www.thedirtbag.com/topsoil-vs-garden-soil-whats-the-difference/&usg=AOvVaw0l9LDfNDRiKb-NBmCukO16J

Ch.5

Sciencing.com "The Effects of Moon Phase on Ocean Tides"

https://www.google.com/url?q=https://sciencing.com/effects-moon-phases-ocean-tides-8435550.html&usg=AOvVaw3MMOb1pyTt3mP-NHZ_LkIt9

Ch.6

Foodal.com "Kitchen Composting 101: How to Repurpose Food Scraps"

https://www.google.com/url?q=https://foodal.com/knowledge/how-to/kitchen-composting-101/&usg=AOvVaw36e9ZXyCkoU0r-2y94XECl

Ch.7

FarmersAlmanac.com "Anthracnose"

https://www.almanac.com/pest/anthracnose

GardeningKnowHow.com "Verticillium Wilt Treatment"

https://www.google.com/url?q=https://www.gardeningknowhow.com/plant-problems/disease/verticillium-wilt-treatment.htm&usg=AOvVaw-0GxFYfeSi43w8bhS24h7DA

BobVilla.com "All You Need to Know about Insecticidal Soap"

https://www.google.com/url?q=https://www.bobvila.com/articles/insecticidal-soap/&usg=AOvVaw3Gd1LN6tdKCHAE8ZDfG0rz

Colorado State University, Colorado "Root Weevils"

https://www.google.com/url?q=https://extension.colostate.edu/topic-areas/insects/root-weevils-5-551/&usg=AOvVaw0S1VxI8hx8eEX54X-aCstSZ

Gardeners.com "Root Maggots"

https://www.google.com/url?q=https://www.gardeners.com/how-to/root-maggot/5312.html&usg=AOvVaw3eLEQgskiOdMA5aDN6vkDU

GardeningKnowHow.com "Root Maggot Control"

https://www.google.com/url?q=https://www.gardeningknowhow.com/plant-problems/pests/insects/root-maggot-control.htm&usg=AOvVaw-1tAfqj-h1Bz-sZMyBCBH-D

FineGardening.com "Effective Deer Deterrents"

https://www.google.com/url?q=https://www.finegardening.com/article/effective-deer-deterrents&usg=AOvVaw2rvXR2itKdJBgumL9SiAEd

Ch.8

TheGardenWebsite.com "Crop Rotation, Succession, and Companion Planting"

https://www.thegardenwebsite.com/vegetable-gardening-organic.html

TheSpruce.com "When to Harvest Vegetables"

https://www.thespruce.com/when-to-harvest-vegetables-1403402

FoodCrumbles.com "The Science of Colors in Fruits and Vegetables"

https://foodcrumbles.com/colours-in-fruits-vegetables/

Ch.9

Canning

Better Homes and Gardens, BHG.com "Pressure Canning Basics"

https://www.bhg.com/recipes/how-to/preserving-canning/pressure-canning-basics/

Clemson University, College of Agriculture, Forestry, and Life Sciences "Factsheet: Canning Foods at Home":

https://hgic.clemson.edu/factsheet/canning-foods-at-home/

The University of Georgia, National Center for Home Food Preservation "Freezing"

https://nchfp.uga.edu/how/freeze/blanching.html

The University of Georgia, National Center for Home Food Preservation "Drying Fruit"

https://nchfp.uga.edu/publications/uga/uga_dry_fruit.pdf

TheKitchn.com "How to Quick-Pickle Any Vegetable"

https://www.thekitchn.com/how-to-quick-pickle-any-vegetable-233882

LiveEatLearn.com "The Ultimate Guide to Quick Pickled Vegetables"

https://www.liveeatlearn.com/quick-pickled-vegetables/

Tinctures

MotherEarthNews.com "Making Your Own Herbal Medicine, Tinctures, and Infusions"

https://www.motherearthnews.com/natural-health/making-your-own-herbal-medicine-tinctures-and-infusions-zbcz1507

TraditionalMedicinals.com "The Basics: Herbal Tonics"
https://www.traditionalmedicinals.com/articles/plants/the-basics-herbal-tonics/

Bonus
RareSeeds.com "18 Jours Radish"
https://www.rareseeds.com/store/vegetables/radishes/de-18-jours-radish
FarmersAlmanac.com "Radishes- Planting, Growing, and Harvesting Radishes"
https://www.almanac.com/plant/radishes#:~:text=For%20a%20spring%20planting%2C%20sow,in%20rows%2012%20inches%20apart.

All photos by Luke Potter

99+ EASY HOME CANNING RECIPES

How to Preserve Your Harvest, Live Greener, Eat Healthier, Feed Your Family & Prepare for Hard Times

BY
LUKE POTTER

THE URBAN FARMER

Luke Potter

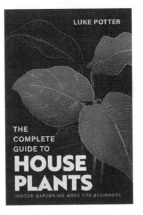

Other books by Luke Potter

Available worldwide on Amazon

INTRODUCTION to 99+ EASY HOME CANNING RECIPES

My Story

I've dedicated my adult life to gardening and preserving my harvest. I learned these life skills from my Canadian-born grandmother, who raised two daughters on her own during The Great Depression and WWII. For her, gardening and home canning was not a hobby. It meant food and survival for her family. My mom continued the family traditions, and I learned in the kitchen at her feet. My first job was on a farm. It was demanding work and little pay, but I learned how things grow and what to do with the harvest to make it last all year. To this day, nothing makes me happier than when I'm growing and canning my own food.

Many of these home canning recipes were handed down from generation to generation on hand-written recipe cards. So that you know, they all meet or exceed modern-day food safety standards. These are tried-and-true recipes that are simple to follow even if you've never canned before. I teach many of these same recipes to children in my homeschool canning classes. If they can do it, so can you!

I've tried and evaluated many different recipes during many decades of home canning, but these easy recipes simply produce the most delicious, jaw-dropping results! Nothing beats the genuine flavor of home-grown green beans or tomatoes in the dead of winter. Plus, you'll have an emergency backup supply of nutritious food for your family if, for some reason, you can't get to the grocery store or there are food shortages – either natural, fabricated or disaster-related

So, let's roll up our sleeves, get our aprons on and dive right in. I guarantee you'll enjoy the satisfying Zen-like process of home canning and take tremendous pride in the results!

Introduction to Canning Food

Home canning, also known colloquially as "putting up food" or processing, is the method of preserving foods, especially fruits, vegetables, and meats, by packing them into glass jars and then heating the jars to create a vacuum seal and killing the organisms that would otherwise cause spoilage.

Two methods are used in home canning. One is the hot water bath for foods high in acid or sugars like tomatoes and jams. The other requires a pressure canner for low acid foods like meats, stews, carrots, and green beans. Food properly processed and stored in canning jars has a stable shelf life of 18 months or longer without refrigeration.

Mason jars were developed in 1858 by John Mason. Soon other companies began manufacturing canning jars, but they are all commonly referred to as Mason jars regardless of the manufacturer. They are available in a variety of sizes in either wide-mouth or regular mouth styles.

For the hot water bath method, you simply need a large pot with a lid, deep enough, so your jars will be covered with an inch or two of boiling water. You'll also need a rack to keep your jars off the bottom of the pot to prevent breakage. For pressure canning, you'll need a pressure canner. They are available in various sizes. The capacity will determine the number of jars it will hold. When manufacturer directions are followed, they are entirely safe to use.

History of Home Canning

It used to be that homemakers canned fresh fruits and vegetables for consumption during the winter months before modern farming techniques and global transportation made fresh produce available year-round. Nowadays, many people practice home canning for the same reasons because it extends and preserves the harvest. Plus, if you have an abundant garden, and you should after reading my book How to Grow Vegetables in Pots & Containers, there are only so many tomatoes, beans, and cucumbers you can eat when faced with a harvest of bushels of fresh produce. And it simply makes meal prep easier. You have a ready stockpile of prepared food on hand. If you want a bowl of tomato soup, just reheat a pint. You did all the prep work months before. Want some pickles? Just open the pantry or cupboard. Can't make it to the market because of a blizzard, hurricane, or disaster? Your family won't go hungry because you prepared in advance. When I can at home, I'm reminded of the fable of the ant and the grasshopper. The ant prepared for the winter while the grasshopper played and fiddled the summer away. When winter came, and he had no food to eat, the ant turned him away, and the grasshopper starved. The moral being, be prepared. There's a time for work, and there's a time for play. I always joke with my neighbors that they know which house has food stored up when the zombie apocalypse comes!

Like millions of others, perhaps you took up home gardening and canning during the recent pandemic - just like our ancestors had done during earlier times of national struggle and food shortages. Let's take a brief historical look at the history of home canning before diving into the recipes.

Napoleonic Wars – Malnutrition

Since before written history, humans have preserved food by drying, smoking, salting, and fermenting. Home canning in glass jars is a relatively recent development in the long history of food preservation.

Napoleon said, "An army travels on its stomach." Meaning that without a consistent supply of food, either when his naval forces were at sea or his troops were thousands of miles from home marching towards Russia, they were destined to fail. It is believed, more of Napoleon's troops died of malnutrition and disease during his ill-fated Russian campaign than perished from battle.

Napoleon offered a prize to the person who could develop a method of safe food preservation for his constantly traveling military forces. The winner of the reward was Nicholas Appert. He developed a technique of heat-processing food in glass jars and bottles. Some claim that the first "bottling" was invented by Napoleon's troops, who would ladle hot soup into empty wine bottles and carry them into battle or on to the next encampment. The troops sealed these bottles with corks, wire, and paraffin.

US Civil War – A Nation Divided

During the US Civil War, glass jars with glass lids, rubber rings, and a wire and bale locking mechanism were developed, making it easier for homemakers, and the war machine, to preserve the harvest while supplying the troops on both sides of the battle. These locking jars became the standard for home canning for nearly 100 years.

WWI – War Gardens

In 1915, Alexander Kerr invented the modern-day two-piece metal lid and screw band to seal glass canning jars. This is the sealing method that we still utilize today. Also, during WWI, the first "War Gardens" began in the United States, United Kingdom, Canada, Australia, and Germany. In these nations at war, citizens, including school children, were encouraged, through public campaigns, to plant vegetable gardens to supplement their rations, allowing more food to be diverted to the troops. Gardening was also encouraged to boost morale. Citizens planted gardens in both public parks and private residences. Just like the recent pandemic, many people grew gardens for the first time. It is estimated that over five million War Gardens were planted in the United States alone.

Faced with abundant harvests, homemakers learned to can what they could not consume, give away, or preserve by other means. Coupled with the technological advances introduced by the Ball and Kerr companies, home canning enjoyed its first boom.

The Great Depression – Hard Times

Following a period of economic vitality, The Great Depression and The Dust Bowl devasted America in the 1930s. Grain became scarce as the topsoil blew away in the Great Plains. Without feed, livestock was slaughtered or died. Another disaster created another surge in home canning, and it was simply cheaper to grow and can your own food. Homemakers in the Dust Bowl states resorted to pickling and canning nettles to keep their families alive. Hard times required folks to become more self-reliant to survive.

WWII – Victory Gardens

Another World War – this one was more extensive in scale. War Gardens were renamed Victory Gardens to boost morale and lower the military's cost of food. At the height of the War in 1943, there were 18 million Victory Gardens in the United States – 12 million in cities and 6 million on farms. Even First Lady Eleanor Roosevelt had a Victory Garden planted at the White House. During the War, gardening was considered a patriotic duty.

"A Victory Garden is like a share in an airplane factory. It helps win the War and it pays dividends too." Claude Wickard, U.S. Secretary of Agriculture

And with all those gardens, and the mass production of glass canning jars by Ball, Atlas, Kerr, and others, home canning surged to new heights. In 1943, home canning peaked with more than 4 billion jars processed. The sheer amount of home-grown food was awe-inspiring. By 1944, home production of fruits and vegetables equaled what was commercially grown. After the War, home gardening declined as the population moved to the suburbs, and kitchen gardens were replaced with the well-manicured lawns of the 1950s and 1960s. Home canning also declined with the mass marketing of home freezers. Of course, some people continued to garden and practice home canning to preserve their harvest.

1970s – Back to Basics

With gas shortages, double-digit inflation, and the back-to-basics movement, home canning regained popularity in the 1970s.

Pandemic – Self-reliance

In 2020, a worldwide pandemic appeared out of nowhere. And the lockdowns coincided with the start of the gardening season. Stores and nurseries were ordered closed. Walmart cordoned off their gardening section as "non-essential." Seeds became unavailable, except through mail order companies, which quickly sold out. It is estimated that home gardening increased by 300% during the coronavirus pandemic. People were isolated in their homes, unable to work, and had time on their hands. Plus, everyday items were simply unavailable. Meat, eggs, and everyday food items were rationed. With the fear of food shortages, people took up home gardening. Once again, a crisis compelled people back to nature. Spending time in the sun, working in the dirt, and tending our gardens was therapeutic and nurturing when the world seemed to be falling apart.

Vitamin D boosted our immune systems. Sunlight relieved depression. And the pandemic gardeners learned to can their harvest so their pantries would be well-stocked. Their families would not go hungry. Many of these first-time gardeners and canners vowed to become life-long gardeners and home canners. They realized how quickly things can go awry and that it pays to be prepared.

Preppers – Survival

In the 21st century, a new movement began to take hold. Harkening back to the Cold War Era, people, fearing the uncertainty of the future, witnessing social and political unrest, and the erosion of civil liberties, began preparing for when SHTF and society as we know it collapses. Survivalists, or preppers, began living off-grid, homesteading, building bomb shelters, gathering weapons, practicing low-tech life skills, and stockpiling food. These forward-thinking individualists raise chickens, livestock and grow and preserve their food. There are food preservation books specifically marketed to preppers and survivalists.

Conclusion

"In times of great stress or adversity, it's always best to keep busy, to plow your anger and your energy into something positive." Lee Iacocca

I'm convinced there is something inherent in our human DNA instructing us to grow and preserve food in times of great stress and adversity. It's our ancient primal survival instinct at work. And because of that, there will always be home gardeners. There will always be home canners. The cities may collapse. The grid may go down. There may be war. But we will grow food. And our families will not go hungry because we have learned how to preserve our abundant harvests. Join me on this self-reliant, sustainable journey. You'll never look back.

PLANT A GARDEN
for VICTORY

POST MAY 1ST. TO 15 TH. WAR PRODUCTION CO-ORDINATING COMMITTEE

PLANT A VICTORY GARDEN

OUR FOOD IS FIGHTING

A GARDEN WILL MAKE YOUR RATIONS GO FURTHER

THE BASICS

The Science

Let's begin with a science lesson. Food spoils because of the presence of molds, yeast, and bacteria. They exist in nature and are on the food, in water, air, and soil - even in the canning jars we use. Canning stops their action by the application of heat and the removal of air from the jars. The heat kills molds, yeast, and bacteria in the food and jars. The vacuum-sealed lid is airtight and prevents micro-organisms from entering the jar after canning. This makes canned goods shelf-stable without refrigeration for 18 months or longer.

Boiling water stops the action of yeasts and molds. Short exposure to boiling water will neutralize the enzymes found in all vegetables, fruits, and meats. Unless the actions of enzymes are stopped, they can bring about unwanted changes such as discoloration, softened texture, loss of flavor, and destruction of Vitamin C.

Bacteria are more challenging to destroy. There are several types of bacteria, some of which are more heat resistant. Like tomatoes and many fruits, acidic foods help prevent the growth of bacteria and are the easiest to can. If not destroyed by heat during the canning process, yeast and many bacteria can grow in a sealed jar. A sure sign that bacteria or yeast is present is the seal has popped, the lid is not secure, and there is an odor or discoloration. This means you did not use sufficient heat during the canning process, and the food has spoiled. If you notice any of these indicators, dispose of the food at once, and sterilize the jar. DO NOT taste test suspicious canned food to see if it has spoiled. You'll risk botulism. With home canning, it's better safe than sorry. To avoid problems like spoilage, always process food the full time suggested in the recipes, adjusting for your altitude. Use the hot water bath method or pressure canner method as shown in the recipe.

Start Fresh

You can't make a silk purse out of a sow's ear, so start by selecting vegetables, fruits, and meats in excellent condition. Fruits and vegetables that are overripe may not process correctly. Produce with blemishes, soft spots, or rotten spots may spoil your entire product, so make sure to cut these out and discard them. Process meats as soon as possible to avoid spoilage. The quality of fruits and vegetables deteriorates quickly, so I like to harvest and be ready to can immediately. Prepare your canner and jars and gather all your supplies in advance of harvesting, and you'll capture the maximum garden-fresh flavor and nutrition.

And make sure to read the recipe thoroughly before beginning so you'll know what to have on hand, how to proceed, the method to use, and the time required from start to finish. When you plan ahead, you'll find home canning is easy, fun, and therapeutic. You'll experience a Zen-like delight as you see your pantry fill up with jars of healthy, nutritious food. You'll feel a well-earned sense of pride in your accomplishment.

CANNING METHODS

Canning is one of the best ways to preserve food easily and quickly. It's also a low-tech operation that requires only a few standard kitchen instruments to be successful. The most important thing about canning is to make sure you select high-quality canning jars that have seals and lids in good condition. Ensure the jars have no chips or cracks, as these can cause breakage during the canning process. At a minimum, clean your jars thoroughly with dish soap and hot water before use. Or use a food-grade sanitizer. I run mine through the dishwasher cycle using hot water before canning to ensure no fungi or bacteria contaminate the contents.

Steps for Hot Water Bath Canning

Hot water bath canning is a suitable method for preserving high-acid foods. This includes most fruits and pickled vegetables. Low-acid foods run the risk of developing the bacterial spore that causes botulism. You'll need to add citric acid to safely can or use a pressure canner for canning low-acid vegetables and all meats.

The first step is to heat your clean, sterile jars in a large pot of hot water deep enough to cover the jars fully. Fill the jars and kettle with water and put them on low heat. Place the lids and bands in water in a saucepan over low heat until you are ready to use them. Remember, you can only use lids once. You can reuse the bands and jars indefinitely.

Preparing Fruit and Vegetables for Canning

There are two ways to preserve your harvest using the hot water bath: raw and heated. The raw pack method is self-explanatory. You'll simply chop the fruit or vegetable up enough to fit in the jar and fill the rest with boiling water or syrup. Heating the fruits and vegetables to boiling before putting them in the jars yields a better flavor and color. You can use the liquid from heating to fill the canning jar. The heating process reduces the risk of your preserves shrinking and leaving too much space at the top of the jar.

A canning rack keeps the bottom of the jars from touching the pot, which can cause excessive heat and may break your jars. If you don't have a canning rack, you can use a pressure canner insert, a cake cooling rack, or even a folded kitchen towel to prevent the jars from breaking.

You'll want to find a recipe specifically for the type of fruits and vegetables you're canning. There will be a recommended headspace in the jar that prevents over or under-filling. Using a jar lifter, remove one jar at a time from the hot water kettle and drain the water back into the pot. Immediately fill the jar, making sure to use a rubber spatula to scrape around the inside of the jar to free trapped air bubbles.

Wipe the rims, place the lids and pressure bands on the jars, and tighten until just finger tight. You don't want to overtighten the bands because the jars can explode. Air needs to escape during the canning process. Set the jar on the canning rack before getting the next jar from the hot water. Don't let the jars touch on the canning rack.

If you are canning raw fruit and vegetables, start with the water hot but not boiling. Fruits and vegetables heated first should go into softly boiling water. Add enough boiling water to ensure at least one inch of depth above the jars.

Raise the temperature to a steady, rolling boil, then cover and set a timer according to your recipe. When the processing is finished, turn off the heat, remove the lid, wait 5 minutes, and gently remove each jar from the water. Place them on an elevated rack or dry cloth at least one inch apart. This will prevent sudden temperature changes that can result in jar breakage or even dangerous explosions. Do not touch the pressure rings or metal lids. Let the cans cool on their own before handling. Don't forget to label and date them.

Pressure Canner Method

The pressure canner method of canning is the only safe way to can low-acid foods like most vegetables. This is also how you preserve meat, poultry, and seafood. You'll prepare for canning in a pressure canner just the same as for canning in the hot water bath, and the difference is that you'll put only two or three inches of water in the pressure canner rather than submerging the jars.

Once the pressure canner is filled with jars ready for canning, lock the lid in place. Turn the heat on high and let the temperature rise quickly. This will rapidly increase the pressure in the cooker. When steam begins to hiss from the vent pipe, set your timer for 5-10 minutes, then place the gauge in place. Most recipes call for 10 pounds pressure. Lower the burner slightly until the gauge "jiggles" 3-4 times per minute. This lets the pressure build gradually, making it easier to settle the pressure at the proper temperature. There are modern pressure canners that don't work with a weighted gauge. Follow the manufacturer's directions for the pressure canner you are using.

Follow the guidelines in your recipe for the length of time to process your harvest in a pressure canner. Most fruit and vegetable recipes will require 20-45 minutes per pint - longer for quarts. When the time is up, turn off the heat and move the pressure canner off the burner if possible. Do not remove the vent cap or try to open the lid. Pressure will gradually decrease. You'll leave the cooker alone for 30-45 minutes or longer, depending on the style, size, and thickness of your cooker.

Once you remove the lid, gently lift the jars from the canner using a jar lifter. Arrange them on a cooling rack, or dry dish towel, at least one inch apart, and let them cool. You'll hear a "ping" as the jars cool, showing you have a successful seal. After the jars are thoroughly cooled, check the seal by gently pressing on the metal lid, and it should not pop up or down. Refrigerate any cans that didn't seal properly. You can remove the bands and label your jars. It's a good idea to write down the date you canned the contents. That way, you are practicing proper food rotation when consuming your harvest.

Each of the recipes in this book specifies the canning method, processing time, and specific instructions.

Processing Times Guide

For successful and safe home-canning, using either method, you need to adjust processing times based on the altitude of your location. Use this chart:

Times listed are for 0 to 1,000 feet above sea level

Increase by 5 minutes for 1,001 feet to 3,000 feet

Increase by 10 minutes for 3,001 feet to 6,000 feet

Increase by 15 minutes for 6,001 feet to 8,000 feet

Increase by 20 minutes for 8,001 feet to 10,000 feet

You can check your elevation at: https://whatismyelevation.com

GLOSSARY & ABBREVIATIONS

Altitude = The height of your residence in relation to sea level.

Alum = A colorless astringent compound available online or in the spice section.

Bands = The metal rings used to secure lids on canning jars.

Blanching = Brief immersion of food in boiling water.

Brine = Salted water used in food preservation.

Cup = 8 ounces or 237 ml

ClearJel = A food starch used for thickening in canning.

Cold-pack/Raw-pack = When raw, uncooked food is added to canning jars.

Finger tight = Hand tightening without the use of a tool.

Hard boil/Rolling boil = A boiling liquid that cannot be stirred down.

Headspace = Space in a canning jar between the food or liquid and the lid.

High-acid = A food or product with a pH of less than 4.6.

Hot-pack = When food is partially or fully cooked before adding to canning jars.

Jelly = A sweet spread of fruit juice, sugar, and sometimes pectin that is typically transparent.

Canning salt = Often sold as canning salt, kosher salt, or pickling salt. These are salts containing no iodine, which are used for canning.

lb = Pound or 16 ounces or 2.2 kg

Lemon juice = Use either freshly squeezed or bottled.

Lids = The metallic lids used for canning. Single use only. You cannot reuse them.

Low-acid = A food or product with a pH of more than 4.6.

Marmalade = A preserve made typically from citrus fruit.

Mason jar = Any airtight glass jar with a screw-top used for home canning.

oz = Ounces

Pectin = An extract from ripe fruits used as a setting agent in jams and jellies. Sold in either liquid or powdered form.

Pickle Crisp = Calcium chloride used as a firming agent in pickling.

Pint = 16 ounces or 473 ml

PSI = Pound-force per square inch

Quart = 32 ounces or .95 liter

Relish = A cooked and pickled product made of chopped vegetables, fruits, etc., used as a condiment.

Simmer = When food is cooked at a temperature just below boiling.

Skimming = The removal of impurities from the surface of a liquid while it is cooking.

Soft boil = When the surface of a liquid being heated is barely moving with occasional tiny bubbles rising to the surface.

Sterilize = To make something free from bacteria or other living organisms.

tsp = Teaspoon or 5 ml

Tbsp = Tablespoon or 15 ml

SOUPS & STEWS

When you can a big batch of your favorite soup or stew, you'll always have a meal ready. Simply reheat and enjoy the garden-fresh flavors!

Comfort Food Chicken Soup

The cure for what ails you!

INGREDIENTS

- 16 cups chicken stock (store-bought or homemade)
- 3 cups diced cooked chicken
- 1½ cups peeled, sliced, or diced carrots
- 1½ cups chopped celery
- 1 cup finely chopped yellow or white onions
- Canning salt and freshly ground black pepper to taste
- 3 chicken or vegetable bouillon cubes (optional)

YIELD

8 pints or 4 quarts

Variations

Substitute 3 cups diced, cooked turkey in place of chicken.
Add rice, orzo, or noodles when reheating.

RECIPE

1. In a large stainless-steel saucepan, combine all ingredients. Bring to a boil over medium-high heat. Reduce heat and boil gently for 30 minutes. Add salt and pepper to taste. Add bouillon cubes if using.
2. Using a jar funnel, ladle hot soup into hot jars, leaving 1-inch headspace.
3. Wipe rims with a paper towel moistened with vinegar, add lids and bands. Hand-tighten.
4. Carefully place jars on rack in pressure canner. Attach and secure canner lid. Heat until canner starts hissing, then add gauge and begin timing after the first jiggle. Process pints for 75 minutes and quarts for 90 minutes at 10 pounds pressure. Adjust timing for higher altitudes.
5. Remove canner from heat. Allow pressure to decrease naturally.
6. Remove lid. Remove jars from the canner after 5 minutes. Cool on a wire rack or kitchen towel. Remove bands, label jars, and store them in a cool, dark place.

Traditional Soup Stock

Prepare ahead and have it on hand when you're ready to make soup or homemade gravy.

INGREDIENTS

- Bones, skin, trimmings of meat, poultry, or fish
- 1 onion chopped
- 1 celery stalk chopped
- 1 carrot chopped
- Water
- Canning salt

YIELD

Varies

RECIPE

1. Prepare pressure canner, jars, and lids.
2. Add bones, skin, and trimmings of meat, game, fish, or poultry to a large stainless-steel stockpot. Add one onion, 1 stalk of celery, and 1 carrot. Add water to cover and 1-2 tsp canning salt to taste. Bring to a boil, reduce heat and simmer for 1-2 hours. Add more boiling water if needed.
3. Using a colander, strain the liquid stock into a large bowl. Discard bones and vegetables. Meat pieces may be added to stock if desired.
4. Using a jar funnel, pour the stock into jars. Wipe rims, add lids and bands, and process pints for 45 minutes at 10 pounds pressure or 3 hours in a boiling hot water bath.

Vintage Clam Chowder

A staple of Down East families. Add cream or milk when reheating to make New England-style clam chowder.

INGREDIENTS

- 4 peeled, diced potatoes
- 1 lb fresh clams, rinsed, shelled, and chopped finely
- 2 large onions chopped fine
- 2 stalks celery chopped
- ½ tsp paprika
- 2 Tbsp butter
- Canning salt and freshly ground black pepper to taste

YIELD

3-4 pints

Luke's Variations

- Substitute 1 lb cut-up skinless fish for clams to make fish chowder.
- Add 1 or 2 large peeled, chopped tomatoes to make Manhattan-style clam chowder.

RECIPE

1. In a large stainless-steel saucepan, mix all ingredients. Bring to a boil over medium-high heat. Reduce heat and boil gently for 15 minutes stirring often to prevent sticking.

2. Using a jar funnel, ladle hot chowder into hot jars, leaving 1-inch headspace.

3. Wipe rims with a paper towel moistened with vinegar. Add lids and bands. Hand-tighten.

4. Carefully place jars on rack in pressure canner. Attach and secure canner lid. Heat until canner starts hissing, then add gauge and begin timing after the first jiggle. Process pints for 90 minutes at 10 pounds pressure. Adjust timing for higher altitudes.

5. Remove canner from heat. Allow pressure to decrease naturally.

6. Remove lid. Remove jars from the canner after 5 minutes. Cool on a wire rack or kitchen towel. Remove bands, label jars, and store them in a cool, dark place.

Homestyle Beef Stew with Vegetables

Dinty who? Serve this on a crisp, cold night with some crusty bread to sop up the gravy!

INGREDIENTS

- 4-5 lbs stew beef cut into cubes
- 12 cups peeled, cubed potatoes
- 8 cups thickly sliced carrots
- 3 cups chopped celery
- 3 cups chopped onions
- 5 tsp canning salt
- 1 tsp dried thyme
- Freshly ground black pepper to taste
- Boiling water

YIELD

14 pints or 7 quarts

Luke's Variations

- Don't peel carrots for a more rustic style stew.
- Use petite carrots whole or cut in half depending on size.
- Substitute beef bone broth for boiling water.
- Use 3 cups whole peeled pearl onions instead of chopped onions.

RECIPE

1. Prepare pressure canner, jars, and lids.
2. Heat oil over medium-high heat and brown beef cubes on all sides in a large skillet, adding more oil as needed. Drain oil after browning.
3. Add beef and all other ingredients to a large stainless-steel pot. Add boiling water to cover. Bring to a boil, occasionally stirring to prevent sticking. Reduce heat and simmer until stew begins to thicken.
4. Using a jar funnel, ladle hot stew into hot jars, leaving 1-inch headspace.
5. Wipe rims with a paper towel moistened with vinegar. Add lids and bands. Hand-tighten.
6. Carefully place jars on rack in canner. Attach and secure canner lid. Heat until

Safety Notice

Do not dredge beef cubes in flour or corn starch before browning since it prevents the heat from penetrating the meat evenly during the canning process. You can add some flour or corn starch when reheating if you prefer a thicker gravy.

canner starts hissing. Allow the steam to escape the vent for 5-10 minutes, add gauge and begin timing after the first jiggle. Process pints for 75 minutes and quarts for 90 minutes at 10 pounds pressure. Adjust timing for higher altitudes.

7. Remove canner from heat. Allow pressure to decrease naturally.

8. Remove lid. Remove jars from the canner after 5 minutes. Cool on a wire rack or kitchen towel. Remove bands, label jars, and store them in a cool, dark place.

Homestead Prepper Split Pea Soup

Economical and nutritious. Excellent for camping or survival food when you lose power. A fantastic way to use leftover holiday ham.

INGREDIENTS

- 2 cups dried split peas
- 8 cups water
- 1½ cups sliced t
- 1 cup chopped onion
- 1 cup diced cooked ham
- 1 bay leaf
- ¼ tsp ground allspice
- Canning salt & freshly ground black pepper to taste

YIELD

5 pints

Luke's Variations

- I prefer yellow split peas, but you can substitute green split peas if you prefer.
- Don't peel carrots for a more rustic style stew.
- Use petite carrots whole or cut in half depending on size.
- Use 1 cup whole peeled pearl onions instead of chopped onions.
- If you don't have leftover ham, use a ham steak cut into small cubes.

Luke's Tip: Use a stick blender to puree the mixture making it as smooth as you wish.

RECIPE

1. Add peas and water to a large stainless-steel saucepan. Bring to a boil over medium-high heat. Reduce heat, cover, and boil gently for 1 hour.
2. Prepare pressure canner, jars, and lids.
3. Remove from heat and puree peas if a smoother consistency is desired.
4. Add all other ingredients to peas. Bing to boil, stirring often. Reduce heat and simmer gently for 30 minutes stirring often to prevent sticking. After 30 minutes, add boiling water if the soup is too thick. Remove bay leaf.
5. Using a jar funnel, ladle hot soup into hot jars, leaving 1-inch headspace.
6. Wipe rims with a paper towel moistened with vinegar. Add lids and bands to finger tight. Do not overtighten.
7. Carefully place jars on rack in canner. Attach and secure canner lid. Heat until canner starts hissing. Allow the steam to escape the vent for 5-10 minutes, add gauge and begin timing after the first jiggle. Process pints for 75 minutes and quarts for 90 minutes at 10 pounds pressure. Adjust timing for higher altitudes.
8. Remove canner from heat. Allow pressure to decrease naturally.
9. Remove lid. Remove jars from the canner after 5 minutes. Cool on a wire rack or kitchen towel. Remove bands, label jars, and store them in a cool, dark place.

Classic Tomato Soup

This is a vintage recipe from the 1940s or earlier. The recipe calls for flour and butter, which is not recommended based on modern food safety standards. You can substitute ClearJel for the flour. I also added lemon juice to further acidify the contents.

INGREDIENTS

- 18 cups peeled, cored, chopped tomatoes
- 2 medium onions peeled and chopped
- 1 stalk celery chopped
- 5 sprigs chopped parsley
- 1 bay leaf
- 4 Tbsp flour (optional)
- 4 Tbsp butter (optional)
- 1 Tbsp canning salt
- 3 Tbsp granulated sugar
- 1 tsp pepper
- 1 tsp lemon juice per pint

YIELD

Varies

RECIPE

1. Prepare hot water bath canner, jars, and lids.
2. In a large stainless-steel pot, combine tomatoes, onions, celery, parsley, and bay leaf. Bring to boil over medium-high heat, stirring often to prevent scorching. Reduce heat and simmer for 45 minutes.
3. Remove from heat and pour through a sieve. Discard seeds, onions, celery, and herbs.
4. Melt butter, whisk in flour, or ClearJel, add a little of the hot tomato juice. Whisk until smooth. Add mixture to tomato juice in a large stainless-steel pot. Bring to boil and reduce heat to simmer.
5. Add salt, sugar, and pepper. Mix well. Pour through a sieve again for a smoother consistency.
6. Using a jar funnel, ladle hot soup into hot jars, leaving 1-inch headspace. Add 1 tsp lemon juice to each jar.
7. Wipe rims with a paper towel moistened with vinegar. Add lids and bands to finger tight.
8. Process in a hot water bath for 20 minutes. Adjust timing for higher altitudes.
9. Remove canner from heat. Remove lid. Remove jars from the canner after 5 minutes. Cool on a wire rack or kitchen towel. Remove bands, label jars, and store them in a cool, dark place.

Italian Bread Soup

Place a slice of toasted garlic-rubbed Italian bread in the bottom of the bowl before serving. Drizzle with extra virgin olive oil and sprinkle with freshly shaved or grated Parmesan cheese for a taste of Tuscany. Mamma Mia!

INGREDIENTS

- 1 cup dried cannellini beans
- 3 Tbsp extra virgin olive oil
- 1 cup chopped onion
- ½ cup chopped leeks
- ½ cup diced carrots
- ½ cup diced celery
- 1 Tbsp minced garlic
- 1 tsp crushed dried rosemary
- 2 cups peeled, cored, chopped tomatoes
- 2-3 cups cabbage cut into strips
- 2 Tbsp canning salt
- 1 medium peeled, diced potato
- 1 medium sliced zucchini
- 2 cups Swiss chard cut into strips
- Freshly ground black pepper (to taste)

YIELD

4 quarts

RECIPE

1. Prepare pressure canner, jars, and lids.
2. Rinse beans under cool water. Place in a large bowl and add 3 cups boiling water. Soak beans for 1 hour. Drain and set aside.
3. Heat olive oil in a large stainless-steel stockpot over medium heat. When hot, add onions, leeks, carrots, and celery. Cook for 3-5 minutes, then add garlic and rosemary. Cook, stirring to prevent scorching, for an additional 2 minutes.
4. Add beans, tomatoes, cabbage, salt, and 8 cups boiling water to stockpot. Bring to a boil over medium-high heat. Reduce heat, cover with a lid and simmer for one hour, occasionally stirring to prevent sticking.

5. Add potatoes, zucchini, and chard. Simmer covered for an additional 30 minutes. Season with canning salt and freshly ground pepper.
6. Using a jar funnel, ladle hot soup into hot jars, leaving 1-inch headspace.
7. Wipe rims of jars with a paper towel moistened with vinegar. Add lids and bands to finger tight.
8. Place jars on rack in canner. Attach and secure canner lid. Heat until canner starts hissing. Allow the steam to escape the vent for 5-10 minutes, add gauge and begin timing after the first jiggle. Process pints and quarts for 90 minutes at 10 pounds pressure. Adjust timing for higher altitudes.
9. Remove canner from heat. Allow pressure to decrease naturally.
10. Remove lid. Remove jars from the canner after 5 minutes. Cool on a wire rack or kitchen towel. Remove bands, label jars, and store them in a cool, dark place.

Leek and Potato Soup

Add a little cream when reheating to make a cream soup. Sprinkle with toasted croutons or saltines and enjoy!

INGREDIENTS

- 5 medium potatoes peeled and cubed
- 3-4 cups thinly sliced leeks
- 5 cups vegetable or chicken stock
- Canning salt (to taste)
- Freshly ground black pepper (to taste)

YIELD

6 pints

Note

- Refer to the stock recipe in this book. You may also use store-bought stock but it's so easy to make it yourself!

RECIPE

1. Prepare pressure canner, jars, and lids.
2. Peel and dice potatoes. Rinse under cool water. Slice leeks.
3. Start by layering leeks, then potatoes, then leeks in each jar. Continue layering, leaving 1-inch headspace.
4. Add stock to each jar, leaving 1-inch headspace.
5. Add canning salt and freshly ground pepper to taste to each jar.
6. Wipe rims of jars with a paper towel moistened with vinegar. Add lids and bands to finger tight.
7. Carefully place jars on rack in canner. Attach and secure canner lid. Heat until canner starts hissing. Allow the steam to escape vent for 5-10 minutes, add gauge and begin timing after the first jiggle. Process pints and quarts for 35 minutes at 10 pounds pressure. Adjust timing for higher altitudes.
8. Remove canner from heat. Allow pressure to decrease naturally.
9. Remove lid. Remove jars from the canner after 5 minutes. Cool on a wire rack or kitchen towel. Remove bands, label jars, and store them in a cool, dark place.

Meatless Spaghetti Sauce with Vegetables

Delicious and super-easy to make! Adjust the recipe based on the pounds of tomatoes you have on hand.

INGREDIENTS

- 30 lbs fresh tomatoes (plum tomatoes preferred)
- ¼ cup extra virgin olive oil
- 1 cup chopped onion
- 5 garlic cloves peeled
- 1 cup chopped green bell pepper
- 1 lb sliced mushrooms
- 4½ tsp canning salt
- 2 tsp freshly ground black pepper
- 4 Tbsp dried parsley
- 2 Tbsp dried oregano
- 1 Tbsp dried basil
- Red pepper flakes to taste
- ¼ cup packed brown sugar

YIELD

9 pints

RECIPE

1. Prepare pressure canner, jars, and lids.
2. Peel and core tomatoes.
3. Cook tomatoes over medium-high heat for 20-30 minutes, stirring often.
4. Add vegetables to tomatoes. Add seasonings. Once the sauce begins to bubble, stir in the brown sugar. Reduce heat and simmer uncovered until the sauce is reduced by about half. Stir often to prevent scorching.
5. Ladle hot sauce into hot jars using a jar funnel, leaving 1-inch headspace.
6. Wipe rims of jars with a paper towel moistened with vinegar. Add lids and bands to finger tight.
7. Carefully place jars on rack in canner. Attach and secure canner lid. Heat until canner starts hissing. Allow the steam to escape vent for 5-10 minutes, add gauge and begin timing after the first jiggle. Process pints and quarts for 20 minutes at 10 pounds pressure. Adjust timing for higher altitudes.
8. Remove canner from heat. Allow pressure to decrease naturally.
9. Remove lid. Remove jars from the canner after 5 minutes. Cool on a wire rack or kitchen towel. Remove bands, label jars, and store them in a cool, dark place.

Chili con Carne

A crowd pleaser! Top with shredded cheese and hot pepper rings
before serving!

INGREDIENTS

- 3 cups dried red kidney or pinto beans
- 5½ cups water
- 5 tsp canning salt, divided
- 3 lbs ground beef or pork
- 1½ cups chopped onion
- ½-1 cup seeded and chopped pepper of your choice (adjust the amount to your liking)
- 1 tsp freshly ground black pepper
- 3-6 Tbsp chili powder
- 2 quarts peeled, cored tomatoes

YIELD

9 pints

RECIPE

1. Prepare pressure canner, jars, and lids.
2. Wash beans thoroughly. Place in a saucepan or a large bowl and add cold water to submerge them. Soak 12-18 hours. Drain beans and rinse again.
3. Peel and core tomatoes.
4. Combine beans with 5½ cups cold water and 2 tsp canning salt. Bring to a boil, reduce heat, and simmer for 30 minutes. Drain.
5. Brown ground meat, onions, and peppers. Drain fat, then add seasonings and tomatoes. Add beans and simmer for 5 minutes.
6. Ladle into hot jars using a jar funnel, leaving 1-inch headspace.
7. Wipe rims of jars with a paper towel moistened with vinegar. Add lids and bands to finger tight.
8. Carefully place jars on rack in canner. Attach and secure canner lid. Heat until canner starts hissing. Allow the steam to escape the vent for 5-10 minutes, add gauge and begin timing after the first jiggle. Process pints and quarts for 75 minutes at 10 pounds pressure. Adjust timing for higher altitudes.
9. Remove canner from heat. Allow pressure to decrease naturally.
10. Remove lid. Remove jars from the canner after 5 minutes. Cool on a wire rack or kitchen towel. Remove bands, label jars, and store them in a cool, dark place.

Meatless Chili

Perfect for vegetarians and vegans. Serve it at your next Super Bowl party!

INGREDIENTS

- 3 cups dried red kidney beans
- 1 Tbsp canning salt
- 2 cups chopped onion
- 1 cup diced sweet red bell pepper
- 3 Tbsp chili powder
- 1 tsp freshly ground black pepper
- 8 cups tomato juice
- ½ cup tomato paste
- 2 tsp dried thyme
- 2 tsp ground cumin
- 6 garlic cloves, peeled, minced
- ¼ cup fresh parsley, chopped

YIELD

9 pints

RECIPE

1. Add dried kidney beans to a large bowl. Cover with water and soak overnight. In the morning, drain beans, rinse under cool water, and place in a stainless-steel saucepan. Add fresh water and bring to a boil over medium-high heat. Reduce heat and simmer for 30 minutes until beans split in half. Drain well and set aside.
2. Prepare pressure canner, jars, and lids.
3. In a large stainless-steel saucepan, add all ingredients except beans. Bring to a boil over medium-high heat. Add beans and stir thoroughly. Return to a boil. Reduce heat and simmer for 10 minutes.
4. Stir well, ladle hot chili into hot jars using a jar funnel, leaving 1-inch headspace. Remove air bubbles with a rubber spatula, adding more chili if necessary.
5. Wipe rims of jars with a paper towel moistened with vinegar. Add lids and bands to finger tight.
6. Carefully place jars on rack in canner. Attach and secure canner lid. Heat until canner starts hissing. Allow the steam to escape the vent for 5-10 minutes, add gauge and begin timing after the first jiggle. Process pints for 75 minutes at 10 pounds pressure. Adjust timing for higher altitudes.
7. Remove canner from heat. Allow pressure to decrease naturally.
8. Remove lid. Remove jars from the canner after 5 minutes. Cool on a wire rack or kitchen towel. Remove bands, label jars, and store them in a cool, dark place.

New England Boiled Dinner

Enjoy this traditional taste of St. Patrick's Day any day of the year without all the fuss! Simply reheat and serve!

INGREDIENTS

- 4-5 lb brisket
- 6 cups white potatoes
- 2 cups carrots
- 1 cup turnips or beets (optional)
- 2-3 onions
- ½ head green cabbage
- Pickling spice
- Freshly ground black pepper
- Water

YIELD

6-7 quarts

RECIPE

1. Prepare pressure canner, jars, and lids.
2. Trim as much fat from brisket as possible. Discard fat. Cut brisket into 1-inch chunks.
3. Prepare potatoes and carrots. Cut into 1-inch cubes. Peel and cube turnips or beets. Peel and cut onions into chunks. Slice cabbage into wedges that will fit in your jars.
4. Layer brisket and vegetables into jars, leaving 1-inch headspace.
5. Add ¼ tsp pickling spice to each quart jar. Add freshly ground black pepper to each jar to taste.
6. Add boiling water to each jar, leaving 1-inch headspace.
7. Wipe rims of jars with a paper towel moistened with vinegar. Add lids and bands to finger tight.
8. Carefully place jars on rack in canner. Attach and secure canner lid. Heat until canner starts hissing. Allow the steam to escape vent for 5-10 minutes, add gauge and begin timing after the first jiggle. Process pints for 75 minutes and quarts for 90 minutes at 10 pounds pressure. Adjust timing for higher altitudes.
9. Remove canner from heat. Allow pressure to decrease naturally.
10. Remove lid. Remove jars from the canner after 5 minutes. Cool on a wire rack or kitchen towel. Remove bands, label jars, and store them in a cool, dark place.

Vegetable Soup

This is a great way to preserve your garden vegetables when they're at their peak!

INGREDIENTS

- 8 cups peeled, cored, and chopped tomatoes
- 6 cups peeled and diced potatoes
- 6 cups sliced carrots
- 4 cups bush or pole beans cut into 1-inch pieces
- 4 cups corn kernels
- 2 cups chopped celery
- 2 cups chopped onions
- 6 cups water
- 2 tsp canning salt
- 1 tsp freshly ground black pepper
- ½ cup chopped parsley (use much less if using dried)
- 1 Tbsp chopped rosemary (use less if using dried)

YIELD

7 quarts

Luke's Variations

Use trimmed, washed, un-peeled baby carrots for a more rustic soup.
Add 3 cloves minced garlic.
Use 3 cups white potatoes and 3 cups sweet potatoes.

RECIPE

1. Prepare pressure canner, jars, and lids.
2. Combine all prepared vegetables and water in a large stainless-steel pot. Add seasonings and bring to a boil over medium-high heat, stirring often.
3. Reduce heat to medium-low and simmer uncovered for 30 minutes, stirring often.
4. Using a jar funnel, ladle hot soup into hot jars, leaving 1-inch headspace. Remove air bubbles with a rubber spatula and add more soup if needed.
5. Wipe rims of jars with a paper towel moistened with vinegar. Add lids and bands to finger tight.
6. Carefully place jars on rack in canner. Attach and secure canner lid. Heat until canner starts hissing. Allow the steam to escape the vent for 5-10 minutes, add gauge and begin timing after the first jiggle. Process quarts for 85 minutes at 10 pounds pressure. Adjust timing for higher altitudes.
7. Remove canner from heat. Allow pressure to decrease naturally.
8. Remove lid. Remove jars from the canner after 5 minutes. Cool on a wire rack or kitchen towel. Remove bands, label jars, and store them in a cool, dark place.

JUICES

During WWI, the Great Depression, and WWII, fresh fruits were often unavailable for most of the year. But by canning fruit juices, homemakers were able to add variety to their winter diets. Nowadays, juicing has become commonplace year-round. But modern fruit production is dependent on agribusiness and pesticides, petroleum-based shipping, and preservatives to supply fresh fruit year-round. When you return to the ways of our ancestors, you can have fresh, organic, home-grown fruit juices year-round. If you've never tried canning fruit juices, you're missing out!

Cranberry Juice

Try serving this with Thanksgiving dinner. Or use it when making your favorite cocktail!

INGREDIENTS

- 4 cups whole organic cranberries
- 4 cups water
- 2/3 cup granulated sugar

YIELD

4-5 pints

RECIPE

1. Prepare hot water bath canner, jars, and lids.
2. Wash and remove any stems from 4 cups organic cranberries. Add to a medium stainless-steel saucepan with 4 cups water.
3. Bring to a boil, reduce heat, and softly boil over medium heat for 15 minutes. Strain juice through a dampened jelly bag or several layers of moistened cheesecloth. Do not squeeze bag.
4. After most of the juice has dripped into a bowl, return the juice to the saucepan, and add sugar, stirring to dissolve. Bring to a boil, then ladle hot juice into hot jars using a jar funnel, leaving ½-inch headspace.
5. Wipe rims with vinegar moistened paper towel. Center lids on jars. Add bands and finger-tighten.
6. Using a jar lifter, carefully place jars in the canner with a rack in place. Make sure they are completely covered with water. Add more boiling water if needed. Cover and return to a boil. Process for 10 minutes.
7. Remove from heat. Remove lid. Wait 5 minutes, then remove jars and place on a wire rack or kitchen towel. Allow to cool, listen for pings, label, and store.

Spicy Vegetable Juice Cocktail

Add a pickle spear or a celery stalk to make the perfect Bloody Mary or Bloody Maria or drink your vegetables as is!

INGREDIENTS

- 8 lbs ripe tomatoes
- 1 cup chopped celery
- ½ cup chopped onion
- 6 Tbsp bottled or freshly squeezed lemon juice
- 2 Tbsp granulated sugar
- 1 Tbsp Worcestershire sauce
- 2 tsp prepared horseradish
- 1 tsp canning salt
- Freshly ground black pepper
- ¼ tsp hot sauce (to taste)

YIELD

4 pints

RECIPE

1. Prepare hot water bath canner, jars, and lids.
2. Wash tomatoes. Core and remove stem ends. Chop tomatoes and add to a large stainless-steel saucepan.
3. Add celery and onions. Bring to a boil over medium heat, stirring often to prevent scorching. Cover and simmer for about 20 minutes until tomatoes are soft.
4. Pour mixture through a sieve or colander, discarding solids. Measure 12 cups juice and return to saucepan. Bring to a boil, reduce heat and simmer uncovered for 20 minutes. Stir in lemon juice, sugar, Worcestershire sauce, horseradish, salt, pepper, and hot sauce. Return to boiling and simmer uncovered for 15 minutes.
5. Using a jar funnel, ladle hot juice into hot jars, leaving ½-inch headspace.
6. Wipe rims with vinegar moistened paper towel. Center lids on jars. Add bands and finger-tighten.
7. Using a jar lifter, carefully place jars in the canner with a rack in place. Make sure they are completely covered with water. Add more boiling water if needed. Cover and return to a boil. Process for 35 minutes.
8. Remove from heat. Remove lid. Wait 5 minutes, then remove jars and place on a wire rack or kitchen towel. Allow to cool, listen for pings, label, and store.

Concord Grape Juice

This is an excellent way to preserve an abundant grape harvest.

INGREDIENTS

- 7-8 lbs Concord grapes
- 2½ cups water
- ½-1 cup granulated sugar (optional)

YIELD

8 pints

RECIPE

Day 1

1. Wash grapes and remove them from stems. Measure 17 cups of grapes and add them to a large stainless-steel saucepan. Add water, cover, and simmer for 15 minutes, stirring occasionally.
2. Remove from heat and mash grapes using a potato masher. Strain through a damp jelly bag or several damp layers of cheesecloth over a large bowl. Cover and refrigerate for 24 hours which will allow sediment to settle.

Day 2

1. Prepare hot water bath canner, jars, and lids.
2. Restrain juice and discard solids. You can strain through a coffee filter, jelly bag, or cheesecloth. Discard sediment.
3. In a large stainless-steel pot, combine grape juice and sugar (optional). Heat to almost boiling, stirring to dissolve the sugar. Remove from heat and skim off any foam that has formed. Discard foam.
4. Using a jar funnel, ladle hot juice into hot jars, leaving ½-inch headspace.
5. Wipe rims with vinegar moistened paper towel. Center lids on jars. Add bands and finger-tighten.
6. Using a jar lifter, carefully place jars in the canner with a rack in place. Make sure they are completely covered with water. Add more boiling water if needed. Cover and bring to a boil. Process for 10 minutes.
7. Remove from heat. Remove lid. Wait 5 minutes, then remove jars and place on a wire rack or kitchen towel. Allow to cool, listen for pings, label, and store.

Pineapple Juice

Refreshing and perfect for serving with ham at Easter.

INGREDIENTS

- Pineapples
- Water

YIELD

Varies

RECIPE

1. Prepare hot water bath canner, jars, and lids.
2. Peel as many pineapples as you wish to juice. Grind using a food grinder or food processor fitted with a metal blade.
3. Place in a large stainless-steel saucepan adding just enough water to cover. Bring to a boil over medium-high heat, stirring often. Reduce heat to medium and boil softly for 10 minutes.
4. Strain through a damp jelly bag or several damp layers of cheesecloth over a large bowl and using a jar funnel, at once ladle hot juice into hot jars, leaving ½-inch headspace.
5. Wipe rims with vinegar moistened paper towel. Center lids on jars. Add bands and finger-tighten.
6. Using a jar lifter, carefully place jars in the canner with a rack in place. Make sure they are completely covered with water. Add more boiling water if needed. Cover and bring to a boil. Process for 10 minutes.
7. Remove from heat. Remove lid. Wait 5 minutes, then remove jars and place on a wire rack or kitchen towel. Allow to cool, listen for pings, label, and store.

Grapefruit Juice

Great way to start the day! You've got to move quickly to preserve the fresh taste of the juice, so have everything prepared in advance.

INGREDIENTS

- Grapefruits

YIELD

Varies

RECIPE

1. Prepare hot water bath canner, jars, and lids. Bring water to a boil and keep covered.
2. Wash the grapefruit. Cut in half and extract the juice using a conical-shaped juicer. Strain out seeds and pulp. Move quickly. The quality of the grapefruit juice deteriorates quickly when exposed to air so fill one jar at a time. Leave ½-inch headspace.
3. Wipe rims with vinegar moistened paper towel. Center lids on jars. Add bands and finger-tighten.
4. Using a jar lifter, carefully place jars in the boiling water bath with a rack in place. Make sure they are completely covered with water. Add more boiling water if needed. Cover and return to a boil. Process for 20 minutes.
5. Remove from heat. Remove lid. Wait 5 minutes, then remove jars and place on a wire rack or kitchen towel. Allow to cool, listen for pings, label, and store.

Apple Juice
A tasty way to keep the doctor away!

INGREDIENTS
- 24 lbs apples, stemmed and chopped
- 8 cups water

YIELD
12 pints

RECIPE
1. Prepare apples by combining apples with water in a large stainless-steel saucepan. Bring to a boil over medium-high heat. Reduce heat and boil gently, stirring often, until apples are soft.
2. Strain through a damp jelly bag or several damp layers of cheesecloth over a large bowl. Allow to drip for 2-3 hours. Do not squeeze bag.
3. Prepare hot water bath canner, jars, and lids.
4. Return juice to a large stainless-steel saucepan. Heat over medium heat until almost boiling. Maintain juice at this temperature for 5 minutes.
5. Using a jar funnel, ladle hot juice into hot jars, leaving ½-inch headspace.
6. Wipe rims with vinegar moistened paper towel. Center lids on jars. Add bands and finger-tighten.
7. Using a jar lifter, carefully place jars in the canner with a rack in place. Make sure they are completely covered with boiling water. Add more boiling water if needed. Cover and return to a boil. Process for 10 minutes.
8. Remove from heat. Remove lid. Wait 5 minutes, then remove jars and place on a wire rack or kitchen towel. Allow to cool, listen for pings, label, and store.

FRUITS

Before modern transportation and refrigeration, fresh fruit was available seasonally. Homemakers canned their harvests when fresh fruit was in season to enjoy the taste and health benefits all year long.

Fruit Cocktail

Traditionally, a delicious treat in the middle of winter when fresh fruits weren't available.

INGREDIENTS

- 5¼ cups light syrup*
- 1 pineapple
- 3 lbs peaches
- 3 lbs pears
- 1 lb fresh cherries
- 1 lb seedless grapes, any variety

YIELD

9 pints

RECIPE

1. Prepare light syrup. Keep hot but not boiling.
2. Prepare hot water bath canner, jars, and lids.
3. Prepare the pineapple by slicing off the bottom and the green top. Slice off the skin and discard. Remove eyes with a sharp paring knife. Cut pineapple in half lengthwise and then cut each half in half again. Slice off and discard core from each quarter. Cut pineapple into bite-sized chunks. Measure 3 cups and set aside.
4. Peel, pit, and cut peaches into similar-sized chunks. Measure 8½ cups peaches. Set aside.
5. Peel, core, and cut pears into chunks. Measure 6½ cups pears. Immerse pear chunks into a bowl of lemon water until ready to use to reduce discoloration.
6. Cut cherries in half and discard pits. Measure 2½ cups cherries. Set aside.
7. Remove the stems from grapes. Keep whole. Measure 3 cups grapes. Set aside.
8. In a large stainless-steel pot, add all fruits. Add hot light syrup and bring to a boil over medium-high heat, stirring often.
9. Immediately, ladle hot fruits and light syrup into hot jars using a jar funnel. Leave ½-inch headspace. Add more syrup as needed leaving ½-inch headspace. Wipe rims of jars with a paper towel dipped in vinegar.

10. Center lids on jars. Add bands and finger-tighten.
11. 11. Using a jar lifter, carefully place jars in the canner with a rack in place. Make sure they are completely covered with water. Add more boiling water if needed. Cover and bring to a boil. Process for 20 minutes.
12. 12. Remove from heat. Remove lid. Wait 5 minutes, then remove jars and place on a wire rack or kitchen towel. Allow to cool, listen for pings, label, and store.

*Light Syrup Recipe

Dissolve 1¼ cups granulated sugar in 5 cups water. Heat over medium heat until sugar dissolves.

Whole Berry Cranberry Sauce

Easy to make and so much better than store-bought. When you make it ahead of time, it's one less thing to worry about on Thanksgiving Day! It also makes a thoughtful gift if you're invited to someone's home for Thanksgiving or Christmas dinner.

INGREDIENTS

- 4 cups granulated sugar
- 4 cups water
- 8 cups fresh cranberries

YIELD

4 pints

Luke's Variation

Add the grated zest of one orange to the sauce during the last few minutes of cooking.

RECIPE

1. Prepare hot water bath canner, jars, and lids.
2. In a large stainless-steel saucepan, combine sugar and water. Bring to a boil over high heat, stirring to dissolve sugar. Boil hard for 5 minutes.
3. Rinse cranberries under cool water and remove any stems. Add to boiling sugar/water mixture and return to a boil. Reduce heat and boil gently. Stir occasionally until all berries burst. This should take about 15 minutes.
4. Immediately ladle hot sauce into hot jars using a jar funnel. Leave ¼-inch headspace. Remove air bubbles with a rubber spatula. Wipe rims of jars with a paper towel dipped in vinegar.
5. Center lids on jars. Add bands and finger-tighten.
6. Using a jar lifter, carefully place jars in the canner with a rack in place. Make sure they are completely covered with water. Add more boiling water if needed. Cover and bring to a boil. Process for 15 minutes.
7. Remove from heat. Remove lid. Wait 5 minutes, then remove jars and place on a wire rack or kitchen towel. Allow to cool, listen for pings, label, and store.

Applesauce

In addition to apple cider, dried apples, and apple butter, this is a traditional way to preserve your apple harvest so it lasts all year! Although you can make applesauce from any variety of apples, my favorites for this recipe are McIntosh and Rome Beauty.

INGREDIENTS

- 8 lbs cooking apples, cored and quartered
- 2 cups water
- ¼ cup freshly squeezed lemon juice
- 1 cup granulated sugar

YIELD

6 pints

RECIPE

1. Prepare hot water bath canner, jars, and lids.
2. In a large stainless-steel saucepan, combine prepared apples, water, and lemon juice. Bring to a boil over medium-high heat, stirring to prevent scorching. Reduce heat to medium-low and simmer covered for 30 minutes until apples are tender, stirring often.
3. Press apples through a sieve or food mill to remove skins and seeds over a large bowl. Return pulp to pan, add sugar, stirring to dissolve and return to a boil. Add more boiling water, if necessary, to achieve desired consistency.
4. Immediately, ladle hot applesauce into hot jars using a jar funnel. Leave ½-inch headspace. Remove air bubbles with a rubber spatula. Wipe rims of jars with a paper towel dipped in vinegar.

5. Center lids on jars. Add bands and finger-tighten.
6. Using a jar lifter, carefully place jars in the canner with a rack in place. Make sure they are completely covered with water. Add more boiling water if needed. Cover and bring to a boil. Process pints for 15 minutes and quarts for 20 minutes.
7. Remove from heat. Remove lid. Wait 5 minutes, then remove jars and place on a wire rack or kitchen towel. Allow to cool, listen for pings, label, and store.

Cinnamon and Brown Sugar Applesauce

In Step 2, add 2 broken cinnamon sticks to apples. Simmer as directed. Remove sticks before pressing through the sieve. Replace granulated sugar with ¾ cup dark brown sugar.

Perfect Peaches

Enjoy this delightful taste of summer all year long! Serve with freshly whipped cream.

INGREDIENTS

- Fresh peaches
- Ascorbic acid
- Light syrup*

YIELD

1-1½ pounds of fresh peaches per pint

RECIPE

1. Prepare hot water bath canner, jars, and lids.
2. Immerse whole peaches in boiling water for 1 minute. Remove with a slotted spoon and immerse peaches in ice water. Skins should slip off easily. Halve and pit peaches. Slice into wedges if desired. Treat with ascorbic acid to prevent browning. (See note below.)
3. In a large stainless-steel saucepan, combine peaches and light syrup. Bring to a boil over medium-high heat, stirring to prevent scorching.
4. Immediately, ladle hot peaches and syrup into hot jars using a jar funnel. Leave ½-inch headspace. Remove air bubbles with a rubber spatula. Add more syrup if necessary, leaving ½-inch headspace.
5. Wipe rims of jars with a paper towel dipped in vinegar.
6. Center lids on jars. Add bands and finger-tighten.

7. Using a jar lifter, carefully place jars in the canner with a rack in place. Make sure they are completely covered with water. Add more boiling if needed. Cover and bring to a boil. Process pints for 20 minutes and quarts for 25 minutes.
8. Remove from heat. Remove lid. Wait 5 minutes, then remove jars and place on a wire rack or kitchen towel. Allow to cool, listen for pings, label, and store.

Note

Ascorbic acid can be found in most markets and stores that stock canning supplies. Follow package directions to prevent the browning of fruits during the canning process like peaches and apples.

*Light Syrup Recipe

Dissolve 1¼ cups granulated sugar in 5 cups water. Heat over medium heat until sugar dissolves.

Blueberries

Follow the same steps to can currants, elderberries, gooseberries, and huckleberries.

INGREDIENTS

- Blueberries
- Light syrup*

YIELD

1-3 pounds of berries for each quart

RECIPE

1. Prepare hot water bath canner, jars, and lids.
2. Immerse blueberries in hot but not boiling water and simmer for 30 seconds. Drain.
3. Fills jars with berries and hot syrup, leaving ½-inch headspace.
4. Wipe rims of jars with a paper towel dipped in vinegar.
5. Center lids on jars. Add bands and finger-tighten.
6. Using a jar lifter, carefully place jars in the canner with a rack in place. Make sure they are completely covered with water. Add more boiling water if needed. Cover and bring to a boil. Process both pints and quarts for 15 minutes.
7. Remove from heat. Remove lid. Wait 5 minutes, then remove jars and place on a wire rack or kitchen towel. Allow to cool, listen for pings, label, and store.

*Light Syrup Recipe

Dissolve 1¼ cups granulated sugar in 5 cups water. Heat over medium heat until sugar dissolves.

Pears

Select just ripe, unblemished pears with no soft or mushy spots.

INGREDIENTS

- Fresh pears
- Ascorbic acid
- Light syrup*

YIELD

2-3 pounds of fresh pears per quart

RECIPE

1. Prepare hot water bath canner, jars, and lids.
2. Peel, halve, and core pears. Treat with ascorbic acid to prevent browning. Drain and set aside.
3. In a large stainless-steel saucepan, prepare light syrup over medium heat. When sugar is completely dissolved, add pear halves and simmer uncovered for 5 minutes.
4. Immediately, ladle hot pears and syrup into hot jars using a jar funnel. Leave ½-inch headspace. Remove air bubbles with a rubber spatula. Add more syrup if necessary, leaving ½-inch headspace.
5. Wipe rims of jars with a paper towel dipped in vinegar.
6. 6. Center lids on jars. Add bands and finger-tighten.
7. Using a jar lifter, carefully place jars in the canner with a rack in place. Make sure they are completely covered with water. Add more boiling water if needed. Cover and bring to a boil. Process pints for 20 minutes and quarts for 25 minutes.
8. Remove from heat. Remove lid. Wait 5 minutes, then remove jars and place on a wire rack or kitchen towel. Allow to cool, listen for pings, label, and store.

Note

Ascorbic acid can be found in most markets and stores that stock canning supplies. Follow package directions to prevent the browning of fruits during the canning process like peaches and apples.

*Light Syrup Recipe

Dissolve 1¼ cups granulated sugar in 5 cups water. Heat over medium heat until sugar dissolves.

Old-Fashioned Red Cinnamon Apples

Just like great-grandma used to make!

INGREDIENTS

- Apples
- Cinnamon
- Red food coloring
- Light syrup*

YIELD

Varies

RECIPE

1. Prepare hot water bath canner, jars, and lids.
2. Prepare the light syrup in a large stainless-steel saucepan. Flavor the syrup with cinnamon to taste and add a few drops of red food coloring. Keep syrup warm while preparing apples.
3. Peel and core apples. Cut into quarters and add to warm syrup as you complete each apple.
4. When all apples have been added to the syrup, bring to a boil over medium-high heat. Reduce heat and cook for 3-5 minutes.
5. Using a jar funnel, ladle hot apples and syrup into hot jars. Leave ½-inch headspace. Remove air bubbles with a rubber spatula. Add more syrup if necessary, leaving ½-inch headspace.
6. Wipe rims of jars with a paper towel dipped in vinegar.
7. Center lids on jars. Add bands and finger-tighten.
8. Using a jar lifter, carefully place jars in a boiling water bath. Make sure they are completely covered with water. Add more boiling water if needed. Cover and return to a boil. Process pints for 25 minutes.

9. Remove from heat. Remove lid. Wait 5 minutes, then remove jars and place on a wire rack or kitchen towel. Allow to cool, listen for pings, label, and store.

*Light Syrup Recipe

Dissolve 1¼ cups granulated sugar in 5 cups water. Heat over medium heat until sugar dissolves.

PIE FILLINGS

The next time you want to make a pie or turnover, you simply have to make the pastry crust and fill!

Easy as Apple Pie Filling

The taste of home!

INGREDIENTS

- 1 lemon
- 10-12 lbs apples (about 24)
- 5½ cups granulated sugar
- 1½ cups ClearJel
- 1 Tbsp cinnamon
- ½ tsp nutmeg
- ¼ tsp ground cloves
- 5 cups apple juice
- 2½ cups cold water
- ¾ cup lemon juice

YIELD

7 quarts

RECIPE

1. Prepare hot water bath canner, lids, and jars.
2. Fill 2 large bowls with cold water and add half the juice of 1 lemon to each.
3. Peel, core, and cut apples into wedges. Immediately immerse apple pieces into the lemon water to prevent browning.
4. Drain the apples reserving the lemon water. In a stainless-steel saucepan, bring the lemon water to a boil. Measure 24 cups apples. Working in batches, add the apples to boiling water, cooking 1 minute per batch. Remove cooked apples with a slotted spoon to a large bowl. Cover with a cloth to keep the apples hot.
5. When apples are done, drain the saucepan. Add sugar, ClearJel, and spices. Stir in apple juice and 2½ cups cold water. Bring to a boil over medium-high heat, stirring constantly until the mixture begins to thicken. Add lemon juice and boil for 1 more minute. Stir in apples.

230

6. Using a jar funnel, ladle hot filling into hot, sterilized jars leaving about 1-inch headspace.
7. Wipe down rims of jars with a paper towel moistened with vinegar.
8. Add lids and bands to finger tight.
9. Carefully place jars on rack in canner. Cover and return to a boil. Process quarts for 25 minutes.
10. Remove canner from heat. Remove cover. After 5 minutes, remove jars from the canner using a jar lifter. Cool on a wire rack or kitchen towel. Remove bands, label jars, and store them in a cool, dark place.

Note

The best apples for this recipe include Honey Crisp, Golden Delicious, Gaia, and Granny Smith.

Mom's Strawberry Rhubarb Pie Filling

A family favorite in my home for many generations – sweet and tart!

INGREDIENTS

- 3 large apples
- 1 Tbsp grated orange rind
- ¼ cup freshly squeezed orange juice
- 7 cups sliced rhubarb
- 2 cups granulated sugar
- 4 cups strawberries

YIELD

5 pints

RECIPE

1. Prepare hot water bath canner, lids, and jars.
2. In a large stainless-steel saucepan, combine apples, peeled, and diced, orange zest, and orange juice. Stir to coat apples. Stir in rhubarb sliced in 1-inch pieces and sugar. Bring to a boil over medium-high heat, stirring often to prevent scorching. Reduce heat and boil gently for about 15 minutes until rhubarb is tender. Add hulled, halved strawberries and their juice and return to a boil. Remove from heat.
3. Using a jar funnel, ladle hot pie filling into hot, sterilized jars leaving about 1-inch headspace. Remove air bubbles with a rubber spatula.
4. Wipe down rims of jars with a paper towel moistened with vinegar.
5. Add lids and bands to finger tight.
6. Carefully place jars on rack in canner. Cover and return to a boil. Process quarts for 15 minutes.
7. Remove canner from heat. Remove cover. After 5 minutes, remove jars from the canner using a jar lifter. Cool on a wire rack or kitchen towel. Remove bands, label jars, and store them in a cool, dark place.

Note

I suggest cooking apples such as Granny Smith, Rome Beauty, or Golden Delicious.

Blueberry Pie Filling

Serve at a summer picnic or family reunion!

INGREDIENTS

- 3 quarts water
- 8 quarts fresh blueberries
- 8 cups granulated sugar
- 3 cups ClearJel
- 9 cups cold water
- 2/3 cup lemon juice

YIELD

7 quarts

RECIPE

1. Prepare hot water bath canner, lids, and jars.
2. Rinse and drain blueberries under cool water. Remove any remaining stems. In a large stainless-steel saucepan, bring 3 quarts of water to a boil. Working in batches, add 8 cups of blueberries at a time to the boiling water for 30 seconds. Remove berries with a slotted spoon to a large bowl.
3. When finished, drain the pot, and add sugar and ClearJel. Add 9 cups cold water, stirring until dry ingredients dissolve. Bring to a boil over medium-high heat, stirring constantly. Add lemon juice and boil for 1 more minute. Remove from heat. Add blueberries all at once and stir to coat.
4. Using a jar funnel, ladle hot filling into hot, sterilized jars leaving about 1-inch headspace.
5. Wipe down rims of jars with a paper towel moistened with vinegar.
6. Add lids and bands to finger tight.
7. Carefully place jars on rack in canner. Cover and return to a boil. Process quarts for 30 minutes.
8. Remove canner from heat. Remove cover. After 5 minutes, remove jars from the canner using a jar lifter. Cool on a wire rack or kitchen towel. Remove bands, label jars, and store them in a cool, dark place.

Meatless Mincemeat Pie Filling

Perfect fruity filling for pies, cookies, and tarts. And vegan-friendly!

INGREDIENTS

- 6 cups apples
- 1 large lemon
- 2 medium oranges
- 4 cups seedless raisins*
- 2 cups currants
- 4 tsp cinnamon
- 1½ tsp nutmeg
- 1½ tsp ground cloves
- 1½ tsp allspice
- 1 tsp canning salt
- 3-4 Tbsp ClearJel
- ½ cup granulated sugar
- 6 Tbsp unsweetened applesauce
- 3 tsp rum extract (optional)

YIELD

4 pints

RECIPE

1. Quarter and core apples. Do not peel. Grind in an old-fashioned food grinder using the medium-coarse blade. Set aside in a large ceramic or glass bowl.
2. Quarter lemon and oranges. Remove all seeds but leaves rinds intact. Grind and add to ground apples.
3. Grind 2 cups of raisins and add to bowl.
4. Add the rest of the raisins (whole) and all other ingredients to the bowl. Stir well. Cover and refrigerate for 1 week.
5. After 1 week, prepare jars, lids, and hot water bath canner.
6. Heat pie filling until hot but not boiling over medium-low heat, stirring often.
7. Using a jar funnel, ladle heated pie filling into hot, sterilized jars leaving ½-inch headspace. Remove air bubbles with a rubber spatula.
8. Wipe down rims of jars with a paper towel moistened with vinegar.
9. Add lids and bands to finger tight.
10. Carefully place jars on rack in canner. Cover and return to a boil. Process pints for 20 minutes, adjusting for altitude.
11. Remove canner from heat. Remove cover. After 5 minutes, remove jars from the canner using a jar lifter. Cool on a wire rack or kitchen towel. Remove bands, label jars, and store them in a cool, dark place.

*You can use 2 cups regular seedless raisins and 2 cups golden raisins, also known as sultana raisins, if you prefer.

Old-Fashioned Green Tomato Mincemeat Pie Filling

This is a vintage recipe using beef suet.

INGREDIENTS

- 1½ pints chopped tart apples
- 1 pint chopped green tomatoes
- 2 tsp cinnamon
- 1 tsp canning salt
- 1 tsp allspice
- 1 tsp ground cloves
- 3 cups granulated sugar
- 1 lb raisins*
- ¼ cup vinegar
- 1 cup chopped beef suet

YIELD

Uncertain because my grandma didn't specify on her recipe card!

RECIPE

1. Prepare hot water bath canner, jars, and lids.
2. Peel, core, and chop apples.
3. Mix all ingredients in a large stainless-steel saucepan. Bring all ingredients to a boil over medium-high heat, stirring constantly. Reduce heat to medium-low and simmer until thick, stirring often.
4. Using a jar funnel, ladle heated pie filling into hot, sterilized jars leaving ½-inch headspace. Remove air bubbles with a rubber spatula.
5. Wipe down rims of jars with a paper towel moistened with vinegar.
6. Add lids and bands to finger tight.
7. Carefully place jars on rack in canner. Cover and return to a boil. Process pints and quarts for 25 minutes, adjusting for altitude.
8. Remove canner from heat. Remove cover. After 5 minutes, remove jars from the canner using a jar lifter. Cool on a wire rack or kitchen towel. Remove bands, label jars, and store them in a cool, dark place.

*You can use one-half pound regular seedless raisins and one-half pound golden raisins, also known as sultana raisins, if you prefer.

Peach Pie Filling

It makes a great pie or cobbler!

INGREDIENTS

- 1 cinnamon stick broken in half
- 2 tsp whole cloves
- 12 cups peeled, pitted, sliced peaches
- 2 cups peeled, cored, finely chopped apples
- 2 2/3 cups granulated sugar
- 1 cup seedless golden raisins
- 2 Tbsp grated lemon zest
- ½ cup lemon juice
- ¼ cup white vinegar
- ½ tsp ground nutmeg

YIELD

4 pints

RECIPE

1. Prepare hot water bath canner, jars, and lids.
2. Create a spice bag by tying cinnamon and cloves in a cheesecloth square.
3. Mix all ingredients in a large stainless-steel saucepan. Bring all ingredients to a boil over medium-high heat, stirring constantly. Cover and reduce heat to medium-low and simmer, stirring often, until thickened. Remove spice bag.
4. Using a jar funnel, ladle hot pie filling into hot, sterilized jars leaving 1-inch headspace. Remove air bubbles with a rubber spatula.
5. Wipe down rims of jars with a paper towel moistened with vinegar.
6. Add lids and bands to finger tight.
7. Carefully place jars on rack in canner. Cover and return to a boil. Process for 15 minutes, adjusting for altitude.
8. Remove canner from heat. Remove cover. After 5 minutes, remove jars from the canner using a jar lifter. Cool on a wire rack or kitchen towel. Remove bands, label jars, and store them in a cool, dark place.

Pumpkin or Squash Pie Filling

Use in place of store-bought pumpkin or squash pie filling to finish off your Thanksgiving dinner in style!

INGREDIENTS

- 10 lbs pumpkin or 10 lbs acorn, Hubbard, or butternut squash

YIELD

6 pints

RECIPE

1. Prepare pressure canner, jars, and lids.
2. Cut pumpkin or squash into medium size chunks. Peel and discard peels.
3. Add chunks to a stainless-steel saucepan with just enough water to cover. Bring to a boil over medium-high heat, then lower heat to medium and cook, covered, until fork-tender.
4. Drain liquid and process in a food processor fitted with a metal blade until smooth.
5. Using a jar funnel, fill jars leaving ½-inch headspace. Remove air bubbles with a rubber spatula.
6. Wipe down rims of jars with a paper towel moistened with vinegar.
7. Add lids and bands to finger tight.
8. Place jars on rack in canner. Attach and secure canner lid. Heat until canner starts hissing. Allow the steam to escape the vent for 5-10 minutes, add gauge and begin timing after the first jiggle. Cover and process at 10 pounds pressure for 15 minutes after first jiggle adjusting for altitude.
9. Remove canner from heat. After pressure drops, remove the lid. After 5 minutes, remove jars from the canner using a jar lifter. Cool on a wire rack or kitchen towel. Remove bands, label jars, and store them in a cool, dark place.

Luke's Suggestion

I prefer the taste and flavor of squash pie over pumpkin pie. Try it if you've never had it, and you'll never go back!

FYI

All pumpkins are members of the squash family, but not all squash are pumpkins. Pumpkins are round, thick-skinned squash. The more you know.

To Make Pie

1. Empty 1 pint canned pumpkin or squash into a large mixing bowl.
2. Mix ¾ cup granulated sugar, 1 tsp cinnamon, ½ tsp salt, ½ tsp ground ginger, ¼ tsp ground cloves in a separate bowl. Then stir into filling.
3. Beat 2 eggs slightly. Stir well into the filling.
4. Gradually add 1 12oz can evaporated milk stirring until filling is smooth.
5. Pour pie filling into 9-inch unbaked 1 crust pie shell. Bake at 425 degrees for 15 minutes, then reduce heat to 350 degrees and bake 40-45 minutes until a knife inserted comes out clean.
6. Cool on a wire rack for several hours. Serve with whipped cream.

VEGETABLES

Bursting with nutrients, canning your home-gown vegetables is easy and the results are delicious!

Ma's Classic Green Beans

There's an old black and white picture taken of me in 1958 when I was 2 years old, hoeing beans in the family vegetable garden. Over 60 years later, and I'm still at it! This family recipe preserves the classic taste of green beans and becomes the main ingredient for the perfect green bean casserole for Thanksgiving!

INGREDIENTS

- Beans
- Canning salt (optional)

YIELD

Varies

Luke's Variations

You can use any variety or color of string bean, bush bean, or pole bean for this recipe.

RECIPE

1. Harvest and rinse freshly gathered young, tender, crisp beans under cold running water. Drain.
2. Trim ends. Leave whole or cut into 2-inch pieces.
3. Pack tightly into hot, sterilized jars leaving about 1-inch headspace.
4. Add ½ tsp of canning salt to each pint jar.
5. Add boiling water to each jar, leaving 1-inch headspace.
6. Add lids and bands. Hand-tighten.
7. Carefully place jars on rack in pressure canner. Attach and secure canner lid. Heat until canner starts hissing, then add

vent and begin timing. Process pints for 20 minutes and quarts for 25 minutes at 10 pounds pressure. Adjust timing for higher altitudes.

8. Remove canner from heat. Allow pressure to decrease naturally.

9. Remove lid. Remove jars from the canner after 5 minutes. Cool on a wire rack or kitchen towel. Remove bands, label jars, and store them in a cool, dark place.

Stewed Tomatoes and Vegetables

Because this recipe calls for low acid vegetables, it must be processed in a pressure canner. My mom served this as a vegetable side dish and added a dab of butter to each bowl before serving us. Add to casseroles!

INGREDIENTS

- 16 cups peeled, cored, chopped tomatoes (any types)
- 1 cup celery
- ½ cup chopped onion (any type)
- ¼ cup chopped seeded green bell pepper
- 1 Tbsp granulated sugar
- 2 tsp canning salt
- Freshly ground black pepper to taste
- Bottled lemon juice

YIELD

7 pints

Luke's Variation

To easily peel tomatoes, score an X on the bottom of each tomato using a sharp knife. Drop them in a pot of boiling water for 60 seconds. Remove with a slotted spoon and drop them in ice water. The peels will then slide off easily!

RECIPE

1. In a large stainless-steel saucepan, add tomatoes, celery, onion, green pepper, sugar, salt, and pepper. Bring to a gentle boil over medium heat, stirring often to prevent sticking. Cover and boil gently for about 10 minutes.

2. Add 1 tsp lemon juice to each pint jar to acidify the contents.

3. Pack hot tomato/vegetable mixture into hot jars using a slotted spoon, leaving 1-inch headspace. Add juice from the saucepan to cover. Using a rubber spatula, remove air bubbles. Wipe rims with a paper towel soaked in vinegar. Center lids, add bands, and finger-tighten.

4. Using a jar lifter, gently place jars in the pressure canner. Adjust water level if necessary and lock lid. Bring to boil until steam escapes, vent for 5-10 minutes, add gauge, and process jars at 10 pounds pressure for 15 minutes.

5. Turn off heat and allow pressure to return to zero. Remove lid, wait 10 minutes, then remove from canner. Cool, label, and store jars.

Vintage Stewed Tomatoes and Vegetables

Back in the day, instead of using a pressure canner, homemakers simply processed low acid foods for a longer processing time in a hot water bath. This recipe calls for the vegetables to be raw packed instead of precooked. I added lemon juice to the recipe to further acidify the contents.

INGREDIENTS

- 8 cups peeled cored tomatoes cut into chunks
- 4 Tbsp chopped green pepper
- 4 Tbsp chopped onion
- 8 Tbsp chopped celery
- 2 tsp celery salt
- 2 tsp sugar
- ½ tsp canning salt
- Bottled lemon juice

YIELD

6-7 pints

RECIPE

1. Measure all vegetables after chopping and mix in a large bowl.
2. Pack into sterilized jars leaving ½-inch headspace.
3. Add 1 tsp lemon juice to each pint jar to further acidify the contents.
4. Using a rubber spatula, remove air bubbles. Wipe rims with a paper towel moistened with vinegar. Center lids, add bands, and finger-tighten.
5. Process in boiling water bath for 45 minutes.
6. Remove canner from heat. Remove lid, wait 10 minutes, then remove jars from canner. Cool, label, and store jars.

Whole Kernel Corn

Enjoy the taste of summer all year long! Warm up with some butter, and salt, and it's like eating corn on the cob! Or use in soups, shepherd's pie, casseroles, add to a salad, etc.

INGREDIENTS

- 12 ears corn, shucked with kernels removed
- Canning salt

YIELD

6 8oz jars

RECIPE

1. Shuck corn, remove silks.
2. Using a knife or corn cob stripper or cutter, remove kernels from the cob.
3. Add kernels to clean, hot jars leaving 1-inch headspace.
4. Add ¼ tsp canning salt to each 8oz jar or ½ tsp to a pint jar.
5. Add boiling water to each jar leaving 1-inch headspace.
6. Wipe rims, add lids and bands.
7. Place jars on rack in canner. Attach and secure canner lid. Heat until canner starts hissing. Allow the steam to escape the vent for 5-10 minutes, add gauge and begin timing after the first jiggle. Process at 10 pounds pressure for 55 minutes for 8oz jars and pints, 85 minutes for quart jars.
8. Turn off heat and allow pressure to return to zero. Remove lid, wait 10 minutes, then remove from canner. Cool, label, and store jars.

Easy Creamed Corn

New England favorite! You'll need about 4 ears of corn for each pint.

INGREDIENTS

- 12 ears corn
- Canning salt (optional)

YIELD

3 pints

RECIPE

1. Shuck corn, remove silks, wash ears.
2. Blanch ears in a large pot of boiling water for 3-5 minutes.
3. Using a serrated knife or corn cob stripper, remove kernels from the cob.
4. Scrape cobs with a knife to extract pulp and milk.
5. Add kernels, pulp, and milk to a large bowl. Measure. For every 2 cups corn mixture, add 1 cup boiling water.
6. Add to a large stainless-steel saucepan, bring to boil, reduce heat and boil gently for 3 minutes.
7. Ladle mixture into pint jars, leaving 1-inch headspace. Add ½ tsp canning salt to each jar if desired.
8. Wipe rims, add lids and bands.
9. Place jars on rack in canner. Attach and secure canner lid. Heat until canner starts hissing. Allow the steam to escape the vent for 5-10 minutes, add gauge and begin timing after the first jiggle. Process pints for 85 minutes at 10 pounds pressure.
10. Turn off heat and allow pressure to return to zero. Remove lid, wait 10 minutes, then remove from canner. Cool, label, and store jars.

Green Peas

Fresh home-canned green peas are far superior to their supermarket counterpart.

INGREDIENTS

- Sweet green peas
- Canning salt (optional)

YIELD

2¼ lbs pea pods for each pint jar

Luke's Variations

Follow the same steps and process for the exact time for black-eyed peas, field peas, or crowder peas.

RECIPE

1. Select plump, young pea pods. Rinse under cold water. Shell,
2. rinse peas again.
3. Loosely fill jars with peas leaving 1-inch headspace.
4. Add ½ tsp canning salt to each pint jar.
5. Add boiling water to each jar, leaving 1-inch headspace.
6. Wipe rims, add lids and bands.
7. Place jars on rack in canner. Attach and secure canner lid. Heat until canner starts hissing. Allow the steam to escape the vent for 5-10 minutes, add gauge and begin timing after the first jiggle. Process 40 minutes at 10 pounds pressure for both pint and quart jars.
8. Turn off heat and allow pressure to return to zero. Remove lid, wait 10 minutes, then remove from canner. Cool, label, and store jars.

Winter Squash

Use Blue Hubbard, acorn, or butternut squash. Do not use summer squash.

INGREDIENTS

- Winter squash
- Boiling water
- Canning salt (optional)

YIELD

2¼ lbs squash for each quart jar

RECIPE

1. Prepare pressure canner, jars, and lids.
2. Peel and cut the squash into chunks. Place in a stainless-steel saucepan. Add enough water to cover and bring to a boil over medium-high heat. Boil for 2 minutes. Do not overcook.
3. Drain and discard cooking water. Add squash to jars leaving 1-inch headspace. Add boiling water to cover, leaving 1-inch headspace. Add ½ tsp canning salt if desired.
4. Wipe rims, add lids and bands.
5. Place jars on rack in canner. Attach and secure canner lid. Heat until canner starts hissing. Allow the steam to escape the vent for 5-10 minutes, add gauge and begin timing after the first jiggle. Process pints for 55 minutes and quarts for 90 minutes at 10 pounds pressure adjusting for altitude. Turn off heat and allow pressure to return to zero. Remove lid, wait 10 minutes, then remove jars from canner using a jar lifter. Cool, label, and store jars.

Carrots

Just drain the liquid and warm the carrots up with some butter and salt for a delicious side dish!

INGREDIENTS

- Carrots
- Canning salt (optional)

YIELD

1-1½ lbs of carrots for each pint jar

RECIPE

1. Wash carrots. Peel and wash again.
2. Leave small carrots whole or slice or dice larger carrots.
3. Pack carrots into hot jars, leaving 1-inch headspace.
4. Add ½ tsp canning salt to each pint jar.
5. Add boiling water to each jar, leaving 1-inch headspace.
6. Wipe rims, add lids and bands.
7. Place jars on rack in canner. Attach and secure canner lid. Heat until canner starts hissing. Allow the steam to escape the vent for 5-10 minutes, add gauge and begin timing after the first jiggle. Process pints for 25 minutes at 10 pounds pressure.
8. Turn off heat and allow pressure to return to zero. Remove lid, wait 10 minutes, then remove from canner. Cool, remove bands, label, and store jars.

Greens

This recipe works for all leafy greens, including beet, Swiss chard, spinach, mustard, kale, and collard greens.

INGREDIENTS

- Leafy greens
- Canning salt (optional)

YIELD

2 lbs of fresh, tender leaves for each pint jar

RECIPE

1. Wash greens well in several changes of cold water. Trim and discard tough stems.
2. In a large stainless-steel pot of boiling water, add greens, 1 pound at a time until they wilt.
3. Drain greens and chop on a cutting board. Fill jars leaving 1-inch headspace.
4. Add ½ tsp canning salt to each pint jar.
5. Add boiling water to each jar leaving 1-inch headspace.
6. Wipe rims, add lids and bands.
7. Place jars on rack in canner. Attach and secure canner lid. Heat until canner starts hissing. Allow the steam to escape the vent for 5-10 minutes, add gauge and begin timing after the first jiggle. Process pints for 70 minutes at 10 pounds pressure adjusting for altitude.
8. Turn off heat and allow pressure to return to zero. Remove lid, wait 10 minutes, then remove from canner. Cool, remove bands, label, and store jars.

Beets

This traditional recipe is quick and easy to prepare.

INGREDIENTS

- Beets
- Granulated sugar
- Canning salt

YIELD

1-1½ pounds of beets for each pint jar

RECIPE

1. To prepare beets, leave the roots and two inches stem intact. Scrub thoroughly to remove dirt. Place in a saucepan and bring to boil. Reduce heat and cook until tender. Remove beets and run under cold water. Slip off the skins, remove stem, and taproot. Leave small beets whole or slice or quarter larger beets.
2. Prepare canner, jars, and lids.
3. Add prepared beets to hot jars leaving 1-inch headspace. Add 1 tsp canning salt and 1 tsp granulated sugar to each jar. Add boiling water to each jar, leaving 1-inch headspace.
4. Wipe rims with a paper towel moistened with vinegar. Add lids and bands to finger tight.
5. Place jars on rack in canner. Attach and secure canner lid. Heat until canner starts hissing. Allow the steam to escape the vent for 5-10 minutes, add gauge and begin timing after the first jiggle. Process pints for 30 minutes at 10 pounds pressure.
6. Turn off heat and allow pressure to return to zero. Remove lid, wait 10 minutes, then remove from canner. Cool, remove bands, label, and store jars.

Okra

Use only small, crisp, brightly colored pods.

INGREDIENTS

- Okra
- Canning salt (optional)

YIELD

¾-1 pound of okra for each pint jar

RECIPE

1. To prepare okra, wash, and drain. Remove stem and blossom ends without cutting into the pods. Leave whole or cut into 1-inch slices.

2. Add okra and hot water to a stainless-steel saucepan. Bring to a boil over medium-high heat and boil for 2 minutes. Drain and discard cooking liquid.

3. Add hot okra to hot jars leaving 1-inch headspace. Add ½ tsp canning salt to each jar (optional). Pour boiling water into each jar, leaving 1-inch headspace.

4. Wipe rims with a paper towel moistened with vinegar. Add lids and bands to finger tight. Add jars to pressure canner.

5. Place jars on rack in canner. Attach and secure canner lid. Heat until canner starts hissing. Allow the steam to escape the vent for 5-10 minutes, add gauge and begin timing after the first jiggle. Process pints for 25 minutes and quarts for 40 minutes at 10 pounds pressure.

6. Turn off heat and allow pressure to return to zero. Remove lid, wait 10 minutes, then remove from canner. Cool, remove bands, label, and store jars.

Sweet Potatoes

What would Thanksgiving be without sweet potato casserole or sweet potato pie?

INGREDIENTS

- Sweet Potatoes
- Boiling water
- Canning salt (optional)

YIELD

2½ lbs sweet potatoes for each quart jar

RECIPE

1. Prepare pressure canner, jars, and lids.
2. Wash and boil sweet potatoes for 15-20 minutes. Cool slightly. Remove skins and cut them into uniform-sized chunks.
3. Pack into hot jars, leaving 1-inch headspace. Add boiling water to cover, leaving 1-inch headspace. Add ½ tsp canning salt per jar if desired.
4. Wipe rims, add lids and bands.
5. Place jars on rack in canner. Attach and secure canner lid. Heat until canner starts hissing. Allow the steam to escape the vent for 5-10 minutes, add gauge and begin timing after the first jiggle. Process pints for 65 minutes and quarts for 90 minutes at 10 pounds pressure adjusting for altitude. Turn off heat and allow pressure to return to zero. Remove lid, wait 10 minutes, then remove jars from canner using a jar lifter. Cool, label, and store jars.

White, Red and Yellow Potatoes

Warm up, drain, add butter, salt, pepper, and mash. Delicious!

INGREDIENTS

- Potatoes
- Boiling water
- Canning salt (optional)

YIELD

2½ lbs potatoes for each quart jar

RECIPE

1. Prepare pressure canner, jars, and lids.
2. Wash potatoes. Peel and wash again. Leave small potatoes whole. Cut larger potatoes into uniform chunks. Place in a stainless-steel saucepan. Add enough water to cover and bring to a boil over medium-high heat. Boil for 5-10 minutes. Do not overcook.
3. Drain and discard cooking water. Add potatoes to jars leaving 1-inch headspace. Add boiling water to cover, leaving 1-inch headspace. Add ½ tsp canning salt to each jar.
4. Wipe rims, add lids and bands. Using a jar lifter, place in a pressure canner. Process pints for 35 minutes and quarts for 40 minutes at 10 pounds pressure adjusting for altitude. Turn off heat and allow pressure to return to zero. Remove lid, wait 10 minutes, then remove jars from canner using a jar lifter. Cool, label, and store jars.

JELLIES, JAMS, FRUIT BUTTERS & MARMALADES

Canning jelly is fun and easy! You'll create beautiful, canned goods in every shade of the rainbow! You can make mouth-watering jellies out of fruits, juices, vegetables, and even herbs and flowers. Jelly, unlike jams and preserves, is clear and firm when sliced. Most jelly recipes require the addition of pectin for the liquid to gel. Jellies make colorful gifts!

Concord Grape Jelly

Use a combination of fully ripe and slightly under-ripe Concord grapes for the best results.

INGREDIENTS

- 3½-4 lbs Concord grapes
- ½ cup water
- 6¾ cups granulated sugar
- 1 3oz pouch liquid pectin

YIELD

7 8oz jars

RECIPE

1. Wash grapes and remove stems. Crush grapes, one cup at a time in a large stainless-steel saucepan. Add water. Bring to a boil over medium-high heat. Reduce heat and simmer, covered, for about 10 minutes.

2. Using a damp jelly bag or colander lined with several layers of moistened food-grade cheesecloth, pour cooked grapes and juice into a jelly bag or colander. Let drain for about 2 hours. Do not squeeze bag or cheesecloth. Measure 4 cups of prepared grape juice into a large bowl. Cover and refrigerate the juice for 12-24 hours.

3. Strain chilled juice through a damp jelly bag or colander lined with moistened cheesecloth a second time. Place juice in a large stainless-steel saucepan. Add sugar all at once. Bring to a full rolling boil over medium-high heat, stirring often to prevent scorching. When the mixture cannot be stirred down, add liquid pectin all at once. Boil hard for 1 minute, stirring constantly. Remove from heat and skim off foam with a large spoon. Discard foam.

4. Immediately ladle hot jelly into hot jars using a jar funnel. Leave ¼-inch headspace. Wipe rims of jars with a paper towel dipped in vinegar.

5. Center lids on jars. Add bands and finger-tighten.

6. Using a jar lifter, carefully place jars in a hot water bath canner with a rack in place. Make sure they are completely covered with water. Add more boiling water if needed. Add lid and return to a boil. Process for 10 minutes, adjusting for altitude.

7. Remove from heat. Remove lid. Wait 5 minutes, then remove jars and place on a wire rack or kitchen towel. Allow to cool, listen for pings, label, and store.

Granny's Apple Jelly

First, make apple juice from fresh apples, any variety, or a mixture. Then, make your jelly!

INGREDIENTS

- 5-6 lbs apples
- 1 package 1.75oz regular powdered fruit pectin
- 7 cups granulated sugar

YIELD

7 8oz jars

RECIPE

Prepare Apple Juice

1. Wash apples. Remove stem and blossom ends. Place quartered apples, skin, and core intact in a large stainless-steel saucepan. Add about 5 cups cold water. Bring to a boil over high heat, stirring often. Reduce heat and simmer, covered loosely, for about 30 minutes until apples are soft.
2. Remove from heat. Crush apples slightly using a potato masher.
3. Transfer apple pulp and juice to a dampened jelly bag or a colander lined with several layers of dampened cheesecloth over a deep bowl. Let drip for 4 hours or overnight. Do not squeeze bag or cheesecloth.

Making Jelly

1. Prepare hot water bath canner, lids, and jars.
2. In a deep stainless-steel saucepan, add apple juice. Whisk in pectin until thoroughly dissolved. Bring to a boil over high heat, stirring often to prevent scorching. Add sugar all at once and return to a full rolling boil stirring constantly. Boil hard for about 1 minute. Remove from heat and quickly skim off foam with a large spoon. Discard foam.

3. Immediately ladle hot jelly into hot jars using a jar funnel. Leave ¼-inch headspace. Wipe rims of jars with a paper towel dipped in vinegar.
4. Center lids on jars. Add bands and finger-tighten.
5. Using a jar lifter, carefully place jars in the canner with a rack in place. Make sure they are completely covered with water. Add more boiling water if needed. Cover and bring to a boil. Process for 10 minutes.
6. Remove from heat. Remove lid. Wait 5 minutes, then remove jars and place on a wire rack or kitchen towel. Allow to cool, listen for pings, label, and store.

Crabapple Jelly

Use 5-6 lbs crabapples in place of regular apples to make the apple juice. Follow all other steps

Rose Hip Jelly

Collect the hips from wild beach roses after the first frost to make this old-fashioned sweet and tart favorite.

INGREDIENTS

- 2 quarts rose hips
- 6 cups water
- ½ cup freshly squeezed lemon juice
- 1 1.75oz package regular powdered pectin
- ½ tsp butter to reduce foaming
- 3½ cups granulated sugar

YIELD

5 8oz jars

RECIPE

1. Rinse rose hips. Remove stem end. Place in a large stainless-steel pot and add 6 cups water. Bring to a boil, then reduce heat and simmer covered for 1 hour.

2. Using a potato masher, mash the rose hips into a pulp. Transfer pulp and juice to a dampened jelly bag or a colander lined with several layers of dampened cheesecloth over a deep bowl. Let drip for 1-2 hours until you have 3 cups strained juice. Do not squeeze bag or cheesecloth.

3. Prepare hot water bath canner, lids, and jars.

4. Add 3 cups of rose hip juice, lemon juice, and powdered pectin to a deep stainless-steel saucepan. Whisk in the pectin until thoroughly dissolved. Add the sugar all at once, stirring to dissolve. Then add the butter (optional). Bring to a full rolling boil stirring constantly. Boil hard for 1 minute. Remove from heat and quickly skim off foam with a large spoon. Discard foam.

5. Immediately ladle hot jelly into hot jars using a jar funnel. Leave ¼-inch headspace. Wipe rims of jars with a paper towel dipped in vinegar.

6. Center lids on jars. Add bands and finger-tighten.

7. Using a jar lifter, carefully place jars in the canner with a rack in place. Make sure they are completely covered with water. Add more boiling water if needed. Cover and bring to a boil. Process for 10 minutes.

8. Remove from heat. Remove lid. Wait 5 minutes, then remove jars and place on a wire rack or kitchen towel. Allow to cool, listen for pings, label, and store.

Fresh Blueberry Jelly

First, make blueberry juice from fresh blueberries. Include some slightly under-ripe berries to enhance natural pectin content. Discard over-ripe, mushy berries. Then, make your jelly!

INGREDIENTS

- 2 quarts fresh blueberries
- 4 cups water
- 2 pouches 3oz each liquid pectin
- 12 cups granulated sugar

YIELD

12 8oz jars

RECIPE

1. Place blueberries in a large stainless-steel pot. Crush berries using a potato masher. Add water and bring to a boil over medium-high heat, stirring often. Reduce heat to medium and cook, uncovered, for 45 minutes. Line a colander with four layers of moistened cheesecloth and place over a bowl or use a moistened jelly bag with a stand. Place pulp and liquid in colander or jelly bag. Let drip for 1 hour or until you have 6 cups of blueberry juice.

2. Pour juice back into the pot. Gradually stir in sugar until it dissolves. Bring to a boil over high heat, stirring constantly. Stir in pectin. Bring to a rolling boil that cannot be stirred down and stir constantly for 1 minute.

3. Remove from heat and quickly skim off foam with a large spoon. Discard foam.

4. Immediately ladle hot jelly into hot jars using a jar funnel. Leave ¼-inch headspace. Wipe rims of jars with a paper towel dipped in vinegar.

5. Center lids on jars. Add bands and finger-tighten.

6. Using a jar lifter, carefully place jars in a hot water bath canner with a rack in place. Make sure they are completely covered with water. Add more boiling water if needed. Cover and return to a boil. Process for 5 minutes.

7. Remove from heat. Remove lid. Wait 5 minutes, then remove jars and place on a wire rack or kitchen towel. Allow to cool, listen for pings, label, and store.

Strawberry Jelly

You'll get more juice from your strawberries if you freeze them for 24-48 hours. Thaw in the refrigerator, then mash and pour in a jelly bag.

INGREDIENTS

- 4-5 quarts fresh strawberries
- 1 1.75oz package regular powdered fruit pectin
- 4½ cups granulated sugar
- ½ tsp butter (to reduce foaming)

YIELD

5 8oz jars

RECIPE

1. Place thawed strawberries in a large stainless-steel pot. Crush berries using a potato masher. Line a colander with four layers of moistened cheesecloth and place over a bowl or use a moistened jelly bag with a stand. Pour pulp and liquid into the colander or jelly bag. Let drip for 2-4 hours or until you have 3½ cups of strawberry juice.
2. Pour juice back into the pot. Whisk in powdered pectin and butter. Bring to a boil over medium-high heat, stirring often. Add sugar all at once and return to a rolling boil that cannot be stirred down. Boil hard, stirring constantly for 1 minute.
3. Remove from heat and quickly skim off foam with a large spoon. Discard foam.
4. Immediately ladle hot jelly into hot jars using a jar funnel. Leave ¼-inch headspace. Wipe rims of jars with a paper towel dipped in vinegar.
5. Center lids on jars. Add bands and finger-tighten.
6. Using a jar lifter, carefully place jars in a hot water bath canner with a rack in place. Make sure they are completely covered with water. Add more boiling water if needed. Cover and return to a boil. Process for 10 minutes.
7. Remove from heat. Remove lid. Wait 5 minutes, then remove jars and place on a wire rack or kitchen towel. Allow to cool, listen for pings, label, and store.

Hot Sriracha Pepper Jelly

Hot and sweet! Serve it with crackers, cheese, and fruits at your next party.

INGREDIENTS

- 12oz sriracha peppers (about 8-10)
- 2 cups apple cider vinegar
- 6 cups sugar
- 2 3oz pouches liquid pectin
- Green food coloring (optional)

YIELD

5 8oz jars

RECIPE

1. Remove stems. Place peppers and 1 cup apple cider vinegar in a food processor or blender. Puree.
2. Add 6 cups sugar and 1 cup apple cider vinegar to a large stainless-steel pot. Add pureed pepper mixture. Add a few drops of green food coloring if desired. Stir well.
3. Bring to boil over high heat. Boil hard for 10 minutes. Stir often.
4. Add 2 pouches of liquid pectin all at once. Stir and return to a full boil. Stir constantly for 1 minute.
5. Remove from heat and skim off foam. Discard foam. Using a jar funnel, pour into jars leaving ¼-inch headspace. Wipe rims, add lids and bands to finger tight.
6. Using a jar lifter, place jars in a hot water bath canner. Cover. Return to a full boil. Process for 10 minutes.
7. Remove pot from heat source. Remove cover. After 5 minutes, remove jars to cooling rack or towel.
8. Cool, label, and store jars.

Banana Pepper Jelly: Use 12oz yellow banana peppers instead of sriracha peppers. Use a few drops of yellow food coloring if desired.

Hot Hungarian Pepper Jelly: Use 12oz Hungarian wax peppers instead of sriracha peppers.

Jalapeno Jelly: Use 12oz jalapeno peppers instead of sriracha peppers.
Or mix and match any combination of peppers using 12oz total.

Fresh Herb Jelly

Not all jellies are sweet. Savory jellies can be served with cheese and crackers or as a glaze for meat, poultry, or fish.

INGREDIENTS

- 2 cups coarsely chopped parsley, basil, thyme, dill, or any combination of fresh herbs
- 1½ cups unsweetened apple juice
- 1 cup water
- 1 cup white wine vinegar
- 1 1.75oz package powdered pectin
- 5¼ cups granulated sugar
- Food coloring (optional)

YIELD

5 8oz jars

Luke's Variations

Add a few drops of green food coloring to the jelly mixture when it is cooking.

Note

Using white wine vinegar allows the flavor of the herbs to take center stage.

RECIPE

1. Combine herbs, apple juice, water, and vinegar in a large stainless-steel saucepan. Bring to a boil over medium heat. Remove from heat, cover, and let steep for 30 minutes. Stir, pressing down on herbs to extract flavor and oils.

2. Transfer herbs and liquid to a moistened jelly bag or strain through several layers of damp cheesecloth into a large bowl. Let drip for 30 minutes or longer. Do not squeeze bag.

3. Prepare hot water bath canner, jars, and lids.

4. Transfer strained juice to a large stainless-steel saucepan. Whisk in powdered pectin until fully dissolved. Bring to a bowl over medium-high heat, stirring often. When boiling, add sugar all at once, stirring constantly to dissolve. When mixture reaches a full rolling boil, time for 1 minute stirring constantly. Remove from heat and skim off foam. Discard foam.

5. Using a jar funnel, pour hot jelly into hot jars, leaving ¼-inch headspace. Wipe rims with a paper towel moistened with vinegar. Add lids and bands to finger tight.

6. Using a jar lifter, place jars in a boiling water bath. Cover. Return to a full boil. Process for 10 minutes.

7. Remove canner from heat. Remove cover. After 5 minutes, remove jars to cooling rack or towel.

8. Cool, label, and store jars.

Lemon and Lavender Jelly

Make this in the summer when your herb garden is in bloom!

INGREDIENTS

- 3-4 lemons
- 1 1/3 cups boiling water
- 2 Tbsp fresh just-opened lavender flowers (or 1 Tbsp dried lavender flowers crushed)
- 4¼ cups granulated sugar
- 1 3oz pouch liquid pectin

YIELD

4 8oz jars

RECIPE

1. Remove 2 Tbsp lemon zest. Squeeze ¾ cup juice from the lemons. In a large glass bowl, add zest, lemon juice, lavender flowers, and boiling water. Cover with a cloth and let stand 1 hour.
2. Prepare hot water bath canner, jars, and lids.
3. Strain mixture through a fine sieve. Discard peel, pulp, and flowers.
4. Transfer strained liquid to a large stainless-steel saucepan. Add the sugar and bring to a full boil over high heat, stirring constantly. Stir in liquid pectin and return to a full rolling boil that cannot be stirred down. Boil hard for 1 minute, stirring constantly.
5. Remove from heat and skim off foam. Discard foam.
6. Using a jar funnel, pour hot jelly into hot jars, leaving ¼-inch headspace. Wipe rims with a paper towel moistened with vinegar. Add lids and bands to finger tight.
7. Using a jar lifter, place jars in a boiling water bath. Cover. Return to a full boil. Process for 5 minutes.
8. Remove canner from heat. Remove cover. After 5 minutes, remove jars to cooling rack or towel.
9. Cool, label, and store jars.

Patten's Farm Stand Strawberry Jam

In the late 1970s, my first job was on a strawberry farm. I earned 7 cents a quart for picking strawberries. A few summers later, the pay was increased to 10 cents a quart. One day I picked 100 quarts which meant I earned $10 for 8+ hours in the hot, summer sun. But it was worth it because earning my own money allowed me to buy a tape recorder, record albums, and my own school clothes. While working on the farm, I learned how to make this mouth-watering strawberry jam from the berries I had just picked. Your whole family will love this delicious, fresh-tasting jam. The taste of nostalgia!

INGREDIENTS

- 3¾ cups crushed hulled strawberries
- 4 Tbsp lemon juice
- 7 cups granulated sugar
- 1 tsp butter (to reduce foaming)
- 1 3oz pouch liquid pectin

YIELD

8 8oz jars

RECIPE

1. In a large, deep pan, combine crushed strawberries and their juice, lemon juice, and sugar. Add butter. Stir constantly over high heat until it comes to a full rolling boil that cannot be stirred down. Stir in pectin all at once. Return to a rolling boil and boil hard, stirring constantly for 1 minute. Remove from heat.
2. Skim foam off the surface with a large spoon. Discard foam. Your liquid should be clear with pieces of fruit.
3. Ladle hot jam into hot jars. Leave ¼-inch headspace. Wipe down rims of jars with a paper towel dipped in vinegar.
4. Center lids on jars. Add bands and finger-tighten.
5. Using a jar lifter, carefully place jars in a hot water bath canner with a rack in place. Make sure they are completely covered with water. Add more boiling water if needed. Add lid and bring to a boil. Process for 10 minutes.
6. Remove from heat. Remove lid. Wait 5 minutes, then remove jars and place them on a kitchen towel or wire rack. Allow to cool, listen for pings, label, and store.

Blueberry Jam

Not everyone has a garden or a farm. But you can still preserve the taste of summer all year long when you buy fresh ingredients from a local farm stand or pick-your-own. This recipe is simple and delicious!

INGREDIENTS

- 4½ cups crushed blueberries (about 3 pints)
- ¼ cup lemon juice
- 7 cups granulated sugar
- 1 tsp butter
- 2 3oz pouches liquid pectin

YIELD

8 8oz jars

RECIPE

1. In a large, deep stainless-steel pan, combine crushed blueberries and their juice, lemon juice, and sugar. Add butter. Stir constantly over high heat until it comes to a full rolling boil that cannot be stirred down. Stir in pectin all at once. Boil hard, stirring constantly for 1 minute. Remove from heat.
2. Skim foam off the surface with a large spoon. Discard foam. Your liquid should be clear with pieces of fruit.
3. Ladle hot jam into hot jars. Leave ¼-inch headspace. Wipe down rims of jars with a paper towel dipped in vinegar.
4. Center lids on jars. Add bands and finger-tighten.
5. Using a jar lifter, carefully place jars in a hot water bath canner with a rack in place. Make sure they are completely covered with water. Add more boiling water if needed. Add lid and bring to a boil. Process for 10 minutes.
6. Remove from heat. Remove lid. Wait 5 minutes, then remove jars and place them on a kitchen towel or wire rack. Allow to cool, listen for pings, label, and store.

Triple Berry Jam

An easy jam made without pectin combining the flavors and colors of 3 summer fruit favorites!

INGREDIENTS

- 3 cups cut-up strawberries
- 1½ cups blueberries
- 1½ cups raspberries
- ¾ cup granulated sugar
- Zest of 1 lemon
- 2 tsp lemon juice
- 1 tsp butter

YIELD

3-4 8oz jars

RECIPE

1. In a large bowl, combine all 3 fruits and sugar. Stir together and allow to sit for 1-2 hours until sugar is dissolved and syrupy.
2. Add mixture to a stainless-steel saucepan and bring to a boil over medium-high heat, stirring often. Reduce heat to medium-low and boil gently for 30-40 minutes until the jam begins to thicken. Mash fruits with a potato masher, then stir in butter, lemon zest and lemon juice. Cook for 5 more minutes. Remove from heat.
3. Skim foam off the surface with a large spoon. Discard foam. Your liquid should be clear with pieces of fruit.
4. Ladle hot jam into hot jars. Leave ¼-inch headspace. Wipe down rims of jars with a paper towel dipped in vinegar.
5. Center lids on jars. Add bands and finger-tighten.
6. Using a jar lifter, carefully place jars in a hot water bath canner with a rack in place. Make sure they are completely covered with water. Add more boiling water if needed. Add the lid and bring to a boil. Process for 10 minutes.
7. Remove from heat. Remove lid. Wait 5 minutes, then remove jars and place them on a kitchen towel or wire rack. Allow to cool, listen for pings, label, and store.

Raspberry Jam

If you want fewer seeds in your raspberry jam, press half or more of the crushed berries through a sieve and discard the seeds.

INGREDIENTS

- 12 cups fresh raspberries
- 1 1.75oz package powdered fruit pectin
- ½ tsp butter (optional)
- 7 cups granulated sugar

YIELD

8 8oz jars

RECIPE

1. Crush raspberries, one cup at a time, in a large stainless-steel saucepan. Continue crushing until you have 5 cups of crushed berries.
2. Stir in pectin and butter (optional) and bring to a full rolling boil that cannot be stirred down, stirring constantly. Once you have reached the rolling boil, time for exactly 1 minute. Remove from heat and skim the foam off the surface with a large spoon. Discard foam.
3. Immediately, ladle hot jam into hot jars. Leave ¼-inch headspace. Wipe down rims of jars with a paper towel dipped in vinegar.
4. Center lids on jars. Add bands and finger-tighten.
5. Using a jar lifter, carefully place jars in a hot water bath canner with a rack in place. Make sure they are completely covered with water. Add more boiling water if needed. Add lid and bring to a boil. Process for 10 minutes.
6. Remove from heat. Remove lid. Wait 5 minutes, then remove jars and place on a wire rack or kitchen towel. Allow to cool, listen for pings, label, and store.

Queen's Jam

This Scandinavian favorite is served on Swedish pancakes and drizzled over ice cream!

INGREDIENTS

- 2 pints fresh raspberries
- 1 pint fresh blueberries
- 1¾ cups granulated sugar
- Juice of one-half lemon

YIELD

3-4 8oz jars

RECIPE

1. Layer raspberries and blueberries in a large stainless-steel saucepan. Crush with a potato masher. Add the sugar, stir well to dissolve the sugar, and let sit for 30 minutes.

2. Add lemon juice. Bring to a full rolling boil that cannot be stirred down, stirring often. Once the jam reaches 220 degrees, remove from heat, and skim the foam off the surface with a large spoon. Discard foam and, at once, ladle hot jam into hot jars. Leave ¼-inch headspace. Wipe down rims of jars with a paper towel dipped in vinegar.

3. Center lids on jars. Add bands and finger-tighten.

4. Using a jar lifter, carefully place jars in a hot water bath canner with a rack in place. Make sure they are completely covered with water. Add more boiling water if needed. Cover and bring to a boil. Process for 20 minutes.

5. Remove from heat. Remove lid. Wait 5 minutes, then remove jars and place on a wire rack or kitchen towel. Allow to cool, listen for pings, label, and store.

New England Apple Cider Butter

Apple butter, cider, and applesauce were old-timey ways of preserving the apple harvest. It wasn't too many generations ago that fall was the only time you could get apples. I suggest using one or a combination of the following varieties if you have a choice: Red Delicious, Yellow Delicious, or Rome.

INGREDIENTS

- 6 lbs apples, peeled, cored, and quartered
- 2 cups apple cider
- 3 cups granulated sugar
- 1½ tsp ground cinnamon
- ½ tsp ground cloves
- ½ tsp ground nutmeg

YIELD

Makes about 4 pints

RECIPE

1. Prepare hot water bath canner, jars, and lids.
2. Mix sugar and spices. Set aside.
3. In a large stainless-steel saucepan, combine apples and apple cider. Bring to a boil over medium-high heat. Reduce heat and boil gently for 30 minutes, stirring occasionally until apples are soft.
4. Cool slightly, then puree apples in a food processor or grinder until smooth. Do not liquefy.
5. Measure 12 cups of apple puree into a large stainless-steel pot. Add sugar/spice mixture and stir until sugar is dissolved. Bring to a boil over medium-high heat, stirring often to prevent scorching. Reduce heat and boil gently until the mixture holds its shape on a spoon.

Luke's Variations

Substitute I cup local honey for the 3 cups of sugar. This recipe will be slightly less sweet.

Traditional Apple Butter

Replace apple cider with 3 cups water. Increase sugar to 5 cups.

6. Immediately ladle hot butter into hot jars using a jar funnel. Leave ¼-inch headspace. Wipe rims of jars with a paper towel dipped in vinegar.

7. Center lids on jars. Add bands and finger-tighten.

8. Using a jar lifter, carefully place jars in a hot water bath canner with a rack in place. Make sure they are completely covered with water. Add more boiling water if needed. Cover and bring to a boil. Process for 10 minutes.

9. Remove from heat. Remove lid. Wait 5 minutes, then remove jars and place on a wire rack or kitchen towel. Allow to cool, listen for pings, label, and store.

Traditional Orange Marmalade

This old-fashioned marmalade recipe has been a family favorite since WWII, when oranges were considered a delicacy in most of the United States.

INGREDIENTS

- 4 oranges (2 cups)
- 3 lemons (1½ cups)
- Granulated sugar

YIELD

Use 8oz or smaller jars

RECIPE

1. Chop oranges and lemons, including rinds, into small chunks. Place in a large bowl and add 6 cups cold water. Cover with a cloth and let sit overnight.
2. Add water and fruit to a large stainless-steel saucepan. Bring to a boil over medium-high heat, stirring often. Reduce heat to medium-low and cook for about 30 minutes until fruits are tender. Remove from heat. Cover and let sit overnight.
3. On the third day, prepare hot water bath canner, jars, and lids.
4. Measure fruit bits and juice. Add to a large stainless-steel saucepan. For each 16oz, add 2 cups granulated sugar stirring as you go to dissolve the sugar.
5. Heat mixture to jelly stage*, about 10 minutes. Remove from heat and skim off foam. Using a jar funnel, pour hot marmalade into hot jars, leaving ¼-inch headspace.

6. Wipe rims, add lids and bands to finger tight.
7. Process in a hot water bath canner for 5 minutes.**
8. Using a jar lifter, remove jars and cool on a wire rack or kitchen towel. Remove bands, label, and store.

*Jelly stage is achieved when the jelly mixture drips off a spoon in a "sheet." The temperature of the jelly should be 220-222 degrees.

**Old recipes don't call for the use of a hot water bath. Home canners usually sealed the jars with paraffin and lids, and the temperature of the hot marmalade was typically enough to seal the jars. Although some still employ this method, it is no longer considered safe by modern food safety standards.

Old-Fashioned Carrot and Orange Marmalade

This old-fashioned marmalade recipe does not call for processing in a hot water bath, but I've added it to meet modern food safety standards. Since these old recipes don't use liquid or powdered pectin, they require a longer cooking time.

INGREDIENTS

- 2 cups uncooked ground carrots
- 1 orange
- 2 lemons
- Granulated sugar
- 3 cups water

YIELD

Use 8oz or smaller jars

RECIPE

1. Prepare hot water bath canner, jars, and lids.
2. Squeeze and extract the juice from the oranges and lemons. Set aside. Grind the rinds using a food grinder or food processor. Add the ground rinds to a large stainless-steel saucepan. Add just enough water to cover. Cook over medium heat for about 30 minutes until tender, stirring often to prevent scorching. Add the ground carrots, stir to blend, and cook an additional 30 minutes. Add the orange and lemon juice. Remove from heat.
3. Measure the mixture and add an equal amount of water. Remeasure. For each cup of this mixture, add 2/3 cup granulated sugar.
4. Return to clean stainless-steel saucepan and bring to a boil over high heat, stirring often, until mixture reaches the jelly stage*. This will take about an hour.
5. Remove from heat and skim off foam. Discard foam. Using a jar funnel, pour hot marmalade into hot jars, leaving ¼-inch headspace.
6. Wipe rims, add lids and bands to finger tight.
7. Process in a hot water bath canner for 5 minutes.

8. Using a jar lifter, remove jars and cool on a wire rack or kitchen towel. Remove bands, label, and store.

*Jelly stage is achieved when the jelly mixture drips off a spoon in a "sheet." The temperature of the jelly should be 220-222 degrees.

Strawberry Lemon Marmalade

Try this instead of syrup on pancakes and waffles!

INGREDIENTS

- 2 lemons
- ½ cup water
- 1/8 tsp baking soda
- 6 cups strawberries (3 cups when crushed)
- 5 cups granulated sugar
- 1 3oz package liquid pectin

YIELD

Makes about 6 8oz jars

RECIPE

1. Prepare hot water bath canner, jars, and lids.
2. Wash and peel the lemons. Set the peeled lemons aside. Scrape off the inner white part of the rind and discard. Slice the lemon peels into very thin strips.
3. In a large stainless-steel saucepan, combine lemon peels, water, and baking soda. Bring to a boil, reduce heat and simmer covered for 20 minutes. Chop lemons, reserving juice, discard seeds, and add lemons and juice to the saucepan. Add crushed strawberries and return to boiling. Reduce heat and simmer covered for 10 minutes.
4. Add sugar all at once. Return to a full, rolling boil stirring constantly. Stir in liquid pectin and return to a full, rolling boil that cannot be stirred down. Boil hard for 1 minute, stirring constantly. Remove from heat and quickly skim off foam. Using a jar funnel, pour hot marmalade into hot jars, leaving ¼-inch headspace.
5. Wipe rims, add lids and bands to finger tight.
6. Process in a hot water bath canner for 5 minutes.
7. Using a jar lifter, remove jars and cool on a wire rack or kitchen towel. Remove bands, label, and store for 2 weeks before serving.

PICKLES & PICKLED VEGETABLES

Pickling began more than 4000 years ago when ancient Mesopotamians began preserving cucumbers in brine to preserve them. We're still enjoying them today!

Grammie's Victory Garden Dill Pickles

This traditional family recipe has been used successfully for 100 years with excellent results! My family never processes the pickles in a hot water bath, and the boiling brine is typically sufficient to seal the lids. But you can process them for 5 minutes in a hot water bath for added peace of mind.

INGREDIENTS

- 2 quarts hot water
- 1 quart white vinegar
- ¾ cup canning salt
- Fresh dill or dill seed
- Garlic cloves
- Peppercorns
- Pickling cucumbers, sliced

YIELD

Makes 6-8 pints

Luke's Secret to Crisper Pickles

Soak cucumber slices in a bowl of salted ice water.

Remove blossom end.

Do not use English cucumbers.

Use right from the garden cucumbers that are not too large, old, mushy, or seedy.

Add 1/8 teaspoon Ball Pickle Crisp Granules to each pint jar before processing. This is calcium chloride and helps make crisp, delicious pickles every time!

RECIPE

1. Prepare hot water bath canner, jars, and lids.
2. Mix 2 quarts of hot water and 1 quart white vinegar in a stainless-steel saucepan. Add ¾ cup canning salt. Bring to a hard boil which cannot be stirred down.
3. Add your cucumber slices to clean hot canning jars. Do not pack them down and leave some headspace for the liquid to be added.
4. Add dill flowers, leaves, stems, or dill seed to each jar. Add one peeled garlic clove to each jar. Add a few whole black peppercorns to each jar.

5. Using a jar funnel, gently pour hot brine over cucumbers in each jar, leaving ½-inch headspace. Use a rubber spatula to remove air bubbles. Add lids and bands. Hand-tighten bands.
6. Using a jar lifter, carefully place each jar in a boiling hot water bath. Make sure the jars are not crowded and are covered with water. Add more boiling water if needed. Cover pot and return to a boil.
7. Process for 5 minutes. Remove from the heat and remove the lid. Wait another 5 minutes, and then using a jar lifter, place each jar upright on a towel or wire rack. Allow to cool completely. Although you could eat these pickles immediately, I suggest waiting a week or two to allow the flavors to develop fully. Be sure to label each jar with what it holds and the date it was canned for long-term storage. Before storing, remove the bands. Do not stack the jars on top of each other.

Old-Fashioned Cucumber and Onion Pickles

My maternal grandmother was born in Canada, and her family brought this traditional recipe with them when they emigrated to Maine in 1920. The recipe calls for peeled cucumbers which is unusual, and it doesn't call for processing in a hot water bath, but I've updated it to follow modern food safety standards.

INGREDIENTS

- Pickling cucumbers
- Onions
- ¼ cup canning salt
- 1 quart apple cider vinegar
- 2 cups brown sugar
- 1 Tbsp dry mustard
- 1 Tbsp turmeric
- 1 Tbsp ClearJel (optional)
- Ball Pickle Crisp (optional)

YIELD

Makes 6-8 pints

RECIPE

1. Wash, peel, and slice cucumbers and onions. Place in a bowl and cover them with ice-cold water and salt. Let stand 12 hours or overnight.
2. Bring vinegar and sugar to a boil. Mix dry mustard, turmeric, and ClearJel. Add a little vinegar to form a paste, then add to boiling vinegar and sugar. Stir well to mix.
3. Drain and rinse cucumbers and onions under cold water. Place vegetables in the brine and boil softly for 5 minutes. Pack into prepared jars, leaving ½-inch headspace. Add brine to cover, remove air bubbles, add sterilized lids and bands to finger tight. Add 1/8 tsp Pickle Crisp to each pint jar.

4. Using a jar lifter, carefully place each jar in a hot water bath canner. Make sure the jars are not crowded and are covered with water. Add more boiling water if needed. Cover pot and return to a boil.

5. After 5 minutes, shut off the heat and remove the lid. Wait another 5 minutes, and then using a jar lifter, place each jar upright on a wire rack or towel. Allow to cool completely. Although you could eat these pickles immediately, I suggest waiting one or two weeks to allow the flavors to develop fully. Be sure to label each jar. Before storing, remove the bands. Do not stack the jars on top of each other.

Bread and Butter Pickles

Just like Grandma used to make!

INGREDIENTS

- 10 cups sliced, trimmed pickling cucumbers
- 4 medium onions sliced thinly
- ½ cup canning salt
- 3 cups white vinegar
- 2 cups granulated sugar
- 2 Tbsp mustard seed
- 1 tsp celery seed
- 1 tsp turmeric
- ¼ tsp Pickle Crisp per pint (optional)

YIELD

5 pints

RECIPE

1. Prepare pickling cucumbers making sure to trim off and discard the blossom end. Combine cucumber slices, onions, and salt in a large glass bowl. Mix. Add ice-cold water, cover, and allow to sit for 2 hours. After 2 hours, drain, rinse with cool water, and set aside.

2. Prepare hot water bath canner, jars, and lids.

3. In a large stainless-steel saucepan, combine vinegar, sugar, and spices. Bring to a boil over medium-high heat, stirring to dissolve sugar. Add cucumbers and onions and return to a boil.

4. Pack cucumbers and onions into hot jars, leaving ½-inch headspace. Using a jar funnel, ladle hot brine to cover, remove air bubbles with a rubber spatula. Add Pickle Crisp if desired.

5. Wipe rims, add lids and bands to finger tight.

6. Using a jar lifter, carefully place each jar in the boiling hot water bath. Make sure the jars are not crowded and are covered with water. Add more boiling water if needed. Cover pot and bring to a boil.

7. Return to a boil and process for 10 minutes. Remove canner from heat and remove the lid. Wait another 5 minutes, and then, using a jar lifter, place each jar upright on a wire rack or towel. Cool, label, and remove bands. Although you could eat these pickles immediately, I suggest waiting one or two weeks to allow the flavors to develop fully.

Watermelon Rind Pickles

Rather than tossing the rinds in the compost pile, make pickles. Give this vintage recipe a try. Waste not, want not!

INGREDIENTS

- Rind of 1 large watermelon
- 4 Tbsp canning salt
- Water
- 8 cups granulated sugar
- 4 cups white vinegar
- 8 tsp whole cloves
- 16 cinnamon sticks
- 1 tsp mustard seed
- Green or red food coloring (optional)

YIELD

Varies

RECIPE

1. Peel and remove all pink and green portions from the rind of 1 large watermelon. Cut rind into 1-inch cubes and soak overnight in 1 quart water mixed with 4 Tbsp canning salt.
2. Next day, drain and add to a large stainless-steel saucepan. Cover with fresh water and cook over medium heat until the rind is almost tender. Drain.
3. Make a cheesecloth spice bag with cloves, cinnamon sticks, and mustard seed. In the saucepan, add sugar, vinegar, and spice bag. Heat the syrup to boiling, then simmer for 15 minutes.
4. Prepare hot water bath canner, jars, and lids.
5. Add rinds to syrup and cook until clear and transparent. Add a few drops of food coloring (optional).
6. Using a slotted spoon, pack rinds into hot jars, leaving ½-inch headspace. Using a jar funnel, ladle hot syrup to cover, leaving ½-inch headspace. Remove air bubbles with a rubber spatula. Add more syrup if needed.
7. Wipe rims, add lids and bands to finger tight.
8. Using a jar lifter, carefully place each jar in a boiling hot water bath. Make sure the jars are not crowded and are covered with water. Add more boiling water if needed. Cover pot and return to a boil.

9. Process for 5 minutes. Remove canner from heat and remove the lid. Wait another 5 minutes, and then using a jar lifter, place each jar upright on a wire rack or towel. Cool, label, and remove bands.

Down East Sour Pickles

Another family recipe. You can be creative with this recipe and slice, quarter, or halve the cucumbers (blossom end removed) or cut into spears. This is an old-fashioned Down East sour pickle. My grandmother poured the hot brine into the jars and added the lids and bands, but I suggest a brief hot water bath to comply with modern food safety standards.

INGREDIENTS

- Cucumbers
- 3 cups vinegar
- 1 cup water
- ¼ cup canning salt
- ¼ cup granulated sugar
- ¼ cup dry mustard
- ¼ tsp Ball Pickle Crisp per pint (optional)

YEILD

Makes 4 pints

Luke's Variation

Add 1/8 tsp mustard seed to each jar.

RECIPE

1. Prepare cucumbers as desired. Add to sterilized canning jars, leaving headspace.
2. Add vinegar, water, salt, sugar, and dry mustard to the pot and bring it to a hard boil.
3. Pour hot brine over cucumbers leaving ½-inch headspace. Add Pickle Crisp to each jar. (optional)
4. Wipe rims, add lids and bands to finger tight.
5. Add jars to a hot water bath canner. Cover. Return to a boil. Process for 5 minutes.
6. Shut off heat and remove the lid. Wait another 5 minutes, and then using a jar lifter, place each jar upright on a wire rack or towel. Cool completely. Although you could eat these pickles immediately, I suggest waiting one or two weeks to allow the flavors to develop fully. Be sure to label each jar with what it holds and the date it was canned for long-term storage. Before storing, remove the bands. Do not stack the jars on top of each other.

Ice Water Pickle Spears

Another vintage recipe that I've adjusted slightly. Serve on a vintage pickle dish at your next dinner party!

INGREDIENTS

- 6 lbs medium cucumbers
- 3 quarts white vinegar
- 3 cups granulated sugar
- 1 cup canning salt
- Mustard seed
- Celery stalks
- Pickling onions
- Ball Pickle Crisp (optional)

YIELD

Use quart jars to accommodate long spears

RECIPE

1. Remove blossom end and slice cucumbers into spears. Scrape off excess seeds.
2. Soak spears in ice water for 3 hours.
3. Add 6 small, peeled pickling onions, 2 stalks trimmed celery, and 1 tsp mustard seed to each jar.
4. Drain cucumbers and pack spears into jars.
5. Mix vinegar, sugar, and salt. Bring to a hard boil.
6. Pour brine solution into jars leaving ½-inch headspace.
7. Add 1 tsp Ball Pickle Crisp to each quart jar.
8. Wipe rims, add lids and bands to finger tight.
9. Add jars to a hot water bath canner. Cover. Return to a boil. Process for 5 minutes.
10. Shut off heat and remove the lid. Wait another 5 minutes, and then using a jar lifter, place each jar upright on a wire rack or towel. Label jars and store them in a cool, dark place.

End of Harvest Pickled Vegetable Mix

This is a great way to make effective use of small amounts of lots of things at the end of the gardening season.

INGREDIENTS

- 3 cups sliced zucchini
- 3 cups sliced, trimmed green or yellow beans
- 1½ cups peeled, sliced carrots
- 2 cups peeled pickling or pearl onions
- 3 green or red bell peppers, seeded and cut into thin strips
- 3 cups apple cider vinegar
- 1 cup brown sugar
- 1 cup granulated sugar
- 2 Tbsp dry mustard
- 2 Tbsp mustard seed
- 5 tsp canning salt
- 1 tsp ground cinnamon
- 1 tsp ground ginger

YIELD

Makes about 5 pints

RECIPE

1. Prepare hot water bath canner, jars, and lids.
2. In a large glass bowl, combine all vegetables. Mix well and set aside.
3. In a large stainless-steel saucepan, combine vinegar, sugars, and all spices. Bring to a boil over medium-high heat, stirring to dissolve sugar. Add vegetable mix and return to a boil. Reduce heat and boil gently for 15 minutes.
4. Using a slotted spoon and a jar funnel, pack hot vegetables into hot jars, leaving ½-inch headspace. Add pickling brine to cover, remove air bubbles using a rubber spatula. Add lids and bands to finger tight.
5. Using a jar lifter, carefully place each jar in the boiling hot water bath. Make sure the jars are not crowded and are covered with water. Add more boiling water if needed. Cover pot and bring to a boil. Process pints for 15 minutes.
6. Shut off heat and remove the lid. Wait another 5 minutes, and then using a jar lifter, place each jar upright on a wire rack or towel. When cool, remove bands, label, and store in a cool, dark place.

Pickled Red Cabbage

Even people who claim they hate cabbage will love this spicy pickled treat!

INGREDIENTS

- 12 lbs red cabbage
- ½ cup canning salt
- ¼ cup whole cloves
- ¼ cup whole allspice
- ¼ cup whole black peppercorns
- ¼ cup celery seed
- 2 cinnamon sticks
- 8 cups red wine vinegar
- 1 cup brown sugar
- ½ cup mustard seed
- ¼ cup ground nutmeg

YIELD

Makes about 9 pints

Luke's Variation

Use green cabbage or a combination of both.

RECIPE

1. Core red cabbage and shred using a very sharp knife or mandoline. Working in batches, place in a colander and rinse under cold water. Transfer to a baking sheet and drain between layers of paper towels for 5-6 hours.
2. Prepare hot water bath canner, jars, and lids.
3. Make a spice bag with cheesecloth. Tie cloves, allspice, peppercorns, celery seed, and cinnamon sticks broken into pieces in cheesecloth.
4. Bring vinegar, brown sugar, mustard seed, nutmeg, and spice bag to a boil over medium-high heat in a large stainless-steel saucepan. Reduce heat and boil gently for 5-10 minutes. Discard spice bag.
5. Pack the cabbage into hot jars, leaving ½-inch headspace. Using a jar funnel, pour the hot pickling liquid over cabbage, leaving ½ inch headspace. Use a rubber spatula to remove air bubbles. Add more liquid if necessary.
6. Wipe rims with a paper towel moistened with vinegar. Add lids and bands to finger tight.
7. Add jars to a hot water bath canner. Cover. Return to a boil. Process for 20 minutes.
8. Shut off heat and remove the lid. Wait another 5 minutes, and then using a jar lifter, place each jar upright on a wire rack or towel. Allow to cool completely. Remove bands, label, and store in a cool, dark place.

291

Dilly Beans

Use a combination of green, yellow, and purple beans for a spectacular effect!

INGREDIENTS

- 3 Tbsp canning salt
- 3 cups white vinegar
- 3 cups water
- 4-5 lbs beans
- 2-3 sweet red bell peppers
- Peppercorns
- Fresh dill
- Garlic cloves

YIELD

Makes about 6 pints

RECIPE

1. Prepare hot water bath canner, jars, and lids.
2. In a large stainless-steel saucepan, combine salt, vinegar, and water. Bring to a boil over medium-high heat. Add beans cut into jar-sized pieces and thinly sliced red pepper strips. Return to a boil. Remove from heat.
3. Place 3-5 peppercorns, a generous sprig of dill, or ½ tsp of dill seed if fresh dill is unavailable, and 1 peeled garlic clove to each jar. Add beans and pepper strips to each jar, leaving ½-inch headspace. Use a rubber spatula to remove air bubbles. Add more liquid if necessary.

4. Wipe rims with a paper towel moistened with vinegar. Add lids and bands to finger tight.
5. Add jars to boiling water bath. Cover. Return to a boil. Process for 10 minutes.
6. Shut off heat and remove the lid. Wait another 5 minutes, and then using a jar lifter, place each jar upright on a wire rack or towel. Allow to cool completely. Remove bands, label, and store in a cool, dark place.

Dilly Carrots

Add to salads, sandwiches, or relish trays. Try using rainbow carrots!

INGREDIENTS

- 6 cups white vinegar
- 2 cups water
- ½ cup canning salt
- Garlic cloves
- Fresh dill or dill seed
- 3½ tsp red pepper flakes (optional)
- 5 lbs carrots
- Peppercorns

YIELD

Makes about 7 pints

RECIPE

1. Prepare hot water bath canner, jars, and lids.
2. Peel carrots and remove ends. Using a mandoline or sharp knife, cut carrots into sticks.
3. In a large stainless-steel saucepan, combine salt, vinegar, and water. Bring to a boil over medium-high heat, stirring to dissolve the salt.
4. Place 1 garlic clove, 3-5 peppercorns, a generous sprig of dill, or ½ tsp of dill seed if fresh dill is unavailable, and ½ tsp red pepper flakes to each jar. Pack carrots into jars, leaving ½-inch headspace. Ladle hot pickling brine over carrots leaving ½-inch headspace. Use a rubber spatula to remove air bubbles. Add more brine if necessary.
5. Wipe rims with a paper towel moistened with vinegar. Add lids and bands to finger tight.
6. Add jars to boiling water bath. Cover. Return to a boil. Process for 10 minutes.
7. Shut off heat and remove the lid. Wait another 5 minutes, and then using a jar lifter, place each jar upright on a towel or wire rack. Allow to cool completely. Remove bands, label, and store in a cool, dark place.

Do Chua (Vietnamese Carrot and Daikon Radish Pickles)

Try these Asian sweet pickles on a sandwich once, and the jar will be empty before you know it!

INGREDIENTS

- 3 cups white vinegar
- 3 cups water
- 1½ cups granulated sugar
- 2 tsp grated ginger root
- 2 lbs carrots
- 2 lbs daikon radish
- 6 whole star anise (optional)

YIELD

Makes about 6 pints

RECIPE

1. Prepare hot water bath canner, jars, and lids.
2. Peel carrots and remove ends. Peel daikon. Using a mandoline or an extremely sharp knife, julienne the carrots and radishes into very thin strips.
3. In a large stainless-steel saucepan, combine sugar, vinegar, water, and ginger root. Bring to a boil over medium-high heat, stirring to dissolve sugar. Add carrot and daikon and stir for 1 minute. Remove from heat.
4. Add 1 star anise (if using) to each jar. Pack hot vegetables into hot jars, leaving ½-inch headspace. Ladle hot pickling liquid into each jar to cover vegetables leaving ½-inch headspace. Use a rubber spatula to remove air bubbles. Add more liquid if necessary.
5. Wipe rims with a paper towel moistened with vinegar. Add lids and bands to finger tight.
6. Add jars to boiling water bath. Cover. Return to a boil. Process for 10 minutes.
7. Shut off heat and remove the lid. Wait another 5 minutes and then, using a jar lifter, place each jar upright on a wire rack or towel. Allow to cool completely. Remove bands, label, and store in a cool, dark place.

Banh Mi (Vietnamese Sandwich) Recipe

Banh Mi is a traditional Vietnamese sandwich sold by street vendors made on a crusty bread roll, or French bread, smeared with mayo. Add your choice of grilled meat and a heap of Do Chua. Top with green onion, coriander/cilantro, and sliced jalapeno peppers. Your new favorite sandwich!

Sweet Pickled Beets

Besides being rich in vitamins and minerals, pickled beets are delicious and heart-healthy!

INGREDIENTS

- 10 whole cloves
- 2 cinnamon sticks
- 2½ cups white vinegar
- 1 cup water
- 1 cup granulated sugar
- 10 cups prepared beets

YIELD

Makes about 6 pints

RECIPE

1. To prepare beets, leave the roots and two inches stem intact. Scrub thoroughly to remove dirt. Place in a saucepan and bring to boil. Reduce heat and cook until tender. Remove beets and run under cold water. Slip off the skins, remove stem and taproot. Leave small beets whole or slice or quarter larger beets.
2. Prepare hot water bath canner, jars, and lids.
3. Make a spice bag with cheesecloth. Tie cloves and cinnamon sticks broken into pieces in cheesecloth.
4. In a large stainless-steel saucepan, bring vinegar, sugar, water, and spice bag to a boil over medium-high heat, stirring to dissolve sugar. Reduce heat and boil gently for 15 minutes. Discard spice bag.
5. Using a slotted spoon and jar funnel, add beets to hot jars, leaving ½-inch headspace. Pour hot pickling liquid over beets leaving ½-inch headspace. Use a rubber spatula to remove air bubbles. Add more liquid if necessary.
6. Wipe rims with a paper towel moistened with vinegar. Add lids and bands to finger tight.
7. Add jars to boiling water bath. Cover. Return to a boil. Process for 30 minutes.

8. Shut off heat and remove the lid. Wait another 5 minutes, and then, using a jar lifter, place each jar upright on a wire rack or towel on the counter. Allow to cool completely. Remove bands, label, and store in a cool, dark place.

Sweet Pickled Beets and Onions: Add 3 cups peeled and thinly sliced Vidalia onions to the pickling liquid and cook as directed in Step 4. Use only 8 cups of prepared beets.

Traditional Fermented Sauerkraut

Fermented foods, like this sauerkraut, are rich in probiotic bacteria. Consumption of fermented foods adds beneficial bacteria and enzymes to your digestive system and enhances the immune system.

INGREDIENTS

- 5 lbs cabbage
- 3½ Tbsp canning salt

YIELD

Makes about 5 pints

Note

You'll need a large crock to ferment the kraut. An extra-large crockpot would suffice.

RECIPE

1. Prepare cabbage by removing the outer leaves. Rinse well under cool water. Quarter the heads and shred cabbage finely.
2. Place 5 pounds of cabbage and canning salt into a large pan and mix with clean hands. Pack salted cabbage into the crock pressing down with a potato masher until the crock is full.
3. Cover with a plate, a weight, and a cloth. Every day, remove the scum as it forms and cover with a clean cloth. Fermentation will be complete in 10-12 days.
4. Once the kraut is thoroughly cured, I suggest taste-testing it. When satisfied with the flavor, pack it into hot, clean jars. Add kraut juice to cover, leaving ½-inch headspace. If you run out of liquid, dissolve 2 Tbsp canning salt in 1 quart water and use that to top off jars.
5. Wipe rims with a paper towel moistened with vinegar. Add lids and bands to finger tight.
6. Process pints in hot water bath canner for 20 minutes.
7. Remove from heat. Remove lid, wait 5 minutes, then remove jars from canner. Cool, remove bands, label, and store jars.

State Fair Pickled Three-Bean Salad

A traditional church picnic and family reunion favorite for generations. Try this award-winning recipe!

INGREDIENTS

- 4½ cups green beans
- 4½ cups yellow beans
- 1 lb lima beans (fresh or frozen)
- 2 cups celery
- 2 cups sliced onions
- 1 large sweet red bell pepper
- Boiling water
- 2½ cups granulated sugar
- 1 Tbsp mustard seed
- 1 tsp celery seed
- 4 tsp canning salt
- 3 cups white vinegar
- 1¼ cups water

YIELD

Makes about 5-6 pints

RECIPE

1. Prepare hot water bath canner, jars, and lids.
2. Trim beans to 1-1½-inch slices. Slice celery into ½-inch slices. Shell lima beans if fresh or defrost if frozen. Peel and thinly slice onions. Core and dice red pepper.
3. Add all vegetables to a large stainless-steel saucepan. Add boiling water to cover. Return to a boil over medium-high heat. Reduce heat and boil gently for 5 minutes to heat vegetables.
4. Meanwhile, in a separate stainless-steel saucepan, prepare your pickling brine. Combine sugar, mustard seed, celery seed, salt, vinegar, and water. Bring to a boil over medium-high heat, stirring to dissolve sugar. Reduce heat and boil gently for 5 minutes.
5. Drain hot vegetables and pack into hot jars, leaving ½-inch headspace. Pour hot pickling liquid over vegetables leaving ½-inch headspace. Use a rubber spatula to remove air bubbles. Add more liquid if necessary.
6. Wipe rims with a paper towel moistened with vinegar. Add lids and bands to finger tight.
7. Add jars to boiling water bath. Cover. Return to a boil. Process pints for 15 minutes.

8. Shut off heat and remove the lid. Wait another 5 minutes and then, using a jar lifter, place each jar upright on a wire rack or towel on the counter. Allow to cool completely. Remove bands, label, and store in a cool, dark place.

No-Cook Pickled Hot Pepper Mix

This vintage recipe doesn't call for processing in a hot water bath. Assuming the lids "ping" you should be fine. To be extra-safe, store in refrigerator or process for 5 minutes in a hot water bath.

INGREDIENTS

- Any combination of hot peppers
- Canning salt
- Water
- White vinegar
- Fresh dill or dill seed
- Grape or oak leaf*
- Garlic clove

YIELD

Varies

Note

Quart jars are an excellent choice to accommodate long banana or Hungarian peppers.

RECIPE

Day One

1. Wash peppers.
2. Cut 2 small slits in each pepper. Place the peppers in a large ceramic bowl or stainless-steel pot.
3. Add 2 quarts of cool water and 1 cup canning salt to the bowl. Submerge peppers using a large plate with a weight on the top to keep peppers submerged in the brine. You can use a Mason jar filled with water as the weight. Set in a cool place overnight.

Day Two

1. Prepare jars and lids.
2. Drain well and pack peppers into hot quart jars.
3. Mix 2 quarts water, ½ cup canning salt, ½ cup vinegar, 1 garlic clove, 1 grape or oak leaf, and a bunch of fresh dill or 1 tsp of dill seed in a large stainless-steel saucepan. Bring to a rapid boil.
4. Pour boiling brine over peppers filling and sealing one jar at a time, leaving ½-inch headspace. Do not remove bands. Label and store.

Optional

5. Using a jar lifter, carefully place each jar in a hot water bath canner. Make sure the jars are not crowded and are covered with water. Add more boiling water if needed. Cover pot and return to a boil. Process for 5 minutes.
6. Shut off heat and remove the lid. Wait another 5 minutes, and then, using a jar lifter, place each jar upright on a towel or wire rack. When cool, remove bands, label, and store in a cool, dark place.

*Black tea leaves, oak leaves, grape leaves, or horseradish leaves all add tannins to the pickle brine resulting in crisper pickles. If you don't have them available, use Ball Pickle Crisp. Use ¾ tsp per pint or 1½ tsp per quart.

Pickled Hot Peppers

This modern recipe calls for processing in a hot water bath. They're great on sandwiches, pizza, anytime you need a kick. You can focus on one type of pepper per jar, jalapeno, for instance, or mix it up for a variety of heat!

INGREDIENTS

- 2 quarts hot peppers, any variety
- 2 cups white vinegar
- 2 cups water
- Canning salt

YIELD

4 pints

Note

If you like a lot of heat, leave most or all the seeds intact.

RECIPE

1. Prepare hot water bath canner, jars, and lids.
2. Rinse peppers under cool water. Remove stem, cores, and some or all the seeds. Slice into ½-inch rings. Or, if you prefer, leave small peppers whole and cut 2 small slits on each side so they don't explode during the canning process.
3. Mix the vinegar and water in a large stainless-steel saucepan. Bring to a boil.
4. Pour boiling brine over peppers leaving ½-inch headspace. Add ½ tsp canning salt to each jar. Remove air bubbles, wipe rims, add lids and bands to finger tight.
5. Using a jar lifter, carefully place each jar in the boiling hot water bath. Make sure the jars are not crowded and are covered with water. Add more boiling water if needed. Cover pot and return to a boil. Process for 5 minutes.
6. Shut off heat and remove the lid. Wait another 5 minutes, and then using a jar lifter, place each jar upright on a wire rack or towel. When cool, remove bands, label, and store in a cool, dark place.

*Black tea leaves, oak leaves, grape leaves, or horseradish leaves all add tannins to the pickle brine resulting in crisper peppers. Discard leaves before adding pickling brine to jars. Or, if you don't have them available, use Ball Pickle Crisp. Use ¾ tsp per pint or 1½ tsp per quart. Add to jars immediately before sealing.

14-Day Sweet Pickles

This vintage recipe takes 2 weeks to prepare, so write the steps down on a calendar. It doesn't call for processing in a hot water bath but use your judgment. Adjust the recipe to suit your desired yield.

INGREDIENTS

- 2 gallons of cucumbers
- 2 cups canning salt
- Water
- 1 Tbsp powdered alum
- 5 pints vinegar
- 6 cups granulated sugar
- 5 tsp celery seed
- 2-3 cinnamon sticks

YIELD

Varies

RECIPE

Day 1: Place cucumbers with blossom end trimmed and sliced lengthwise into a clean crock or large crockpot. Dissolve 2 cups of canning salt in 1 gallon of boiling water and pour over cucumbers. Weigh down cucumbers, so they stay submerged with a plate. Cover and let stand undisturbed for 1 week in a cool place.

Day 8: Drain water and replace with 1 gallon of boiling water, ensuring cucumbers are submerged. Cover and let stand for 24 hours.

Day 9: Drain water and replace with 1 gallon of boiling water mixed with 1 Tbsp of powdered alum. Cover and let stand for 24 hours.

Day 10: Drain again and replace with 1 gallon of boiling water. Let stand for 24 hours, then drain.

Day 11: In a large stainless-steel saucepan, combine 5 pints of vinegar, 6 cups of granulated sugar, celery seed, and cinnamon stick broken into pieces. Bring to a boil and pour this mixture over the cucumbers. Cover and let stand 24 hours.

Day 12: Drain and reserve liquid. Add 1 cup sugar to the reserved liquid. Heat to boiling and repour over pickles. Cover and let stand for 24 hours.

Day 13: Drain and reserve liquid. Add 1 cup sugar to the reserved liquid. Heat to boiling and repour over pickles. Cover and let stand for 24 hours.

Day 14: Drain and reserve liquid. Add 1 cup sugar to the reserved liquid. Reheat to boiling. Pack pickles in sterilized, hot jars. Pour hot syrup over pickles. Wipe rims with a paper towel moistened with vinegar. Add lids, bands, and seal. Allow to cool on a wire rack. If the lids "ping" you have a successful seal.

RELISHES & SALSA

I only included one salsa recipe because it's a fairly new addition to North American diets. Relishes have been around forever and have a variety of uses besides hot dogs and burgers. Relishes may have originated to utilize an abundance of homegrown fruits and vegetables. Relish will take about two weeks to develop maximum flavor.

Taste of Summer Vegetable Salsa

Salsa, long a part of Mexican cuisine, became popular in the United States in Mexican restaurants in the 1980s. So, your grandmother never even heard of it. But I've included it here because of its modern popularity. Plus, it's a great way to use garden tomatoes, onions, peppers, and herbs.

INGREDIENTS

- 7 cups peeled, cored, chopped tomatoes
- 2 cups chopped onion
- 1 cup chopped green bell pepper
- 8 seeded and finely chopped jalapeno or other hot peppers (or less to taste)
- 3 garlic cloves minced
- 1 5.5oz can tomato paste
- ¾ cup white vinegar
- ½ cup chopped cilantro
- ½ tsp ground cumin
- Canning salt and freshly ground black pepper to taste

YIELD

4 pints

RECIPE

1. Add all ingredients to a large stainless-steel saucepan. Bring to a boil over medium-high heat, stirring often. Reduce heat to medium and boil gently for about 30 minutes until the mixture thickens to desired consistency. The more mixture evaporates, the thicker your salsa will be.

2. Meanwhile, prepare a hot water bath canner, jars, and lids.

3. Using a jar funnel, pour hot salsa into jars leaving ½-inch headspace. Wipe rims with a paper towel moistened with vinegar. Add lids and bands to finger tight.

4. Using a jar lifter, carefully place each jar in the boiling hot water bath. Make sure the jars are not crowded and are covered with water. Add more boiling water if needed. Cover pot and return to a boil. Process both 8-ounce and pint jars for 20 minutes. Remove from heat, remove the cover, and remove jars after 5 minutes. Cool on a wire rack, label, and store.

TIPS

You can use any variety of hot pepper. If you want it milder, reduce the number of hot peppers and remove the seeds and veins before chopping. Or for a very mild salsa, eliminate the hot peppers. But, if you like it fiery, include the seeds!

Sweet Relish

Another hand-me-down family recipe from my grandmother. It helps if you have a food grinder. You can often find these at second-hand shops, flea markets, and yard sales. Or use a food processor with a metal blade. Great on hot dogs, burgers, when making deviled eggs, and more!

INGREDIENTS

- 7 cucumbers peeled and cored
- 3 green tomatoes
- 1 green bell pepper cored and seeded
- 1 sweet red bell pepper cored and seeded
- 3 stalks celery
- 3 onions
- ½ head large cabbage
- 3 cups white vinegar
- 1 cup water
- 1 lb brown sugar
- 1 tsp ground clove
- 1 tsp cinnamon
- 2 tsp turmeric
- ½ tsp mustard seed
- 1 Tbsp canning salt

YIELD

8 8oz jars (My grandmother used repurposed mustard jars)

RECIPE

1. Grind all the vegetables. Mix in a large bowl. Sprinkle with 1 Tbsp canning salt. Cover and let stand for 2 hours. Drain liquid and set aside.

2. Bring vinegar, water, and spices to a boil in a large stainless-steel pot. Add all ground vegetables. Return to a boil. Reduce heat and simmer uncovered for 1 hour.

3. Pack into hot jars, leaving ½-inch headspace. Wipe rims with a paper towel moistened with vinegar. Add lids and bands to finger tight.

4. Using a jar lifter, carefully place each jar in a hot water bath canner. Make sure the jars are not crowded and are covered with water. Add more boiling water if needed. Cover pot and return to a boil. Process both 8oz and pint jars for 10 minutes. Remove from heat, remove the cover, and remove jars after 5 minutes. Cool, label, and store.

Dill Relish

This is a great way to use those end-of-season cucumbers and the dill seed you harvested and saved from earlier in the season. Kids love this traditional family favorite!

INGREDIENTS

- 8 lbs pickling cucumbers
- ½ cup canning salt
- 2 tsp ground turmeric
- 4 cups cold water
- 2½ cups finely chopped onions
- 1/3 cup granulated sugar
- 2 Tbsp dill seed
- 4 cups white vinegar

YIELD

7 pints

RECIPE

1. In a food processor or using a food grinder, finely chop cucumbers working in small batches. Transfer to a large bowl.
2. Sprinkle canning salt and turmeric over cucumbers. Mix to blend. Add cold water, cover the bowl, and let stand in a cool place for 2-3 hours.
3. Pour cucumbers into a large colander placed over sink and drain. Rinse with cool water and drain again. Squeeze out excess moisture using your clean hands.
4. Prepare hot water bath canner, jars, and lids.
5. Add drained cucumbers, onions, sugar, dill seed, and vinegar to a large stainless-steel pot. Bring to a boil over medium-high heat, stirring to prevent scorching. Reduce heat and boil gently, uncovered, for 10-15 minutes until relish begins to thicken.
6. Using a jar funnel, ladle hot relish into hot jars, leaving ½-inch headspace. Wipe rims with a paper towel moistened with vinegar, add lids, and bands to finger tight.
7. Using a jar lifter, carefully place each jar in a boiling hot water bath. Make sure the jars are not crowded and are covered with water. Add more boiling water if needed. Cover pot and return to a boil. Process both 8oz and pint jars for 15 minutes. Remove from heat, remove the cover, and remove jars after 5 minutes. Cool, label, and store.

Victory Garden Red Pepper Relish

A pretty and delicious alternative to green relishes, this family favorite is circa WWII.

INGREDIENTS

- 24 sweet red bell peppers
- 7 medium onions (I prefer Vidalia when in season)
- 2 Tbsp mustard seed
- 2 Tbsp canning salt
- 3 cups white vinegar
- 3 cups granulated sugar

YIELD

Use 4oz, 8oz, or pint jars

Note

During WWII, this relish was prepared and packed hot into hot jars. Home canners added the lids and bands, but they did not use a hot water bath. I suggest processing it to meet modern-day food safety standards.

RECIPE

1. In a food processor or using a food grinder, grind peppers and onions. Save the juice.

2. Combine the ground vegetables, juice, and all other ingredients in a large stainless-steel saucepan. Bring to a boil over medium-high heat, stirring to prevent scorching. Reduce heat and boil gently, uncovered, for 30 minutes, stirring often, until the relish begins to thicken.

3. Prepare hot water bath canner, jars, and lids.

4. Using a jar funnel, ladle hot relish into hot jars, leaving ½-inch headspace. Wipe rims with a paper towel moistened with vinegar, add lids, and bands to finger tight.

5. Using a jar lifter, carefully place each jar in the boiling hot water bath. Make sure the jars are not crowded and are covered with water. Add more boiling water if needed. Cover pot and return to a boil. Process 4oz, 8oz, and pint jars for 10 minutes. Remove from heat, remove the cover, and remove jars after 5 minutes. Cool, label, and store

County Fair Corn Relish

Use as a condiment for burgers and hot dogs or as a flavorful side dish for Tex-Mex or Mexican cuisine. Prepare this when sweet corn is in season.

INGREDIENTS

- 4 cups white vinegar
- 1¼ cups granulated sugar
- 2 Tbsp canning salt
- 8 cups corn kernels*
- 2 cups diced red bell pepper
- 2 cups diced green bell pepper
- 2 cups diced celery
- 1 cup finely chopped onion
- 2 Tbsp dry mustard
- 2 tsp celery seed
- 2 tsp ground turmeric
- ¼ cup water
- 2 Tbsp ClearJel

YIELD

12 8oz jars or 6 pints

RECIPE

1. Prepare hot water bath canner, jars, and lids.
2. In a large stainless-steel saucepan, combine vinegar, sugar, and salt. Bring to a boil over medium-high heat, stirring to dissolve sugar. Gradually add all vegetables and stir constantly to prevent scorching. Stir in seasonings while keeping a boil. In a small bowl, mix water and ClearJel with a fork. Stir into the boiling mixture. Reduce heat and boil gently for 5-10 minutes until relish begins to thicken.
3. Using a jar funnel, ladle hot relish into hot jars, leaving ½-inch headspace. Wipe rims with a paper towel moistened with vinegar, add lids, and bands to finger tight.
4. Using a jar lifter, carefully place each jar in a boiling hot water bath. Make sure the jars are not crowded and are covered with water. Add more boiling water if needed. Cover pot and return to a boil. Process both 8oz and pint jars for 15 minutes. Remove from heat, remove the cover, and remove jars after 5 minutes. Cool, label, and store.

*When using fresh corn, blanch ears for 5 minutes in boiling water before removing kernels.

Green Tomato Relish

Another family favorite. This is an excellent recipe for end-of-the-season tomatoes that will not have time to ripen before the first frost.

INGREDIENTS

- 6 cups unpeeled, cored, chopped green tomatoes
- 2 onions finely chopped
- 2 green bell peppers finely chopped
- 1 red bell pepper finely chopped
- ¼ cup canning salt
- 1 tsp ground clove
- 1 tsp celery seed
- 1 cinnamon stick
- 2 cups white vinegar
- 1½ cups brown sugar
- 1 garlic clove finely chopped
- 1 Tbsp dry mustard
- ½ tsp canning salt
- ½ tsp ground ginger

YIELD

6 8oz jars

RECIPE

1. Add prepared tomatoes, onions, peppers, and canning salt to a large glass or stainless-steel bowl. Cover and let stand in a cool place for 12 hours. Drain in a colander. Rinse with cool water, drain, and squeeze out excess moisture with clean hands.

2. Create a spice bag by tying cloves, celery seed, and cinnamon stick (broken in half) in a square of cheesecloth. Set aside.

3. In a large stainless-steel saucepan, mix vinegar, brown sugar, garlic, mustard, remaining salt, ginger, and spice bag. Bring to a boil over medium-high heat, stirring to dissolve sugar and prevent scorching. Add drained tomatoes and return to a boil. Reduce heat and boil gently, stirring often, for about 1 hour. Discard spice bag.

4. Meanwhile, prepare a hot water bath canner, jars, and lids.

5. Using a jar funnel, pour or ladle hot relish into hot jars, leaving ½-inch headspace. Wipe rims with a paper towel moistened with vinegar. Add lids and bands to finger tight.

6. Using a jar lifter, carefully place each jar in the boiling hot water bath. Make sure the jars are not crowded and are covered with water. Add more boiling water if needed. Cover pot and return to a boil. Process for 10 minutes. Remove from heat, remove the cover, and remove jars after 5 minutes. Cool, label, and store.

VINEGARS

Great as a basis for salad dressings, flavored vinegars are easy to make and are a great gift!

Legendary 4 Thieves Vinegar Tonic

Legend has it that during the 18th-century plague epidemic in Europe, a band of thieves robbed the homes and graves of those who were sick and dying of the disease but never fell ill themselves. Their secret? They doused cloth face coverings in a tonic they had created and washed their hands with it after robbing the graves. When finally captured, they shared their secret recipe. This vinegar acts as an antiseptic and to disinfect, repel insects, and boost the immune system when taken as a tonic. You can make it using fresh herbs from your garden and mix and match to suit your needs and tastes.

INGREDIENTS

- Garlic cloves
- Whole cloves
- Cinnamon sticks
- Rosemary
- Thyme
- Oregano
- Sage
- Lavender (optional)
- 32oz organic apple cider vinegar
- Black peppercorns (optional)
- Ginger root (optional)
- Mason jars or decorative bottles with corks or stoppers

YIELD

4 pints

RECIPE

1. Place garlic, cloves, and herbs (fresh or dried) in each jar.
2. Add cinnamon sticks, peppercorns, and grated ginger root to organic apple cider vinegar in a large stainless-steel saucepan. Bring to a gentle boil, reduce heat and simmer for 5-10 minutes. Strain liquid.
3. Pour hot liquid over herbs in jars. Add lids or corks and place in a sunny windowsill and steep for 2-4 weeks.

Luke's Modern Uses

Mix with olive oil to make salad dressing.

Use in a spray bottle for cleaning kitchen/bathroom counters.

Take 1 Tbsp a day as a tonic.

Use on blemishes, cuts, fungal infections.

Apply with a cotton ball to lighten age spots.

Apply to skin to soothe sunburn.

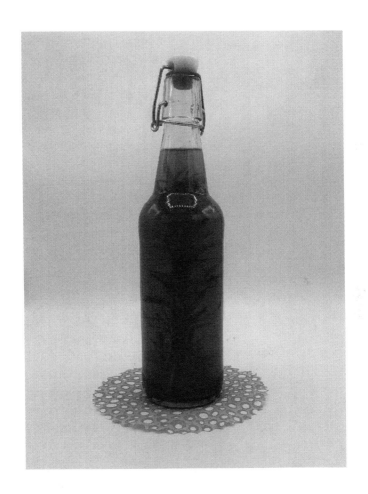

4 Thieves Vinegar

Raspberry Vinegar

Mix with balsamic vinegar for a refreshing salad dressing.

INGREDIENTS

- 4 cups fresh or frozen raspberries
- 5 cups white wine vinegar

YIELD

6 8oz jars

RECIPE

1. Thaw raspberries if frozen. Add thawed or fresh raspberries to a large glass bowl. Add 1 cup of vinegar. Using a potato masher, crush raspberries but do not liquefy. Add the rest of the vinegar, stir, cover, and store in a cool, dark place for 2-4 weeks. Stir every few days. Taste weekly until the desired flavor is achieved.

2. Prepare hot water bath canner, jars, and lids.

3. Using a damp jelly bag or several layers of moistened cheesecloth, drain vinegar and solids over a large stainless-steel saucepan. Do not squeeze. Discard residue. Heat vinegar over medium heat until it is almost boiling.

4. Ladle hot vinegar into hot jars using a jar funnel, leaving ¼-inch headspace. Wipe rims, add lids and bands to finger tight.

5. Using a jar lifter, place jars in a boiling hot water bath, making sure they are covered with water. Cover canner, return to a boil, and process for 10 minutes.

6. Remove from heat, remove the cover, and remove jars after 5 minutes. Cool on a wire rack or kitchen towel. Remove bands, label, and store.

Tarragon Vinegar

Try making this classic flavored vinegar.

INGREDIENTS

- 2 cups white or red wine vinegar
- Fresh tarragon
- Black peppercorns

YIELD

2 8oz jars

Note

Add a handmade label and pretty ribbon if giving as a gift!

RECIPE

1. In a medium stainless-steel saucepan, heat vinegar to just boiling.
2. Place sprigs of fresh tarragon and peppercorns in a sterilized jar.
3. Pour hot vinegar into a jar. Seal with a cork or non-metallic lid. Let steep for 1-2 weeks before using.

Blueberry and Basil Vinegar

Use this flavored vinegar as the basis for a delicious salad dressing.

INGREDIENTS

- 4 cups blueberries
- 4 cups white wine vinegar
- 1 cup fresh basil leaves
- Zest from 1 lemon

YIELD

5 pints

RECIPE

1. In a large glass bowl, add blueberries and 1 cup of vinegar. Lightly mash using a potato masher. Crush the basil leaves using a mortar and pestle or wooden spoon and add to the mixture. Add remaining vinegar and lemon zest. Stir, cover, and store in a cool, dark place for 3-4 weeks stirring every few days. Sample weekly until desired taste is achieved.

2. Prepare hot water bath canner, jars, and lids.

3. In a medium stainless-steel saucepan, heat vinegar to just boiling. Add a few whole, fresh blueberries to each jar.

4. Using a jar funnel, ladle hot vinegar into hot jars, leaving ¼-inch headspace. Wipe rims with a paper towel moistened with vinegar. Add lids and bands to finger tight.

5. Using a jar lifter, carefully place each jar in the boiling hot water bath. Make sure the jars are not crowded and are covered with water. Add more boiling water if needed. Cover pot and return to a boil. Process for 10 minutes. Remove from heat, remove the cover, and remove jars after 5 minutes. Cool, label, and store.

MEAT, POULTRY & FISH

For a desirable finished product, make sure to start with high quality, lean, meat, poultry, or fish.

Canned Chicken

This is one of the easiest recipes ever! Canned chicken is so versatile. You can use it straight out of the jar to make a chicken salad sandwich, toss some on a salad or use it in a soup or casserole. Use it in any recipe that calls for pre-cooked chicken. All you need is chicken, jars, and a few spices! It's that easy and so delicious! I recommend buying boneless, skinless chicken breasts when they're on sale, and you'll always have a supply of protein on hand. Best part? No refrigeration is necessary!

INGREDIENTS

- Boneless, skinless chicken breasts or thighs
- Canning salt
- Freshly ground black pepper

YIELD

Varies

Chicken Bone-in

Canning bone-in chicken may result in more flavor. Use thighs or drumsticks that fit the jars. Cut off excess fat, leave most of the skin intact. Fill jars and follow all other steps. Reduce the processing time for the bone-in chicken to 65 minutes per pint and 75 minutes per quart at 10 pounds pressure adjusting for altitude.

RECIPE

1. Prepare jars, lids, and pressure canner.
2. Cut up chicken into chunks.
3. Pack raw chicken into hot jars, leaving 1-inch headspace.
4. Add ½ tsp per pint or 1 tsp per quart (optional).
5. Add freshly ground pepper (optional).
6. Wipe rims, add lids and bands to finger tight. Do not add water. The chicken will make its own broth.
7. Place jars on rack in canner. Attach and secure canner lid. Heat until canner starts hissing. Allow the steam to escape the vent for 5-10 minutes, add gauge and begin timing after the first jiggle. Process pints for 75 minutes and quarts for 90 minutes at 10 pounds pressure adjusting for altitude.

Luke's Variations

Substitute boneless, skinless turkey breasts or thighs for chicken.
Add 1/8 tsp dried poultry seasoning to each jar.
Add a peeled garlic clove or a few onion slices to each jar.

Canned Chicken

Italian Meatballs in Sauce

Just boil some pasta and all the prep work is done! You can use homemade sauce or store-bought. Your choice.

INGREDIENTS

- Ground beef, pork, veal, turkey, or a combination to your liking
- Dried Italian breadcrumbs
- Dried Italian seasonings
- Canning salt
- Freshly ground black pepper
- Red pepper flakes (optional)
- Homemade or store-bought marinara sauce

YIELD

Varies

Luke's Variations

Substitute tomato juice for the marinara sauce.

Substitute beef bone broth for the marinara sauce.

RECIPE

1. Prepare jars, lids, and pressure canner.
2. Make your favorite meatball recipe. Add breadcrumbs, dried herbs, and seasonings to ground meat. Form into 1½-inch meatballs.
3. In a skillet over medium heat, brown meatballs on all sides. Drain fat.
4. Add meatballs to jar. Do not pack. Leave 1-inch headspace.
5. Using a jar funnel, pour sauce over meatballs leaving 1-inch headspace.
6. Using a rubber spatula, remove air bubbles. Add more sauce if necessary.
7. Wipe rims with a paper towel moistened with vinegar. Add lids and bands to finger tight.
8. Carefully place jars on rack in canner. Attach and secure canner lid. Heat until canner starts hissing. Allow the steam to escape the vent for 5-10 minutes, add gauge and begin timing after the first jiggle. Process pints for 75 minutes and quarts for 90 minutes at 10 pounds pressure. Adjust timing for higher altitudes.
9. Remove canner from heat. Allow pressure to decrease naturally.
10. Remove lid. Remove jars from the canner after 5 minutes. Cool on a wire rack or kitchen towel. Remove bands, label jars, and store them in a cool, dark place.

Chicken a la King

This vintage recipe is delicious served over egg noodles, biscuits, toast, or with a heap of mashed potatoes!

INGREDIENTS

- 1 5-pound chicken
- 4 Tbsp ClearJel
- 1 Tbsp canning salt
- 1 quart chicken broth or homemade stock
- 1 large can sliced mushrooms
- 1 chopped green bell pepper
- 2 Tbsp pimientos or 1 chopped red bell pepper
- Freshly ground black pepper

YIELD

5 pints

Luke's Variations

Substitute turkey for chicken.

Substitute 1 cup fresh green peas for green pepper. Use fresh mushrooms instead of canned mushrooms.

RECIPE

1. Prepare jars, lids, and pressure canner.
2. Cut whole chicken into pieces. Add to large stainless-steel pot. Add water to cover and bring to boil. Reduce heat, cover, and simmer for 1 hour.
3. Remove meat from bones. Discard skin. Cut meat into small pieces.
4. Dissolve ClearJel and salt in a little of the cold broth. Whisk until smooth. Add to the broth or stock and heat over medium heat, stirring constantly until smooth. The sauce will begin to thicken.
5. Add sliced mushrooms, peppers, pimientos, black pepper, and chicken. Heat to boiling, stirring constantly.
6. Using a jar funnel, pour the mixture into hot jars, leaving 1-inch headspace.
7. Using a rubber spatula, remove air bubbles. Add more sauce if necessary, leaving 1-inch headspace.
8. Wipe rims with a paper towel moistened with vinegar. Add lids and bands to finger tight.
9. Carefully place jars on rack in canner. Attach and secure canner lid. Heat until canner starts hissing. Allow the steam to escape the vent for 5-10 minutes, add gauge and begin timing after the first jiggle. Process pints for 75 minutes and quarts for 90 minutes at 10 pounds pressure adjusting for altitude.

10. Remove canner from heat. Allow pressure to decrease naturally.
11. Remove lid. Remove jars from the canner after 5 minutes. Cool on a wire rack or kitchen towel. Remove bands, label jars, and store them in a cool, dark place.

Ground Meat

Convenient to have on hand for soups, stews, sloppy joes, and casseroles since the meat is already cooked and requires no refrigeration.

INGREDIENTS

- 8 lbs ground beef, lamb, pork, chicken, or turkey
- 5 tsp canning salt
- 2 tsp freshly ground black pepper
- 2 medium onions chopped
- 4 garlic cloves chopped finely
- 3 cups beef broth or stock

YIELD

14 pints or 7 quarts

RECIPE

1. Prepare jars, lids, and pressure canner.
2. In a large bowl, combine ground meat, salt, and pepper using your clean hands.
3. Working in batches, brown meat stirring often. Drain fat and set meat aside.
4. Sauté onions and garlic until soft. Mix with browned meat.
5. Heat broth or stock to boiling over medium-high heat, then reduce heat to low.
6. Using a jar funnel, pack the hot meat loosely into the jars, leaving 1-inch headspace.
7. Add hot broth or stock to each jar, leaving 1-inch headspace.
8. Using a rubber spatula, remove air bubbles. Add more liquid if necessary, leaving 1-inch headspace.
9. Wipe rims with a paper towel moistened with vinegar. Add lids and bands to finger tight.
10. Carefully place jars on rack in canner. Attach and secure canner lid. Heat until canner starts hissing. Allow the steam to escape the vent for 5-10 minutes, add gauge and begin timing after the first jiggle. Process pints for 75 minutes and quarts for 90 minutes at 10 pounds pressure. Adjust timing for higher altitudes.

11. Remove canner from heat. Allow pressure to decrease naturally.
12. Remove lid. Remove jars from the canner after 5 minutes. Cool on a wire rack or kitchen towel. Remove bands, label jars, and store them in a cool, dark place.

Venison and Game

If you're a hunter or prepper, this recipe is right up your alley! Make sure to use high-quality, fresh meat for the best results.

INGREDIENTS

- Boneless venison or other game
- Canning salt
- Hot broth or stock
- ClearJel (optional)

YIELD

Varies

Luke's Variations

You can substitute roast beef, lamb, pork, or veal for game meat. Follow all other instructions. Trim fat after roasting and before canning.

RECIPE

1. Prepare jars, lids, and pressure canner.
2. Cut meat into ½ to 1-inch strips long enough to fit into the size jar you are using. Roast at 400 degrees in a preheated oven in a large roasting pan until browned on the outside but still pink on the inside. Remove from oven and set aside.
3. Prepare stock by pouring fat from the roasted meat into a measuring cup. For each tablespoon of fat, add 1 cup of boiling water back to the roasting pan. Bring to boil over medium-high heat, scraping up any meat bits stuck to the pan. Add ClearJel, if desired, to thicken the broth. You can also use premade stock or broth in a pinch.
4. Pack hot meat into hot jars, leaving 1-inch headspace. Add ½ teaspoon canning salt to each pint jar or 1 teaspoon to each quart jar. Using a jar funnel, ladle hot broth over meat to cover, leaving 1-inch headspace.
5. Using a rubber spatula, remove air bubbles. Add more broth if necessary, leaving 1-inch headspace.
6. Wipe rims with a paper towel moistened with vinegar. Add lids and bands to finger tight.
7. Carefully place jars on rack in canner. Attach and secure canner lid. Heat until

canner starts hissing. Allow the steam to escape the vent for 5-10 minutes, add gauge and begin timing after the first jiggle. Process pints for 75 minutes and quarts for 90 minutes at 10 pounds pressure. Adjust timing for higher altitudes.

8. Remove canner from heat. Allow pressure to decrease naturally.

9. Remove lid. Remove jars from the canner after 5 minutes. Cool on a wire rack or kitchen towel. Remove bands, label jars, and store them in a cool, dark place.

Fish

Most people would never think of canning their fresh catch of the day, but you're able to successfully can all fish. Follow the recipe which follows for tuna. Process only in 8oz or pint jars.

INGREDIENTS

- Fresh fish, bones removed if fish is large
- 1 cup canning salt
- 16 cups water

YIELD

Varies

TUNA

The difference when canning tuna is that you don't need to brine the fish before canning. Simply cut the tuna into pieces that will fit in the jars and pack raw. Add ½ teaspoon canning salt per 8oz jar or 1 teaspoon per pint jar. Process both 8oz and pint jars for 100 minutes at 10 pounds pressure. Adjust timing for higher altitudes.

RECIPE

1. Dissolve canning salt in the water to make a salt-water brine in a large bowl or stainless-steel pot. Remove bones and cut fish into pieces that will fit in the jars. Place fish pieces in the brine and soak in the refrigerator for 1 hour. After time has elapsed, drain in a colander for 15 minutes.

2. Prepare jars, lids, and pressure canner.

3. Pack fish in room-temperature jars with the skin facing out, leaving 1-inch headspace. Do not add any liquid.

4. Wipe rims with a paper towel moistened with vinegar. Add lids and bands to finger tight.

5. Carefully place jars on rack in canner. Attach and secure canner lid. Heat until canner starts hissing. Allow the steam to escape vent for 5-10 minutes, add gauge and begin timing after the first jiggle. Process both 8oz and pint jars for 100 minutes at 10 pounds pressure. Adjust timing for higher altitudes.

6. Remove canner from heat. Allow pressure to decrease naturally.

7. Remove lid. Remove jars from the canner after 5 minutes. Cool on a wire rack or kitchen towel. Remove bands, label jars, and store them in a cool, dark place.

OTHER PRESERVATION METHODS

In addition to canning, there are many other popular ways to preserve your harvest, so it lasts all year. What follows is a brief overview.

Freezing

Modern refrigeration began in the early 20th century. Refrigeration helps to preserve food by storing it at low temperatures to slow down the spread of bacteria and decomposition. When separate freezer units were developed, it took refrigeration one step further by freezing water present in meats, fruits, and vegetables into ice crystals, making it unavailable for bacterial microorganisms that need liquid moisture and air to spread. Separate freezer units became popular after WWII.

Many people swear by freezing their harvest for ease and convenience. With rare exceptions, I don't freeze my harvest for several reasons.

1. Frozen food is dependent on a consistent source of electricity or a generator. If you lose your power for a significant period, you'll have to consume 20 gallons of marinara sauce, or else it will go to waste. Canned food is energy independent and can be stored for 18 months or longer, and I've stored some canned items for as long as 4 years. Canned and dehydrated food is the sustainable prepper choice.

2. You can't transport frozen food easily. Suppose there's an impending flood or crisis, and you must leave home in a hurry. Does it make sense to grab an ice chest full of frozen food or a cardboard box packed with canned soups, stews, and meats? In an emergency, you can eat canned food right out of the jar without reheating. The empty jars can also serve a multitude of purposes if you must bug out.

3. You can't mail frozen food to a loved one. Canned goods make thoughtful and appreciated gifts. And can be used to barter.

4. You would need a huge walk-in freezer to store what you can in a pantry, closet, or cupboard.

Drying

Drying, or dehydrating, is the oldest method of preserving food, dating back to prehistoric times, and it's still used today. Once most of the water content is removed, dehydrated foods are lightweight and take up little space, making them easily portable. Dehydrated foods are ideal for hikers, campers, and in an emergency. Add water to rehydrate or eat as is. You can make meat jerky, kale chips, banana chips, sun-dried tomatoes, etc.

Sun & Air

Leaving food in the sun and air causes evaporation of the water content, and this helps prevent bacterial growth as up to 80% of the moisture is removed. This method is free, and it's a traditional and still a popular way to dry herbs, peppers, and tomatoes.

Oven & Electric

You can use an oven on low heat or an electric dehydrator to dehydrate many foods. You need to be careful not to cook the food. Instead, the goal is to remove as much moisture content as possible.

Cold Storage

Back in the day, every farm had a root cellar or underground pantry where produce, especially root crops and fruits, would be stored to extend their usable life. In ancient times, people would bury food in ice or underground during the winter months. Many modern-day preppers employ this technique today. As a child, my family always stored root crops, like potatoes, in our unheated cellar where it was colder.

Salt Curing

When early explorers embarked on voyages that would put them at sea for months, they would pack salt-cured meats and fish in barrels. The meats and fish would be packed in layers with dry salt. The salt drew out moisture, inhibiting the growth of bacteria and slowing the decomposition rate, meaning that certain foodstuffs could last for years if preserved properly. You can also employ salt curing to preserve many herbs. Simply layer the fresh herbs between layers of canning salt in a Mason jar with a lid.

Fermentation

This is another old way of preserving food that is gaining in popularity today. Fermentation is a natural process through which microorganisms like yeast and bacteria convert carbohydrates into alcohol or acids. The alcohol or acids act as a natural preservative and give fermented foods a distinct zest and tartness. It also promotes the growth of beneficial bacteria known as probiotics. Probiotics have been shown to improve immune function as well as digestive and heart health. Pickles and other vegetables can easily be fermented in a specially-designed crock which allows the gases, created during the fermentation process, to escape.

TROUBLESHOOTING

Even experienced home canners still have challenges. Here are some troubleshooting tips for a successful output.

My jars did not seal.

If your jars did not seal properly, there might have been residue left on the rims before you applied the lids. Or you may have overfilled the jars. Refrigerate these jars and consume them promptly.

My pickles are soft or mushy.

So many possibilities. Make sure to slice off the blossom end when preparing cucumbers for pickling. The use of table salt can be an issue so always use canning salt. An improper ratio of vinegar and water could be the culprit. Maybe you used over-ripe cucumbers. Perhaps you packed the cucumbers too tightly in the jar. Maybe your cucumbers were refrigerated for too long. You should always use fresh pickling cucumbers. Soaking cucumbers in ice water, sometimes with salt, will help produce crisper pickles. As found in Ball Pickle Crisp or Xtra Crunch by Mrs. Wages, the use of calcium chloride will help a great deal. You can find these products wherever canning supplies are sold.

My jars leaked and lost liquid during processing.

You may have packed the food too tightly. The bands may have been too loose, or you did not remove air bubbles before applying the lids.

My jelly or jam didn't set correctly and is runny.

If you attempt to double the recipe, it won't set properly. Make 1 batch at a time. Sometimes it may take up to 2 weeks to set correctly. After 2 weeks, you can remake runny jam or jelly by recooking it and reprocessing it following instructions included with the pectin.

My jelly or jam has cloudy globs.

The foam, formed by the air content of the fruit, is minuscule air bubbles. Unless it is skimmed off the surface immediately after removing the jam or jelly from the heat, it will create cloudy globs in your product affecting the appearance. The use of a small amount of butter when cooking the jam or jelly will help reduce foaming. Or use margarine if you're vegan. Simply skim the foam off the surface with a large spoon before ladling the product into the jars.

I didn't get enough juice from the drip bag.

Simply pour sufficient boiling water over the pulp in the drip bag until you accumulate the amount of juice you require. Do not squeeze the bag.

My salsa is runny.

Your tomatoes probably contained a lot of water. Try not to harvest tomatoes immediately after watering or after a rainfall. You can also squeeze the tomatoes after peeling to remove excess moisture and seeds. You can also cook your salsa longer, uncovered, so that additional liquid evaporates until you reach your desired consistency.

My soup or stew is too thick.

Simply add some water when reheating. Or, if you desire a creamy consistency, add some milk or cream when reheating.

I went to open a stored jar, and the lid lifted right off.

Your jar did not seal properly. You may have overfilled the jar. There may have been residue left on the rim of the jar before you applied the lid. There may have been the formation of yeast in the canned product because of improper processing. The food is spoiled and must be immediately discarded. Sterilize the jar and band and safely discard the lid.

CONCLUSION

"Keep calm and can on." Luke Potter

We've come to the end of our home canning journey together, at least for now. We've had fun learning about the history and science of home canning. I hope you can see how easy, economical, and practical home canning can be while enjoying delicious, canned goods with your family and friends. I've included many tips and tricks I've learned over the years that can help you avoid some of the mistakes that are easy to make when you start canning.

As you preserve your own food, you'll find yourself going back to certain recipes repeatedly. Some pages will be earmarked for easy reference. Other pages will be stained with jam. You might make notes in the book or add your own heirloom family recipes in the back. Grandma's recipe cards might be used as bookmarks. Every gardening season means more home canning, and I know you'll come to look forward to those moments you spend in your kitchen just like me. For me and many others, home canning isn't just about the output - it's also about the mental well-being that canning provides. Growing your own food, and then preserving it in the kitchen, seems to chase away clouds of doubt and depression. There are few experiences so simple in life as gardening and home canning that provide you with the self-esteem and confidence that you'll discover by growing and preserving your own food.

Even if you don't have a garden, you can fill your pantry with locally grown fruits and vegetables. Visit your local farmer's market or pick-your-own farms. Stock up on meat when it's on sale and can it. Graciously accept those unwanted zucchinis from your neighbor and make pickles – and then give them a jar. As you've learned in this book, almost anything and everything can be canned successfully when you follow simple instructions. If you can read, you can can.

I could have delved deeper into other food preservation methods, but I'll save those for future books. And if you've struggled with growing your own food in the past, or if you have limited space or experience, refer to Part One of this book, How to Grow Vegetables in Pots & Containers. It's also available as an eBook, paperback, hard cover, and audiobook on Amazon.

I really hope you and your family get to have as much fun as mine when canning season arrives. It's great to get the kids involved so they can learn and pass on these valuable, sustainable life skills. I sincerely hope you take the opportunity to fill your pantry and cupboards with healthy, nutritious home canned food.

The final thought I would like to leave you with before we bid farewell is this - even the smallest pantry is an opportunity for greatness. Treat every situation in life as a new experience. Give it the attention it deserves. Keep an eye on it so it doesn't boil over and wait for the ping! No matter what insurmountable task you are facing, with a bit of love, a little patience, and a little time, you can succeed in anything you do.

I want to give a big thank you to all of you who read this book. I hope you find the content enlightening and that you are motivated to get your pantry and cupboards stocked. There is nothing more satisfying than when you look at what you have accomplished and realize that your family will never go hungry – regardless of what may happen in the future.

If you enjoyed reading this book, please share it with your friends. Consider gifting a copy to a loved one who gardens. And please leave a review on Amazon so that other home canners, preppers, and homesteaders can find the inspiration to preserve their own food. I hope to see you in the canning goods section at the hardware store. I promise, I'll let you take the last box of Mason jars!

Remember, life is abundant!

ABOUT THE AUTHOR

Luke Potter, The Urban Farmer, is a gardener, homeschool teacher, avid home canner and author of gardening and home canning books. He loves to share gardening and canning advice with both expert and first-timers. His goal is to build a sustainable community of like-minded individuals dedicated to feeding their families healthy, organic food while preserving the traditions of our ancestors. Gardeners as close as your neighbor and as far away as Uganda are sharing his lessons with others. He hopes to assist you on your personal journey while attaining the Zen of a more self-reliant lifestyle. His mantra, "Life is abundant," can be applied to all aspects of your life. Join Luke and his growing grassroots movement. He encourages you to learn to reap what you sow while you help make the world a better place for today and tomorrow.

You can contact Luke on Facebook or by email @

luketheurbanfarmer@aol.com

https://luketheurbanfarmer.com

RESOURCES

Canning food processing. (n.d.). Https://Www.Britannica.Com/Topic/Canning-Food-Processing. https://www.britannica.com/topic/canning-food-processing

From salt to cold storage rooms: How we've been preserving food over the years. (2020, May 25). Https://Pindercooling.Com/from-Salt-to-Cold-Storage-Rooms-How-Weve-Been-Preserving-Food-over-the-Years/. https://pindercooling.com/from-salt-to-cold-storage-rooms-how-weve-been-preserving-food-over-the-years/

How did we can? (n.d.). Https://Www.Nal.Usda.Gov/Exhibits/Ipd/Canning/Timeline-Table. https://www.nal.usda.gov/exhibits/ipd/canning/timeline-table

Koehler. (2021, July 21). *It's time to can tuna.* Https://Extension.Wsu.Edu/Graysharbor/2021/07/Time-to-Can-Tuna. https://extension.wsu.edu/graysharbor/2021/07/time-to-can-tuna

Pruitt. (2015, May 21). *The juicy 400-year history of pickles.* Https://Www.History.Com/News/Pickles-History-Timeline. https://www.history.com/news/pickles-history-timeline

Skimming foam from jam: Everything you need to know. (2017, June 21). Http://Nwedible.Com/Skimming-Jam-Foam-Questions. http://nwedible.com/skimming-jam-foam-questions

Troubleshooting common problems with home canned pickles. (n.d.). Https://Extension.Umn.Edu/Preserving-and-Preparing/Pickle-Problems. https://extension.umn.edu/preserving-and-preparing/pickle-problems

Victory Garden. (n.d.). Https://En.Wikipedia.Org/Wiki/Victory_garden. https://en.wikipedia.org/wiki/Victory_garden

What is my elevation? (n.d.). Https://Whatismyelevation.Com. https://whatismyelevation.com

INDEX OF RECIPES

345

My Gardening & Canning Journal

Made in the USA
Middletown, DE
12 February 2024

49605830R00197